FROMMER'S

COMPREHENSIVE TRAVEL GUIDE

BED & BREAKFAST NORTH AMERICA

by Hal Gieseking

PRENTICE
HALL
PRESS

NEW YORK • LONDON • TORONTO • SYDNEY • TOKYO • SINGAPORE

FROMMER BOOKS

Published by Prentice Hall Press
A division of Simon & Schuster Inc.
15 Columbus Circle
New York, NY 10023

ISBN 0-13-333329-9
ISSN 1051-6824

Manufactured in the United States of America

FROMMER'S BED & BREAKFAST NORTH AMERICA
Editor-in-Chief: Marilyn Wood
Senior Editors: Judith de Rubini, Pamela Marshall, Amit Shah
Editors: Alice Fellows, Paige Hughes
Assistant Editors: Suzanne Arkin, Ellen Zucker

CONTENTS _____

PREFACE
THE BEST OF THE B&BS

I want to thank all the readers, owners of B&B homes, and managers of reservation services for all of your suggestions and comments about the first three editions of *Frommer's Bed & Breakfast North America*.

In this fourth edition, we're taking advantage of what we've learned from you.

Many readers wanted to locate the *best* B&Bs in each area. They didn't want to wade through dozens of pages of listings and take potluck on their vacation home for a week or a weekend. They didn't want to drive miles down a country road only to find that the B&B they chose from a few words of description was a decaying wreck.

That's why we asked the top B&B reservation services in the U.S. and Canada to handpick their *best* B&Bs for this new edition—the kinds of places they'd recommend to their own best friends.

These are not necessarily the most expensive. We wanted B&Bs that offered real value for the money, along with luxurious amenities ranging from great breakfasts to unusually helpful hosts—and/or spectacular scenic locations.

It was not possible for us to visit each of the hundreds of prime selections in this book. But each was inspected and hand-picked by the people who know B&Bs best in their own area—the managers of local reservation services who may see dozens of B&B homes in the course of a year. I have relied heavily on these agencies' selections and frequently used their own words to describe their selections. The *real* "insiders" in the booming B&B industry are these managers.

No B&B home or reservation service has ever paid to get into this book. They are listed only because they *earned* the honor.

If you are ever dissatisfied with any B&B home or reservation service included in this book, please write to me. If you find a B&B reservation service or spectacular home, please let me know. (Please see the "B&B Critics" response form at the back of this book.)

We have also listed a number of B&B inns as a convenience to readers.

But now is the time to start planning your own vacation (or business trip) in the "best of the B&Bs." Just turn the page.

Introducing
Bed & Breakfast

1

BED & BREAKFAST—

The *Friendly* Revolution in Travel

- Travel across the U.S. and Canada, and stay in a B&B home for as little as $30 to $50 a night—breakfast included. Or over $200 for a B&B suite with a spa and swimming pool.
- Get "inside" tips from your hosts on the area's best restaurants, shops, stores, sightseeing attractions.
- Make friends as you travel and become "part of the neighborhood," rather than paying guests at a hotel, welcomed only by an occasional bellhop looking for a tip or a desk clerk who may not be able to find your reservation.
- Participate in activities with your host, which can range from shopping the local stores to sailing and lakeside picnics.
- Rather than staying in a cold, impersonal hotel with stain-resistant plastic furnishings, you may wake up in a colonial bedroom filled with antiques.

Many travelers in North America are waking up to the bed-and-breakfast way of travel.

There are now over 20,000 bed-and-breakfast homes operating in the U.S., and the number is climbing almost daily. Many of the states I surveyed reported that the B&B movement was growing so fast they had trouble keeping any list of homes current.

Small wonder. Travelers have discovered what incredible bargains B&B homes can be. The cost of a hotel room in the U.S. has climbed to an average of $70 a night, with many rooms in major cities topping $150 to $200 per night. The B&B homes offer comfortable, home-like lodgings for as little as $30 to $50 per night per single, $30 to $70 per night double. It's true that you can also spend over $200 a night for some B&B rooms, but these are luxury exceptions in choice scenic locations, often with swimming pools, spas, and many other amenities.

But the real reason that the B&B way to travel has caught on is the sheer *friendliness* of many of the hosts. Vacationers and travelers are weary of the impersonality, coldness, and rudeness of many travel personnel. They are tired of passing through some of the most hospitable areas of North America, and meeting no local person other than a bellhop or hotel cashier. People who have become B&B hosts are often outgoing and friendly, and they take real joy in welcoming others into their homes and communities.

This welcome shows up in many ways.

In some California B&Bs you may be greeted on arrival with good local wine and cheeses. In many homes the hosts serve far more than the typical Continental breakfast (juice, roll, coffee/tea). They introduce their guests to the local specialties: not simply bacon and eggs but sourdough pancakes, English scones, fresh-fruit platters, smoked meats, blueberry coffee cake, New England clam cakes, creamed cod on toast, and many other luscious regional surprises you'd never find on a hotel breakfast menu.

Many of the hosts don't treat you like paying guests at all. Stay a few nights and you can practically become part of the family, gathering for cocktails around the fire in the evening with your hosts or even joining them for birthday parties and special local events. The stories I have gathered since I started researching this book indicate just how often hosts go out of their way to make their guests feel welcome.

Many hosts provide laundry facilities. Others will act as your sightseeing guides. Some with small boats or even yachts take guests out on lakes, rivers, and oceans. Many will pick up guests at airports, or bus and train stations. One host provides pajamas and toothbrushes for guests whose luggage may have been lost by the airline. Many are happy to lend you bicycles for local touring, and give you maps, brochures, and directions to interesting sightseeing. Still others give you membership cards to local country clubs, tennis clubs, swimming pools, etc. And when you want some company, they are often happy to oblige with breakfast or end-of-the-day conversations. As I said, this is a *friendly* revolution in travel.

Imagine the advantages of learning firsthand where the best restaurants are—from people who have lived in an area for years. You can learn what are the best times to visit Walt Disney World, which are the least crowded roads for New England leaf watching, which local stores are having sales. In these imperfect times, you also learn which local areas have high crime rates and should be avoided.

The hosts themselves are often fascinating people. Here is a random list of their occupations that I discovered in researching B&B organizations across North America: journalists; investment bankers; linguists; painters; musicians (many); tennis pros; a world-renowned expert on scotch whisky; doctors; lawyers; teachers (many); actors; writers; gardeners; and gracious widows, widowers, and divorced people who love to cook and entertain.

B&B homes are full of surprises, very nice ones. When you check into some hotels you know there's going to be a standard-size bed, a TV set, a scratch-proof, mar-proof dresser, and often the same graphics on the wall from hotel to hotel. But your room in a B&B home may have a cannonball bed from colonial times, a working fireplace, family antiques that span the centuries, and often original artwork on all of the walls. The homes themselves are often unique. A number of B&B homes are listed on the National Historic Register. Others are not really houses at all, but houseboats and yachts in which the hosts welcome you to a floating B&B. There are also working ranches, Boston town houses, New York luxury apartments, and remote Canadian farmhouses.

ABOUT THIS BOOK

B&B travel is not your typical run-of-the-mill travel. Of course you could get a bad B&B—a poorly maintained house, surly people, a stale roll for breakfast. But I've personally encountered all of these problems in modern, expensive hotels, and you probably have too.

B&B travel can be more fun, personal, and relaxing than any kind of traveling you've ever done before. You can meet and make new friends all over the country and the world. You can also save a lot of money.

Talking about savings, think about this. Next time you and

your spouse or friend have breakfast in a top hotel, add up the *total* cost, including the tip to the waiter and local sales tax. That cost alone may just about equal the cost of a typical bed-and-breakfast for two in many parts of the country.

This guidebook was written to help you make the most of your next trip. It contains one of the most comprehensive listings and descriptions of North American B&B reservation services ever published. I have surveyed them frequently to help ensure that I was including the most stable and long-lasting services of this fledgling cottage industry. Some asked if they had to pay to be included in this guidebook. I told them "of course not." My only criterion for their inclusion was how well they were serving the traveling public.

Almost all of these reservation-service organizations are extremely conscientious, personally *pre-inspecting* the B&B homes included in their lists.

This guidebook also contains a listing of some special B&B inns that have come to my attention.

So come join the *friendly* revolution in travel—bed-and-breakfast. You're going to like it!

ANSWERS TO SOME COMMON QUESTIONS ABOUT B&B TRAVEL

Q. *Is B&B travel a new idea?*

A. Not at all. It's one of the oldest. In the 11th century, when monks and other pilgrims were walking to Rome or other holy sites, they frequently stopped overnight at private farms, monasteries, and homes. After breakfast in the morning, they were on their way—the first B&B guests.

In recent years the B&B movement has spread throughout much of Europe. Europeans frequently stop at homes with "Bed & Breakfast" or "Zimmer Frei" (room free) signs posted on the front lawn.

In the American depression years of the 1930s, "tourist homes" sprang up all over the countryside. For as little as $2 you could have a modest room and sometimes an equally modest breakfast.

However, the current B&B movement is much different.

While there are still many modest homes offering a room and breakfast, the quality of most accommodations (and breakfasts) is light-years ahead of early tourist homes.

Q. *I get confused. I see B&B signs on hotels.*

A. It is confusing. Many small inns have taken to calling themselves bed-and-breakfast places. These can be very pleasant, and many of them are listed in this guidebook. But when I say "B&B" I'm talking about a room in a private home with at least a Continental breakfast served to guests.

Q. *Why should I make a reservation through a B&B reservation-service organization? I see lists of individual B&B homes in books and brochures.*

A. You can, of course, make your own reservations directly with a B&B home. Some of these I've seen can be very good. However, because of zoning and other problems with neighbors, often the best B&B homes *never* appear in any public list. The only way you can book them is through a reservation-service organization.

The best of these organizations *pre-inspect* all prospective B&B homes before listing them.

Some of these organizations can occasionally be hard to reach. Many are small "mom and pop," or sometimes just "mom," operations. They have a list of B&Bs, a telephone, and an answering machine. Sometimes you may not be able to reach them until after 6pm at night because the owners of the service work during the day. However, with a little persistence, you can usually get through. Almost all the organizations I have included in this guide have been in existence at least one year.

Q. *Can I use a B&B home for business travel?*

A. Of course—B&Bs are ideal for business travelers who want to reduce costs. The reservation-service organizations included in this directory have listed many of the major corporations that are located near their B&B homes.

B&B homes are also ideal for parents visiting children at college, single women relocating to a new community, skiers, vacationers visiting specific scenic attractions, national parks, and other recreation areas, and everyone who's tired of paying high hotel costs and sometimes getting second-class, impersonal treatment.

Q. *Can I travel with a pet?*

A. Some B&B homes, especially in rural areas, do allow well-behaved dogs and cats to stay with their owners. Always ask about this, however, when you make your reservation. I know of one cat owner who stayed in B&B homes all over the state of Colorado with Tabby joining him for breakfast every morning.

If you are allergic to dogs or cats, be sure to ask if any are in residence in the B&B home before you make your reservation.

Q. *Are there any disadvantages to B&B travel?*

A. Yes. There can be a lack of privacy. Sometimes you and your spouse or friend want to be alone together on vacation; the conversation of even a well-meaning hostess may be more than you want. You also may have to wait in line for a shared bathroom, just like at home if you have a large family. You also may feel guilty staying too long in the shower when you know that others are waiting.

You may find a few B&B homes that are disappointing. Barbara Notarius, president of Bed & Breakfast USA Ltd., reported on her visit to one: "I recently went out on an appointment to visit one prospective B&B for my network. I arrived at the appointed time. The place was beautiful from the outside, handmade by a custom cabinetmaker, very rustic and nestled in the woods by a running stream just outside a desirable country community. When I rang the bell, a woman came to the door and stared at me. I asked for the woman of the house from whom I had the first inquiry many weeks previously. The woman looked at me a bit bewildered and said 'No,' and just stood there. So I asked for the husband who had given me detailed directions only a few days before. Again this woman said 'No,' and continued to look at me. I finally said, 'Who are you? When will the family be back?' Her response was that she was a tenant and the family had had a spat the day before. The wife had left and [the woman] thought the husband had gone off flying shortly before I arrived. Since they obviously had forgotten about the appointment, I asked to have a look at the house anyway. She didn't mind, so in I went. Furniture was practically nonexistent, filth was everywhere, and even the room this woman was renting had only a sleeping bag over a piece of foam, no sheets."

Moral: It's a pretty good idea to have the B&B home inspected and approved by the reservation organization *before* you pull into the driveway.

2

HOW TO FIND BED & BREAKFASTS

- Many of the most fascinating B&B homes never advertise or post a B&B sign.
- New sources of B&B information are springing up almost every week.

This book is the key to hundreds of the better B&B homes throughout the U.S. and Canada.

Why "better"?

Because most of the luxurious or interesting or historic B&B homes won't risk angry confrontations with their neighbors by posting a "Bed & Breakfast" sign on their lawn or advertising in a local publication. Even B&B homes that have received free publicity from a well-meaning reporter have encountered problems from zoning boards, health boards, and sometimes a whole block of people who have exaggerated fears about a "business" operating in the neighborhood.

Also, many B&B hosts feel much more secure if any prospective guests are screened by a reliable reservation-service organization. Otherwise they would be opening their homes to total strangers right off the street.

That's why so many of the really great B&B homes are *never* advertised or publicized. Some of these homes have swimming pools, country antiques, and fireplaces in every room, and beautiful grounds. The way to find them is to call one of the reservation organizations listed in this book.

Use the unique "B&B Finder" cross index at the back of this guide. For example, if you are parents of a son at Atlanta University, you could simply turn to the "Schools and Colleges" section and find which reservation agencies offer B&B accommodations near this school. If you want to attend a Shakespeare play at the Stratford Festival in Ontario, Canada, turn to the "Attractions" section for your B&B reservation service. If you are a business person tired of the plastic sameness and price tags of many hotels, check the reservation listings for a home in the city or area you plan to visit. This service can be particularly valuable for women travelers who enjoy the security and comfort of a home environment when they're out of town.

If you ever do get stuck and can't contact a reservations organization operating in the area you want to visit, there are several alternatives.

First, you can look in the local *Yellow Pages* phone directory. Reservation services and individual bed-and-breakfast homes will be listed under a new, separate "Bed & Breakfast" heading in many directories.

You can also write ahead to local chambers of commerce and state tourism offices (their addresses are listed in this guidebook). Many are now beginning to offer free lists of B&B homes or brochures about individual homes and farms.

Tourist information booths along state highways are also beginning to carry B&B brochures and information.

When you're visiting a resort area, stop in the local tourist office. Some can tell you about local availabilities, and may even be able to book you into a B&B on the spot.

In some rural areas (where neighbors are more tolerant or friendly), you will see "Bed & Breakfast" signs in front of some homes.

You also can now get information about B&B accommodations from the American Automobile Association. In a newsletter to other AAA clubs, the National Travel Department of AAA wrote, "Due to the rapid growth of interest in bed-and-breakfast facilities, we decided to review our method for presenting B&B data to AAA Clubs. In the future, in order to ensure that members receive current information pertaining to reputable B&B referral services, we will provide a listing of only those B&B referral services which screen their listings. In this way, the listing provided to clubs will reflect AAA's concern for property cleanliness, hospitable hosts, and ethical operations." (*Note:* AAA really meant "reservation"—not "referral" agencies.)

As the B&B movement keeps growing (and in some areas it's starting to roar along, picking up new momentum with each day), you'll find more and more sources of information.

When you're traveling in North America, take this guidebook along. It can introduce you to B&Bs all over the U.S. and Canada through a network of reservation-service organizations. It's among the friendliest, most inexpensive ways to travel today.

Want to stay in a B&B inn? You'll find a list of special ones that have come to my attention (listed by state following the B&B reservation-service information in Part II).

Want to stay in one of the finest B&B homes in North America? See the list of *top* B&Bs in each state.

STATE TOURIST OFFICES

Many state tourist offices can supply you with names and addresses of some outstanding B&B homes and inns in their area, as well as good state maps and other travel information. Here is a complete list.

Alabama Bureau of Tourism
and Travel
532 S. Perry St.
Montgomery, AL 36104-4614
205/242-4169

Alaska Division of Tourism
P.O. Box E
Juneau, AK 99811
907/465-2010

Arizona Office of Tourism
1100 W. Washington St.
Phoenix, AZ 85007
602/542-4764

Arkansas Department of
Parks and Tourism
One Capitol Mall
Little Rock, AR 72201
501/682-1087

California Office of Tourism
1121 L St., Suite 103
Sacramento, CA 95814
916/322-2881

Colorado Tourism Board
1625 Broadway, Suite 1700
Denver, CO 80202
303/592-5410

Connecticut Department of
Economic Development
865 Brook St.
Rocky Hill, CT 06067
203/258-4286

Delaware Tourism Office
99 Kings Hwy. (P.O. Box
140)
Dover, DE 19903
302/736-4271

Florida Division of Tourism
Department of Commerce
107 W. Gaines St.
Room 505, Collins Bldg.
Tallahassee, FL 32301
904/488-9187

Georgia Department of
Industry & Trade

30 Peachtree St., NW
P.O. Box 1776
Atlanta, GA 30301
 404/656-3590

Hawaii Department of
 Business and Economic
 Development
State Tourism Office
P.O. Box 2359
Honolulu, HI 96804
 808/548-6007

Idaho Division of Travel
 Promotion
Department of Commerce
State Capitol Building
Boise, ID 83720
 208/334-2470

Illinois Office of Tourism
State of Illinois Center
100 W. Randolf, Suite 3-400
Chicago, IL 60601
 312/917-4732

Indiana Tourism
 Development Division
Department of Commerce
One N. Capitol, Suite 700
Indianapolis, IN 46204
 317/232-8870

Iowa Division of Tourism
Department of Economic
 Development
200 E. Grand Ave.
Des Moines, IA 50309
 515/281-3100

Kansas Department of
 Commerce

Travel and Tourism
 Development Division
400 SW 8th St., 5th Floor
Topeka, KS 66603-3957
 913/296-2009

Kentucky Department of
 Travel Development
Capitol Plaza Tower, 22nd
 Floor
Frankfort, KY 40601
 502/564-4930

Louisiana Office of Tourism
P.O. Box 94291
Baton Rouge, LA 70804-9291
 504/342-8100

Maine Department of
 Economic and Community
 Development
Office of Tourism
189 State St.
State House Station 59
Augusta, ME 04333
 207/289-5710

Maryland Office of Tourism
 Development
Department of Economic &
 Employment Development
217 E. Redwood St., 9th Fl.
Baltimore, MD 21202
 301/333-6611

Massachusetts Office of Travel
 and Tourism
100 Cambridge St.
Boston, MA 02202
 617/727-3205

Michigan Travel Bureau
Department of Commerce

P.O. Box 30226
Lansing, MI 48909
517/373-0670

Minnesota Office of Tourism
375 Jackson Walkway, 250
  Skyway Level
St. Paul, MN 55101
612/296-2755

Mississippi Department of
  Economic Development
Division of Tourism
1301 Walter Sillars Bldg.
P.O. Box 849
Jackson, MS 39205
601/359-3414

Missouri Division of Tourism
P.O. Box 1055
Jefferson City, MO 65102
314/751-3051

Montana Promotion
  Division, Department of
  Commerce
1424 Ninth Ave.
Helena, MT 59620-0411
406/444-2654

Nebraska Travel & Tourism
  Division
Department of Economic
  Development
P.O. Box 94666
301 Centennial Mall South
Lincoln, NE 68509
402/471-3798

Nevada Commission on
  Tourism
600 E. Williams, Suite 207
State Capitol Complex
Carson City, NV 89701

702/885-4322

New Hampshire Office of
  Vacation Travel
105 Loudon Rd.
P.O. Box 856
Concord, NH 03301
603/271-2665

New Jersey Division of Travel
  and Tourism
Department of Commerce &
  Economic Development
20 W. State St., CN 826
Trenton, NJ 08625-0826
609/292-2470

New Mexico Tourism and
  Travel Division
Economic Development and
  Tourism Department
Joseph M. Montoya Bldg.
1100 St. Francis Dr.
Santa Fe, NM 87503
505/827-0295

New York State Department
  of Economic Development
Division of Tourism
One Commerce Plaza
Albany, NY 12245
518/474-4116

North Carolina Department
  of Commerce, Travel &
  Tourism Division
430 N. Salisbury St.
Raleigh, NC 27603
919/733-4171

North Dakota Tourism
  Promotion
Liberty Memorial Building
State Capitol Grounds

Bismarck, ND 58505
701/224-2525

Ohio Division of Travel &
  Tourism
Department of Development
P.O. Box 1001
Columbus, OH 43216-0101
  614/466-8844

Oklahoma Tourism and
  Recreation Department
505 Will Rogers Building
Oklahoma City, OK 73105
  405/521-2406

Oregon Economic
  Development Department
Tourism Division
595 Cottage St. NE
Salem, OR 97310
  503/373-3451
Pennsylvania Bureau of
  Travel Development
Department of Commerce
Room 453 Forum Building
Harrisburg, PA 17120
  717/787-5453

Rhode Island Department of
  Economic Development
Tourism & Promotion
  Division
Jackson Walkway
Providence, RI 02903
  401/277-2601

South Carolina Department
  of Parks, Recreation, and
  Tourism
1205 Pendleton St.
#106, Edgar A. Brown

Building
Columbia, SC 29201
  803/734-0136

South Dakota Department of
  Tourism
P.O. Box 6000
Pierre, SD 57501
  605/773-3301

Tennessee Department of
  Tourist Development
320 Sixth Ave. North
Nashville, TN 37219
  615/741-1904

Texas Tourism Division
Department of Commerce
Capitol Station
P.O. Box 12008
Austin, TX 78711-2008
  512/462-9191

Utah Travel Council
Capitol Hall
300 N. State
Salt Lake City, UT 84114
  801/533-1030

Vermont Travel Division
Agency of Development &
  Community Affairs
134 State St.
Montpelier, VT 05602
  802/828-3236

Virginia Division of Tourism
1021 E. Cary St.
Richmond, VA 23219
  804/786-2051

Washington, DC Convention
  and Visitors Association
1212 New York Ave., N.W.,
  Suite 250

Washington, DC 20005
202/789-7000

Washington Department of
Trade and Economic
Development
Tourism Development
Division
101 General Administration
Building
Bldg. AX-13
Olympia, WA 98504-0613
206/753-5600

West Virginia Department of
Commerce
Tourism/Marketing
2101 Washington St. East
Charleston, WV 25305
304/348-2200

Wisconsin Division of
Tourism
123 W. Washington Ave.
P.O. Box 7970
Madison, WI 53707
608/266-2147

Wyoming Travel Commission
Frank Norris, Jr., Travel
Center
I-25 and College Drive
Cheyenne, WY 82002-0660
307/777-7777

TERRITORIES

American Samoa
Government
Office of Tourism
P.O. Box 1147
Pago Pago, AS 96799
684/699-9280

Guam Visitors Bureau
1200 Bay View Place Pale
San Vitores Rd.
P.O. Box 3520
Agana, Guam 96910
671/646-5278

Marianas Visitors Bureau
P.O. Box 861
Saipan, CM Marianas Islands
96950
670/234-8327

Puerto Rico Tourism
Company
P.O. Box 4435
San Juan, PR 00905
809/721-2400

U.S. Virgin Islands Tourism
Division
P.O. Box 6400
Charlotte Amalie
St. Thomas, USVI 00801
809/774-8784

3

HOW TO BE A B&B GUEST

- Use a reservation-service organization that pre-inspects the homes on its lists.
- Some B&B homes offer free pickup at airports and train and bus stations for travelers without cars.

While enjoying the hospitality and warmth of a typical B&B home may be as easy as saying "Pass the strawberry preserves," finding the right home for you and your family may require a little effort and advance planning.

First, I strongly recommend that you use a reservation service rather than taking pot-luck as you drive along the road or call a home that you've seen listed in a book. Any reservation service worth the fee that it usually receives from each rental (from the B&B host, not from you) will inspect the homes on its list. Or at a very minimum the service will quickly drop any homes that guests have complained about frequently.

It's true that you may occasionally find a gem on your own simply by stopping at a "Bed & Breakfast" sign. But the odds are against you because many of the best B&B homes aren't listed.

I've repeated this warning in other parts of this guide because I truly believe that booking your B&B home through an established reservation-service organization is the simplest, safest, and ultimately the most satisfying way.

However, before you call any reservation service, you should write down your basic needs. In many cases the reservation service will send you a free or low-cost brochure that describes the homes and locations available. You then phone or write the reservation service after you've made the selection. You will usually be required to confirm the reservation by a minimum payment of the first night's rental. Some services may require full payment in advance.

After you have a confirmed reservation from the reservation service, always call the host. This is a very important call because it will be your first contact with this very important person. You can begin to establish a friendship with that first call. Have a map handy so you can ask specific questions about the most direct route to the B&B home. (This is very important—I have been stranded at night in some remote rural areas looking for "the second road on the right.")

Many B&B hosts offer pickup services to carless travelers, free or at a small fee. If you arrive by plane, bus, or train, you may be able to have the host meet you at the airport or station.

It is always a good practice (and often required) that you pay the host any balance due for your entire B&B stay when you arrive. This also saves problems when you check out if the host is away.

Ask about the use of a house key, particularly if your host works and you want access to the house and your room during the day. You may be required to post a key fee.

Ask all about the use of the house and grounds. Some hosts give you kitchen privileges and allow you to fix your own breakfast whenever you're ready. One B&B guest surprised her host by making strawberry pancakes for her husband and the whole host family. "They were pleased," she said later. "But you could tell this wasn't their typical breakfast. They really thought I was serving them dessert."

There may be recreation facilities/equipment in the house and on the grounds—TV sets, stereos, barbecue pits, volleyball nets, swimming pools, sleds, etc. Find out if you're permitted to use them. Many hosts are happy to oblige.

In the house itself, is smoking permitted in your room? In certain areas? Or forbidden throughout the house. Do you have access to the family room, the living room, and the laundry facilities?

Never hesitate to ask if you need certain comfort items—an extra blanket for the bed, extra towels, etc. Some rooms have individual air conditioners or temperature controls. Ask for a demonstration of how to regulate them.

The host may give you a written set of "house rules." Follow them and treat the house as you would your own. Clear communication and common courtesy are the bases for a successful and happy B&B homestay.

Always sign the guestbook when you leave, with any personal comments about what you liked about the visit and your hosts. It's a great keepsake for the hosts. It also can lead to Christmas cards, social notes, and just possibly, a lifelong friendship.

4

HOW TO OPERATE A B&B HOME

- Some hosts make $10,000 and over a year. But the majority earn far less. However, they do make a lot of new friends from around the world.
- Take advantage of possible tax deductions when you use part of your home as a business.
- Expect the unexpected. B&B people have hosted everyone from motion picture and soap opera stars to casual visitors who ask to be married in their home!

A surprising number of people want to become B&B hosts and turn one or two spare rooms in their house into guest rooms. Some are widows, widowers, divorcees, and single people who are burdened by the rising costs and taxes of homeownership. The idea of earning anywhere from $15 to $80 per night for a room (depending on the quality and location of the home) can be very appealing.

Others are simply "empty nesters" whose children have gone off to college or careers and left them with extra rooms and an abnormally quiet house. They like the idea of meeting new people from around the U.S. and the world. Many of these hosts are college professors, doctors, lawyers, world travelers, company presidents, as well as automobile mechanics, shop foremen, secretaries, and bus drivers—a generous cross section of America.

Other people who become B&B hosts are frustrated innkeepers or restaurant owners. Many dream of one day owning their own inn on a mountain or designing their own restaurant serving "new American cuisine." Becoming a B&B host allows a person—at least partially—to satisfy some of these dreams.

However, before you go into this business (and it *must* be a business, not a hobby, if you hope to qualify for possible tax deductions on your house), you should look at the pros and cons with your eyes wide open. You may want to follow Ben Franklin's wise advice. Write down all the positives you can think of on one sheet, all the negative factors on another. Then look at both of them together. You may then quickly see what your decision should be.

Here are some things you should consider:

1. Don't expect to make much money. In fact, one B&B association estimated that only about 10% of the B&B homes make a profit at present. However, as every business person knows, "profit" is relative. You might make attractive and useful improvements in your home, such as new carpeting, drapes, furnishings. You might qualify for depreciation of your house (and furnishings) for tax purposes. And even if the IRS rules that you are pursuing B&B as a hobby, you may still be able to use expenses to offset any income from your B&B. That means you have to make *serious* efforts to rent the room regularly.

2. Look at your home objectively. Does (do) your spare room(s) have a good double or twin beds? Are the furnishings in good condition? Is there adequate closet space? Will your guests have access to a private bath, or will the bathroom be shared with the family and other guests? One knowledgeable hostess said, "Always sleep at least once in the room you plan to use for your B&B service. You may be surprised by street noises, or too bright a light in the early morning streaming in the windows— things you would be aware of only if you stayed in your own room." Often one of the key factors in how often the room is rented is the location of your home. If it's in or near a major interstate highway, a major city, scenic attraction, college, hospital, or major corporations, your chances of renting it regularly increase dramatically. Some reservation agencies have told me that a few B&B homes in really remote areas may only be rented about once a year!

3. Poll your whole family. How do they feel about having guests? Remind them that they may lose some privacy in their own home and that they may have to wait in line to use the bathroom. Everyone may have to cooperate to keep the whole house clean (particularly the bathroom) for the arrival of guests. This may be the time for a good family discussion before you make any decision. Do you have a pet? A dog that protects the home by nipping strangers could cost you a lawsuit.

4. Talk with a good lawyer or someone in local government who is familiar with regulations that may govern B&B operations. The real problem is that zoning laws across the country are often very vague about B&B homes. Some zoning laws seem to permit occasional boarders in a home. At other times riled neighbors, who fear that their property value or privacy may be threatened by strangers coming into the neighborhood, may contact the local zoning board for a ruling. Recently one woman in La Jolla, California, began to operate a B&B business in her home. She posted notices locally. Some incensed neighbors brought suit against her. Although she fought the legal action vigorously, her lawyers eventually advised her to close the business. These zoning laws are in flux all over the nation. However, some B&B homeowners are also winning their cases and getting favorable rulings from zoning boards. This is particularly true in states that are actively encouraging the growth of the B&B movement as a way of stimulating more tourism. Jean Brown, head of Bed & Breakfast International, writes, "Not one of the thousands of host homes I've had has ever been the subject of a complaint to a zoning commission."

Also ask your attorney to check local public health/safety laws/regulations that may apply to any commercial application of your home. For example, some areas may require smoke detectors throughout your home.

5. If you do decide to become a B&B host, you now must decide whether you want to operate independently or want to be connected with a local or national reservation service. *I strongly recommend that you register your home with a reservation service.* If you operate as an independent, you must advertise and promote your home in some ways to attract guests. That could mean putting small ads or generating publicity in local newspapers and magazines. You might even put a small sign in front of your home. Unfortunately all of these activities could raise red flags for your neighbors or local officials. There is another problem. With your phone number on public display in an ad or in one of those books that describes independent B&B homes, you could be subject to unwelcome calls at any time of the day or night. You also would have little opportunity to screen the people who come into your home to spend the night. Instead you would be much better off using a reservation service that does not list your address or phone number in any of their literature. Let the reservation service screen prospective guests. (Before you sign up for any reservation service, ask about their screening activities.) You may want a service that handles all the financial details, even accepting credit-card payments, and forwards a check to you. A service typically charges you a small annual fee to cover administration/advertising costs plus a percentage of each rental (often 20% to 30%). When a service regularly brings you business and conscientiously screens prospective guests, they are more than worth their keep. If the service seems to be choosy about selecting homes for their network and wants to come out for a personal inspection of your home, be thankful! It means, that the service really cares about offering attractive accommodations to the public, and you are in very good hands. Some of the larger services even hold seminars and annual meetings for B&B hosts. This whole business is still in its infancy, and hosts are learning from each other. This guide contains one of the most complete listings of reservation services now operating. Turn to one operating in your area. If none, consider one that offers B&B listings across the U.S.

6. Check your home insurance coverage with your insurance agent. Tell him frankly what you plan to do. Ask what kind of coverage you have and how you would be protected if a paying guest were injured in your home. The standard homeowner's policy may only cover *two* boarders. As the B&B movement grows, the insurance industry is becoming aware of the problems and drafting special new policies. *Warning:* Insurance costs for B&Bs continue to increase—a major new problem.

I have deliberately listed the most negative factors, not to discourage you but to be sure that you understand that becoming a B&B host is not as simple as deciding you want to do it. That decision involves a commitment, and some careful attention to detail to avoid the pitfalls. However, there can be enormous personal rewards. Many of the stories I have heard from B&B hosts have been heartwarming. One host described the young lady who came to their bed-and-breakfast and liked their home so much that she asked to be married there. Other homeowners have met people from around the world who became fast friends. Barbara Notarius, president of Bed & Breakfast USA, Ltd., frequently offers her home as a B&B. She told of her first guest, a retired mining engineer from Australia. He had spent much of his life in remote areas of the world such as New Guinea and had hundreds of stories to tell. Soon Barbara's husband was skipping work so he could drive the guest around town. On another occasion, several of her house guests were musicians. Before they went to bed at night, they gave a chamber concert for Barbara and her family. "What a privilege!" she said.

But hosts also have to learn to be resilient and expect the unexpected. One host received a booking from a young woman for two people. When the two women arrived (one an actress who had recently appeared in a successful avant-garde film), they announced that they were gay and wanted to share a double bed. The hostess accommodated them, and had food for conversation at the next eight bridge parties with her friends. (If you operate a B&B home, you have to decide in advance if you will accept unmarried couples, singles, etc. This is another advantage of using a reservation service that knows your preferences.) Joan Brownhill, president of Pineapple Hospitality reservation service in New Bedford, Massachusetts, tells how she selects B&B homes and hosts: "We sent out a 'Host Home' preliminary packet which tells of our philosophy as an agency. There is a form to be completed that gives a profile of the prospective host, and answers such basic questions as to whether the host will accept children and pets. Two interviewers then visit the home by appointment to check everything out. If it meets the standards we've set, we sign an agreement with the new B&B home. An annual fee to the agency is collected."

Even when you are listed with an agency and want additional guests, there are a number of ways you could discreetly attract a number of guests:

■ If you are close to a local college, call or write the personnel office or office of student housing. Describe your home, its location, and room availability. Often visiting parents need an economical place to stay, especially with today's college costs being what they are. There also may be visiting professors or alumni who would welcome a home atmosphere. You might have some very stimulating guests.

■ Contact the personnel office or corporate travel department of major corporations. Transferees and other visiting employees might make excellent prescreened guests. Women business travelers are particularly receptive to the relaxed B&B concept.

■ Talk with local real estate agents. They may have out-of-town prospects who need a place to stay while looking for a new home. You'll not only earn extra income by providing hospitality, but you may also be making friends with new neighbors.

■ Ask previous guests back. When you find particularly appealing and thoughtful guests, invite them back in the summer or winter. Always keep a guestbook and ask them to write their comments. You may be pleasantly surprised how many Christmas/holiday cards you receive from guests who enjoyed your hospitality. *Note:* If your guest originally came from a reservation-service organization, you should ask them to rebook through this organization rather than directly with you. The few dollars you would lose in commission are more than made up by keeping the goodwill of the reservation service that is advertising and generating business for you.

SOME TIPS FOR HOSTS—

"The Gift of Hospitality"

1. Show room and house and give guests an opportunity to unload their belongings.
2. Offer a drink/beverage and see if anything else is needed.
3. Take care of business, such as collecting money, signing the guestbook and contracts, giving a receipt (preferably within 20 minutes of the guests' arrival).
4. Answer questions and mention nearby attractions.
5. Supply guests with an information sheet containing questions and answers about your local area.
6. Collect brochures on sightseeing for your local area, as well as your state, and have them available for guests.
7. Offer a "Sue's Special": picnic basket breakfast in bed.
8. Collect menus from popular restaurants to leave in the guests' room.
9. Make coffee early. Find out when guests arrive what they prefer to drink in the morning. A Thermos of coffee outside

the door, so the first cup of coffee can be drunk in bed, is a real treat for the real coffee drinker.

10. Put an umbrella stand with loan umbrellas near the door and tell guests about it.

11. Set up a game corner (garage sales are a wonderful source of these and other handy items).

12. Place extra toilet articles (small sample sizes) in drawers.

13. Use liquid soap in the bathroom so that no guest has to use anyone else's soap.

14. Offer a special guest tray including a fruit bowl, drinking glass, tissues, etc.

15. Have on hand books and magazines for your guests to read.

16. A hairdryer, makeup mirror, and curling iron from a garage sale may be lifesavers for your guests.

17. Have newspapers on hand.

18. Have a good map on hand.

19. Copy the section of your local map showing your home and circle your house, restaurants, attractions, movies, etc., and run off enough copies so that each guest can take one with him/her.

20. Collect articles from your newspaper's attractions section and keep in a folder easily available to guests. Copies hold up better than newsprint originals.

21. Collect discount coupons from nearby attractions and restaurants for guests.

22. Save fast-food discount coupons too.

23. Leave a note on the guests' desk or bureau telling where they can order take-out pizza. Let them know if it's all right to eat on your deck or patio.

24. Deliver ice water to the guests' room in the evening.

25. Have iced tea available in the refrigerator or let guests know that they can always boil themselves hot water for tea or instant coffee.

26. Help your guests to feel comfortable in your home. Assure them that they should ask if there is something they need—extra towels, more pillows, etc.

27. Copy your special B&B recipes so guests can take them home.

28. Invite guests to watch you do your hobbies/special-interest activities (such as stained glass, pottery, etc.).

29. If you have a historic home, guests may be interested in its history and architecture. Take a course about tracing the

history of your home and keep the results of your work accessible.

30. See if the historical society or other town group has a walking tour of the community published that your guests can take.

31. Be sensitive to your guests' need for privacy and space. Don't ever make a guest feel that he's there to amuse you. Be available for those who want to talk but in touch enough to recognize when a guest just wants to be left alone.

32. B&B attracts a lot of folks looking for romance. If your setting is conducive to this, encourage it. Offer guests some privacy in front of the fireplace, put out a decanter with a little after-dinner liqueur, etc. Flannel sheets are wonderful in cold climates.

33. Let your guests get to know you as an individual—your way of life, your part of the country.

COMMONLY ASKED QUESTIONS ABOUT HOSTING

Q. *How much should I charge for the room?*

A. The rate depends on several factors. The most important is location. Even a modestly furnished room in a modest house that is close to a popular ski slope can often command a premium rate. The condition of the room, its furnishings, and the general appearance of your home also should be considered. If the room has a private bath instead of a shared bath, you can also charge more. However, you want to be sure that the rate you charge is competitive and doesn't drive business away. Check the rates of other B&B homes in your area. Also, find out the rates of local hotels and motels. Your rate should generally be lower than hotel rates. Travelers expect B&B rates to be bargains.

Q. *What about income tax deductions?*

A. If your home is only used for B&B hosting 14 or fewer nights per year, you may not have to pay any income tax on what you make. However, if a room in your home is rented more than 14 nights a year, then you would have to declare all income. You would also be entitled to deductions that could range from depreciation on your furnishings, fees paid to reservation-service organizations, stamps, phone calls, etc. You also may be able to claim depreciation on your house and a percentage of certain housecleaning/home maintenance costs. You should make (and report) a profit at least two out of every five years or the government may claim your B&B operation is a hobby—not a business—and disallow any business deductions. *Note:* You may be unable to deduct some smaller expenses as a result of the newly revised federal tax law. To avoid problems, work with a good accountant who can help you interpret the current IRS rules.

Q. *Should I tell my neighbors I operate a B&B home?*

A. No. Not unless you are a would-be Perry Mason anxious to plead your case before a local zoning board.

Q. *Should I charge sales tax?*

A. Check with local authorities about this. It may be necessary for you to get a tax number and collect sales tax on all B&B rentals. Don't follow the human tendency to just keep mum about any rentals or income. You could become liable for back taxes and penalties.

Q. *I have to leave for work early in the morning. How can I fix breakfast for guests or give them access to the house should they return while I'm away?*

A. You could leave breakfast ingredients in the refrigerator and give your guests kitchen privileges for a do-it-yourself meal. Some hosts also give their guests a key, charging a "key fee" of $5 or $10 (which is refunded when the guest returns the key). For your own security, you may give the guest a key only to the regular lock, not a deadbolt lock, if you have one. You then have the security of locking the deadbolt without worrying about any unreturned keys that might be floating around.

Q. *What about the possibility of theft? I am letting strangers into my home.*

A. Theft could happen. However, at least so far, B&B guests seem to be an unusually honest group of people. In talking with B&B hosts, I have yet to hear of an incident where a guest has taken as much as a teaspoon. (In contrast, talk with any major-city hotel, which regularly loses a large quantity of towels and room-service silverware and linen in the luggage of departing guests.) You would want to use some common sense in protecting your personal belongings. If your guests have active children, you might want to store away any obvious breakables. You also can get an extra measure of security by having all prospective guests screened by the reservation-service organization. Many of these organizations ask guests for personal references.

Q. *Should I print a "brochure" on my B&B home?*

A. It really isn't necessary. You might want to do a simple letter on your stationery which describes your home and the breakfast you serve, tells of any "house rule" restrictions (such as no smoking, no pets, etc.), and gives directions to your home. Offset print a quantity and send some to your reservation-service organization. Or mail one to the guest who calls and asks for directions or more information.

Q. *Will I make much money as a B&B host?*

A. As I've said before, you probably *won't* make a high income as a host. However, I have been told of hosts who make $10,000 or more a year. Others who are close to scenic attractions, major cities, resort areas, etc., reliably make several hundred extra dollars each month. One hostess recently used her B&B earnings to pay for an all-expense safari in Africa. But there are also some B&B homes in remote locations that are only rented as little as once a year. As the real estate people love to say about selling a house, the three most important factors are location, location, and location.

A LAST NOTE

Much of your reward of being a B&B host will come from meeting other people. Kate Peterson, coordinator of Bed & Breakfast Rocky Mountains, shared this letter she had received from one of her new hosts:

Dear Kate,

Clyde and I just wanted to let you know how delighted we are with our first experience hosting bed-and-breakfast travelers. The couple from Houston left just this morning. I know we have made new friends. They were so comfortable with us that they have already decided to return in June to stay. It's amazing to me that they have even referred some of their friends to us—all this in just the last few days. Yesterday was really special. It was my birthday. When I got home in the afternoon, they had a birthday card and a delicate dried-flower arrangement waiting for me. I was truly touched. Kate, we want to thank you for making this opportunity possible for us and for others. We are looking forward to the next bed-and-breakfast travelers we can serve.

> *Sincerely,*
> *Fairley*

These are the *real* rewards of becoming a B&B host.

(Suggestions from *Rocky Mountains—Bed & Breakfast* hosts, reprinted with the permission of Kate Peterson and Barbara Notarius)

The Top 100 B&B Homes in North America

In the Depression era bed-and-breakfast may have only been a sparsely furnished room and a thin cup of coffee in a modest frame house somewhere along the highway. But today the B&B movement has become the Cinderella of the U.S. travel industry, and the accommodations, services, and thoughtfulness of hosts have created a delightful new way to travel. To help honor these new standards, *Frommer's Bed & Breakfast North America* guidebook has created a new category "The Top 100 B&B Homes in North America."

These selections were made by bed-and-breakfast reservation services. Each was invited to nominate just *one* home, the best home on its list. The men and women who operate these services may see and judge hundreds of homes and are in a unique position to point with pride at a home that rises above the rest.

Some homes are truly spectacular southern mansions that rival *Gone with the Wind*'s Tara. Others are beautiful apartments with skyline views. Still others are more modest rural dwellings with a spectacular mountain or ocean view, unbelievable gourmet breakfasts, or a host who babysits and leaves a glass of sherry and cheeses on a bedstand at night.

Is each a perfect "10"? No, but I think each offers something really special to guests.

There is one confusing element. Some of the B&B homes I have selected call themselves "inns." But I have arbitrarily decided that any B&B operation in a private home is a "B&B home," to distinguish it from the larger commercial inns which are basically small hotels that serve breakfast and also call themselves "B&B inns."

B&Bs change owners and standards can rise and fall. If you stay at any of these homes and are disappointed—or find what you believe is a superior B&B in the same area—you're invited to become one of our "B&B Critics" and write to me with your evaluations and discoveries. The collective judgment of our readers will play a major part in future selections of the **"Top 100."**

But meanwhile you can use this list to help plan a wonderful B&B vacation for yourself and your family all across North America.

Note: In the case of homes nominated by reservations services, I have given only partial addresses. Please contact the service at the phone number listed. Some hosts prefer not to be contacted directly. For homes not listed by reservation services I have provided complete addresses and each host's phone number.

Be sure to check the "Best B&Bs" section of each reservation-service listing. This is designed to give you an edge over other people calling the same reservation service. It describes the B&B homes that the services themselves consider their most appealing. Ask about them. Also you will learn about special services available from many B&B hosts just for the asking.

THE TOP 100 B&Bs IN NORTH AMERICA

Now you can stay at the **most outstanding** B&B homes in North America—each hand-picked by leading reservation-service organizations (RSO's) in the U.S. and Canada as the B&B at the top of their list. See the individual listings for each of the RSO's for complete details on each of these homes.

THE NORTHEASTERN STATES

Lyme, CT—Colonial home in the woods
(nominated by Nutmeg Bed & Breakfast)

New Haven, CT—1770 home
(nominated by Bed & Breakfast Ltd.)

Norfolk, CT—1898 Victorian Tudor home
(nominated by Covered Bridge Bed & Breakfast)

Kennebunkport, ME—"Oldest home in Maine"
(nominated by B&B Reservation Services)

Scarborough, ME—1779 home on the site of an old Native American fort
(nominated by Pineapple Hospitality, Inc.)

Auburn, MA—Georgian farmhouse
(nominated by Folkstone Central Massachusetts Bed & Breakfast)

Barnstable, MA—Barn restoration
(nominated by Bed & Breakfast Cape Cod)

Boston, MA—1863 town house in Copley Square area
(nominated by Bed & Breakfast Associates Bay Colony Ltd.)

Boston, MA—1828 Federal-style town house on Beacon Hill
(nominated by Bed & Breakfast Agency of Boston)

Boston (Brookline), MA—Georgian carriage house
(nominated by Greater Boston Hospitality)

Cheshire, MA—1817 Mansard-style home
(nominated by Berkshire Bed & Breakfast Homes)

Duxbury, MA—Historic salt box home
(nominated by Christian Hospitality)

Falmouth, MA—Cape-style home on the water
(nominated by Be Our Guest Bed & Breakfast)

Newton, MA—1882 Victorian home
(nominated by Host Homes of Boston)

Newton Centre, MA—"Margaret's Room"
(nominated by New England Bed & Breakfast, Inc.)

Orleans, MA—"The Red Geranium Home"
(nominated by Orleans Bed & Breakfast Associates)

Pepperell, MA—Restored 200-year-old Colonial
(nominated by Bed & Breakfast Folks)

Laconia, NH—Contemporary home on Lake Winnisquam
(nominated by New Hampshire Bed & Breakfast)

New York, NY—Penthouse in Midtown Manhattan
(nominated by Aaah! Bed & Breakfast #1 Ltd.)

New York, NY—1884 Victorian brownstone
(nominated by Abode Bed & Breakfast Ltd.)

New York, NY—Loft in Midtown Manhattan
(nominated by Bed & Breakfast Network of New York)

Niagara Falls, NY—White Victorian home
(nominated by Rainbow Hospitality)

North Shore, Long Island, NY—Colonial home
(nominated by A Reasonable Alternative, Inc.)

Sayville, Long Island, NY—Waterfront contemporary
(nominated by Bed & Breakfast of Long Island)

Vernon, NY—1799 Federal homestead
(nominated by Bed & Breakfast Connection)

Newport, RI—1850 home in the Point Section
(nominated by Anna's Victorian Connection)

Newport, RI—Greek Revival mansion
(nominated by Bed & Breakfast of Rhode Island)

Barton, VT—Colonial mansion on Lake Willoughby
(nominated by Vermont Bed & Breakfast)

Stowe, VT—Alpine-style home in Worcester Mountain Range
(nominated by American Country Collection of Bed &
Breakfast Homes and Country Inns)

THE MIDDLE ATLANTIC STATES

Washington, DC—Federal-style home
(nominated by The Bed & Breakfast League/Sweet Dreams &
Toast)

Washington, DC—Victorian mansion on Logan Circle
(nominated by Bed 'n' Breakfast Ltd. of Washington, DC)

New Castle, DE—Historic B&B on a cobblestone street
(nominated by Bed & Breakfast of Delaware)

Lutherville, MD—Victorian home in historic village
(nominated by Amanda's Bed & Breakfast Reservation
Service)

Queenstown, MD—"The House of Burgess"
(nominated by The Traveller in Maryland, Inc.)

Princeton, NJ—Victorian home near the university
(nominated by Bed & Breakfast of Princeton)

Readington, NJ—Restored country barn
(nominated by Bed & Breakfast Adventures)

Elizabethtown, PA—"West Ridge" Guest House
(nominated by Hershey Bed & Breakfast Reservation Service)

Lancaster, PA—Victorian house on the Conestoga River
(nominated by Bed & Breakfast of Lancaster County)

Reading, PA—Victorian mansion
(nominated by Bed & Breakfast of Philadelphia)

Springtown, PA—"Wildernest" B&B in Bucks County
(nominated by Bed & Breakfast of Southeast Pennsylvania)

Valley Forge, PA—22-room Victorian home
(nominated by All About Town—B&B in Philadelphia)

West Chester, PA—Italianate country manor house
(nominated by Guesthouses)

Charleston, SC—1759 carriage house
(nominated by Historic Charleston Bed and Breakfast)

Alexandria, VA—"Home of Washington's brother"
(nominated by Princely Bed & Breakfast Ltd.)

Norfolk, VA—Victorian town house in Ghent area
(nominated by Bed & Breakfast of Tidewater Virginia)

Richmond, VA—1908 restored "Summerhouse"
(nominated by Bensonhouse of Richmond and Williamsburg)

THE GREAT LAKES AREA

Chicago, IL—Studio apartment in center of town
(nominated by Bed & Breakfast/Chicago, Inc.)

Cincinnati, OH—Town house on Mt. Auburn
(nominated by Ohio Valley Bed & Breakfast)

Delaware, OH (near Columbus)—"Delaware Manor"
(nominated by Buckeye Bed & Breakfast)

Sturgeon Bay, WI—Modern home overlooking water
(nominated by Bed & Breakfast Guest Homes)

THE NORTHWEST & GREAT PLAINS

Oelwein, IA—B&B in Amish community
(nominated by Bed & Breakfast in Iowa, Ltd.)

Helena, MT—Victorian home in the state capital
(nominated by Bed & Breakfast Western Adventure)

Laverne, ND—1926 farmhouse in fishing country
(nominated by Oh West B&B)

Hood Canal, WA—Waterfront mansion
(nominated by Traveller's Bed & Breakfast)

Seattle, WA—Hilltop Colonial
(nominated by Pacific Bed & Breakfast)

THE SOUTHEASTERN STATES

Montgomery, AL—"Red Bluff Cottage"
(nominated by Bed & Breakfast Montgomery)

Jupiter, FL—Contemporary a block from the ocean
(nominated by Bed & Breakfast of the Florida Keys, Inc.)

Miami, FL—Luxury cottage
(nominated by Bed & Breakfast Co. Tropical Florida)

Tampa, FL—Waterfront B&B
(nominated by B&B Suncoast Accommodations)

Atlanta, GA—Home in downtown area
(nominated by Atlanta Hospitality)

Atlanta, GA—Tudor home just off Peachtree Road
(nominated by Bed & Breakfast Atlanta)

Thomasville, GA—Victorian mansion
(nominated by Quail Country Bed & Breakfast Ltd.)

Lovington, KY (near Cincinnati)—Amos Shinkle Townhouse
(nominated by author and local residents)

Midway, KY—1795 Federal-style house
(nominated by Bluegrass Bed & Breakfast)

Meridian, MI—B&B home in garden setting
(nominated by Lincoln Ltd. Bed & Breakfast; Mississippi
Reservation Service)

Memphis, TN—Contemporary apartment with river view
(nominated by Bed & Breakfast in Memphis)

THE SOUTHWEST & SOUTH CENTRAL STATES

Calico Rock, AR—Contemporary home in woodland
(nominated by Arkansas & Ozarks Bed & Breakfast)

Boulder, CO—Modernized "miner's cabin"
(nominated by Bed & Breakfast Colorado, Ltd.)

Grand Lake, CO—Hand-hewn log lodge
(nominated by Bed & Breakfast Rocky Mountains)

Lafayette, LA—Antebellum Acadian mansion
(nominated by Southern Comfort Bed & Breakfast
Reservation Service)

New Orleans, LA—Private guest cottages near French
Quarter
(nominated by Bed & Breakfast, Inc. Reservation Service)

New Orleans, LA—Tudor mansion on St. Charles Avenue
(nominated by Peggy Linsay Enterprises)

New Orleans, LA—Private guesthouse with garden view
(nominated by New Orleans Bed & Breakfast)

Branson, MO—Contemporary in "Shepherd of the Hills"
country
(nominated by Ozark Mountain Country Bed & Breakfast)

Kansas City, MO—Southmoreland in Country Club Plaza
(nominated by Bed & Breakfast Kansas City)

Santa Cruz, NM—Old adobe fort restored to B&B
(nominated by Bed & Breakfast of New Mexico)

Hill Country, TX—"The Blackburn House"
(nominated by Bed & Breakfast of Fredericksburg)

San Antonio, TX—Terrell Castle
(nominated by Bed & Breakfast Hosts of San Antonio)

CALIFORNIA & THE WEST

Scottsdale, AZ—Spanish contemporary in Paradise Valley
(nominated by Bed & Breakfast Scottsdale and the West)

Sedona, AZ—Historic ranch estate
(nominated by B&B Reservation Services)

Sedona, AZ—Spanish Colonial home
(nominated by Mi Casa Su Casa)

Tucson, AZ—Hacienda in the foothills of the Santa Catalina
Mountains
(nominated by Old Pueblo Homestays)

La Jolla, CA—B&B one block from the Pacific Ocean
(nominated by El Camino Real Bed & Breakfast)

Napa Valley, CA—1852 Victorian house
(nominated by Wine Country Reservations)

Pasadena, CA—Colonial ranch-style home
(nominated by Eye Openers Bed & Breakfast Reservations)

Pancho Palos Verdes, CA—Colonial ranch on private beach
(nominated by Bed & Breakfast Rent-a-Room)

San Francisco, CA—Queen Anne Victorian
(nominated by Bed & Breakfast International)

San Francisco, CA—B&B on Nob Hill
(nominated by Bed & Breakfast San Francisco)

Santa Rosa, CA—Redwood country home
(nominated by Wine Country Bed & Breakfast)

Whittier, CA—B&B near Disneyland
(nominated by Cohost, America's Bed & Breakfast)

ALASKA & HAWAII

Anchorage, AK—B&B in the downtown area
(nominated by Accommodations Alaska Style—Stay with a
Friend)

Fairbanks, AK—New home near the downtown area
(nominated by Fairbanks Bed & Breakfast)

Big Island of Hawaii, HI—Executive mansion—

setting for famous current movie (nominated by Go Native . . . Hawaii)

Kailua, Oahu, HI—Elegant oceanfront home
(nominated by Bed & Breakfast Hawaii)

Vancouver area, BC, CANADA—Brunswick beach house
(nominated by AB&C Old English Bed & Breakfast Registry)

Vancouver, BC, CANADA—"The Bavarian" large family home
(nominated by Vancouver Bed & Breakfast, Ltd.)

Victoria, BC, CANADA—"Sea Rose" bungalow on the ocean
(nominated by V.I.P. Bed & Breakfast, Ltd.)

Rednersville, Ontario, CANADA—Century-old home
(nominated by Bed & Breakfast Prince Edward County)

Wiarton, Ontario, CANADA—Restored mansion
(nominated by Country Host)

Ottawa, CANADA—Large heritage home near Parliament
(nominated by Ottawa Area Bed & Breakfast)

5

DIRECTORY OF B&B RESERVATION SERVICES AND SELECTED B&B INNS IN NORTH AMERICA

National and Regional B&B
Reservation Services

AMERICAN HISTORIC HOMES BED & BREAKFAST
P.O. BOX 336, DANA POINT, CA 92629

Offers B&B Homes In: 500 locations throughout the United States
Reservations Phone: 714/496-6953
Phone Hours: 9am to 5pm Monday through Friday
Price Range of Homes: On request.
Breakfast Included in Price: Continental or full American; some specialties are cinnamon rolls, freshly ground coffee, smoked meats, fresh-baked breads, and "recipes from the Gold Rush days in Mother Lode Country"
Reservations Should be Made: Two weeks in advance (last minute reservations accepted if possible)

BED & BREAKFAST INTERNATIONAL
1181-B SOLANO AVENUE ALBANY, CA 94706

Offers B&B Homes In: private or commercial accommodations in all areas of California with focus on San Francisco, Carmel, Los Angeles, the Wine Country, coastal, and mountain regions. We also have homes in Las Vegas, Chicago, and Hawaii.
Reservations Phone: Toll free 800/872-4500
Phone Hours: 8:30 to 5pm Monday through Friday and until noon on Saturday
Price Range of Homes: $55 to $125 double occupancy
Brochure Available: Free
Reservations Should Be Made: Two weeks in advance

Best B&Bs
■ This 1880 Queen Anne Victorian home in San Francisco, California, has been exquisitely restored in every detail from the intricate parquet floors and Lycrista wallpaper to the delicate ogee stained-glass win-

dows. Located directly opposite historic Buena Vista Park, it is within easy access to freeways and downtown. (Top 100.)

■ B&B in Pacific Heights, one of San Francisco, California's finest neighborhoods. This two-room cottage is in the back garden of a beautifully restored 1876 Victorian home. It is handsomely decorated, opens onto a patio, and can be entered through a side gate. Many shops and restaurants nearby.

■ Elegant houseboat in Sausalito, across the bay from San Francisco, California, furnished with antiques and a fine art collection. It has water views throughout and a view of Mt. Tamalpais from the kitchen and deck. Restaurants are within walking distance. The rooms are bright, clean, and very comfortably furnished.

■ Exceptional home in Pebble Beach, California, located in one of the most beautiful spots in the U.S. Just off the 17-mile drive in Carmel and a short walk to tidal pools and sandy beach. It is a two-story redwood home furnished in antiques and contains the host's artwork as well.

■ San Diego, California, B&B. Gracious four-bedroom, four-bath home furnished in antiques. It has three fireplaces and a lovely garden patio. It is within walking distance of the ocean, a park, and restaurants. The host was born in Ireland and is very familiar with bed-and-breakfast.

■ A beautifully restored farmhouse in Sonoma, California (wine country), which has historical status and has been photographed for magazines. An old stonecutter's cottage on the property has been renovated for guests. The cottage is in a garden setting, surrounded by countryside studded with giant oaks. It is a short walk to Sonoma Plaza with gourmet restaurants. Wineries are within walking distance and hot springs are nearby.

■ A unique lakefront home in Tahoe City, California, that was built of hand-hewn stone in 1928 by Italian stonemasons. The home is tastefully furnished and has a circular stairway leading to the guestrooms. A ski boat is available by advance arrangements for an additional charge. Restaurants and ski areas nearby.

THE BED & BREAKFAST LEAGUE/SWEET DREAMS & TOAST
P.O. BOX 9490, WASHINGTON, DC 20016

Offers B&B Homes In: Washington, DC, and adjacent suburbs
Reservations: 202/363-7767

Phone Hours: 9am to 5pm Monday through Thursday, to 1pm on Friday

Price Range of Homes: $35 to $100 single, $45 to $105 double

Breakfast Included in Price: Continental, although a few hosts do offer a full breakfast

Brochure Available: Free if you enclose a stamped, self-addressed no. 10 envelope

Reservations Should Be Made: As far in advance as possible (accepts last-minute reservations when possible); two-night minimum

Attractions Near the B&B Homes: All of the attractions of the nation's capital, including the White House, Smithsonian museums, National Gallery of Art, National Zoo, U.S. Capitol

Major Schools, Universities Near the B&B Homes: Georgetown, George Washington, American

Best B&Bs

■ Beautifully preserved 1850 home near the U.S. Capitol in Washington, DC. This Federal-style house has the original woodwork and is furnished with many antiques, Waterford crystal chandeliers, and working fireplaces in the parlor and dining room. The first floor suite has a bedroom with queen-size bed, a living room with double Murphy bed, dining area, complete kitchen, and a large private bath. It has a separate entrance. The master bedroom has a queen-size bed and sitting area with fireplace and a large, two-room bath with Jacuzzi, sauna, and steamroom. The third floor guest suite has one bedroom with an antique double bed. You can walk to the Capitol just two blocks away. There is offstreet parking for two guest cars (an important feature in a crowded neighborhood where a parking spot for the night is a great prize). The hosts are both lobbyists on Capitol Hill. **(Top 100.)**

■ Victorian house in the Capitol Hill section, six blocks from the Capitol in Washington, DC. This B&B offers three guestrooms. One has a king-size bed and shared bath. The other two have one double bed and a shared bath. Both the Eastern Market and Union Station Metro stops are a 12- to 14-minute walk from the house. If you're interested in knowing more about the U.S. space program, this is the place to come. The host is an engineer in the program.

■ Four-story Victorian home in the DuPont Circle area of Washington, DC. The home is furnished with period furniture and the hosts' collection of folk art and porcelain. The guestrooms are large, with high ceilings and wonderful original woodwork along with antique furniture. A full breakfast is served on the deck. Guests are welcome to enjoy the deck, library, and a guest area with a refrigerator and small bar.

■ B&B in Lanier Heights/Adams Morgan section of Washington, DC. Adams Morgan is the hot new restaurant area in a city that loves restaurants. The Federal-style Victorian house has a third floor guest area with two guestrooms, a shared bath, and a small kitchen. Both bedrooms have color TVs and inflatable mattresses for children. Breakfast is served in the first floor dining room with a fireplace and the original plaster ornamentation. The house is a 10-minute walk from the Woodley Park–Zoo Metro stop. Offstreet parking for guests' cars. Your hosts are certainly interesting people. One is an independent film producer, the other an energy consultant.

■ B&B in Woodley Park area of Washington, DC. The National Zoo and a number of embassies are located in this area. In fact, this elegant old house is right across the street from the Swiss Embassy Park and the guestroom windows overlook this park. Want to know about what's new in Washington art? The host works at one of the small museums in the city and is extremely knowledgeable about the city's art scene.

■ Hillside home in the Kent section of Washington, DC. Close to Georgetown and the Potomac River. This B&B is in a secluded, very quiet area. Because the house is built on a hill, it has several levels that provide extra privacy for the guestrooms. The hosts are a defense analyst and an artist.

BED & BREAKFAST U.S.A. LTD.
OLD SHEFFIELD RD., S. EGREMONT, MA 01258

Offers B&B Homes In: All over New York State, Florida, Western Massachusetts, Pennsylvania, and Washington, DC
Reservations Phone: 800/255-7213
Phone Hours: 10am to 9pm Monday to Wednesday, 10am to 5pm Thursday and Friday, 1pm to 4pm Saturday
Price Range of Homes: $20 to $75 single daily, $30 to $225 double daily
Breakfast Included in Price: Continental or full American (juice, eggs, bacon, toast, coffee)
Brochure Available: For $5.25
Reservations Should Be Made: Two weeks in advance (last-minute reservations accepted if possible)

Attractions Near the B&B Homes: Sleepy Hollow Restorations, Lyndhurst Castle, Rye Playland, Caramoor Music Festival, Murcoot Park, Boscobel and Hyde Park mansions, Croton Clearwater Revival, Cold Spring antiquing, Baseball Hall of Fame, Howe Caverns, Corning

Glass, Saratoga, Tanglewood Music Festival, Vanderbilt Mansion, ice caves, plus the attractions of New York City and the Berkshires
Major Schools, Universities Near the B&B Homes: Sarah Lawrence, Iona, Manhattanville, Pace, Vassar, Westchester Community College, SUNY New Paltz, Ithaca College, Cornell, Hamilton & Kirkland, Colgate, Skidmore, Russell Sage, Rensselaer Polytechnic Institute, Elmira College, Columbia

Best B&Bs

■ Federal Colonial mansion in Churchtown, Pennsylvania. This B&B puts you right in the heart of Pennsylvania Dutch Country. You will have plenty of diversions here: a piano, TV, VCR. The breakfast room is filled with antiques. *Insider's Tip:* The host can arrange for you to have dinner with a nearby Amish family, a warm and unusual experience.

CHRISTIAN HOSPITALITY

636 UNION ST., BLACK FRIAR BROOK FARM, DUXBURY, MA 02332

Offers B&B Homes In: The New England states, also in New York, New Jersey, Virginia, Maryland, Tennessee, and Florida
Reservations Phone: 617/834-8528
Phone Hours: 9am to 9pm Monday through Saturday
Price Range of Homes: $35 to $50 single, $35 to $85 double
Breakfast Included in Price: Continental or full American
Brochure Available: Free if you send a stamped, self-addressed no. 10 envelope
Reservations Should Be Made: Two weeks in advance (can accept some last-minute reservations)

Attractions Near the B&B Homes: Historic homes of Boston, the Plymouth, and Cape Cod areas, White Mountains and Green Mountains, Walt Disney World
Major Schools, Universities Near the B&B Homes: Boston College, Gordan College, Stonehill

Best B&Bs

■ Historic salt-box house in Duxbury, Massachusetts. Whatever happened to all of the descendants of the Pilgrims who landed with the Mayflower? We do know about the grandson of Pilgrim George Soule because he built this house in 1708 on grant land from the King of England. As a guest, you can relax in a quiet rural setting on a brick patio, or take a walk on the nearby beach. Gunstalk beams throughout the house remind you of its early origins. Good homey headquarters for a tour of Plymouth, Cape Cod, or Boston. (Top 100.)

■ B&B in Lexington, Massachusetts, near Concord and Boston. You have a view of the Battle Green, site of the first battle for American independence. Hosts of this elegant historic home welcome you with afternoon tea served by a fireplace in the study. Twin stairs lead guests to a second floor sitting room, also with fireplace. The master suite has yet *another* fireplace.

■ B&B in Enfield in the Sunapee Region of New Hampshire. A turn-of-the-century home right on Crystal Lake. You can swim in the lake or walk amidst the pines. A cross-country skiing area is nearby. The host will serve "a real New England breakfast."

■ An 1800 house in Bellows Falls, Vermont. Near Brattleboro and Keene, New Hampshire. Once young school children pranced across the wide oak floors (it was a rural school in the 1920s). After a day of skiing or sightseeing, relax by the library fireplace, sipping a little cider.

■ Red barn B&B in Annapolis, Maryland. Located right on the cove of the Severn River. This barn was built in 1850 and has been restored to a comfortable home with a great room with fireplace. Sit on the private deck overlooking the cove (on nice days breakfast is served on this deck).

■ B&B in Arlington, Virginia. This Victorian home was built in 1899 and now completely restored without losing such touches as a stained-glass butterfly weathervane and period antiques. A convenient place to stay when you're touring Washington, DC.

■ Brownstone triplex in New York City, NY. Close to the Museum of Natural History. *Tip to Business Travelers:* Hosts are involved with a catering business and will arrange for a complete gourmet dinner for you and your guests at a cost of $25 per person, plus the cost of the food. This could be a home-entertaining touch to a business meeting.

■ Island waterfront home in Miami Beach, Florida. In addition to the great water views, the big attraction is the unusual pool—a home for tropical fish and plants as well as people. Also a hot tub nearby. If you come by private boat, you can tie up at their dock.

COHOST, AMERICA'S BED & BREAKFAST
P.O. BOX 9302, WHITTIER, CA 90608

Offers B&B Homes In: Northern and Southern California and in many other states

Reservations Phone: 213/699-8427
Phone Hours: 8am to 9pm daily, or anytime on answering machine
Price Range of Homes: $35 to $55 single, $45 to $75 double
Breakfast Included in Price: Full breakfast; hosts specialize in regional foods, such as a typical Mexican breakfast with huevos rancheros
and tortillas, or country biscuits and gravy with ham and eggs, or
eggs Benedict and fruit compotes
Brochure Available: $1 if you send a stamped, self-addressed no. 10
envelope
Reservations Should Be Made: Two weeks in advance (last-minute
reservations accepted if possible)

Best B&Bs

■ Luxurious home in Whittier, near many of California's top attractions
—from Disneyland and Knotts Berry Farm to Universal Studios. You will
be located just five minutes from California's convenient (and sometimes
frightening) freeway system in an area that is both private and exotic
(with numerous plants). You will have a great view of the greater Los
Angeles area from the deck, including Long Beach and Catalina Island.
Breakfast is Southern-style and really special here, with bacon, sausage
or ham, eggs, potatoes or grits, and fresh fruit—or sometimes mixed
with regional California specialties such as huevos rancheros, tortillas,
and yogurt parfaits. The host will arrange pickup at the airport (at
prices competitive with those of local bus service), plan and escort
tours, take care of babies, provide laundry service, and even host patio
brunches or dinners for guests. Complimentary refreshments served include wine and hors d'oeuvres. Your room has extra long beds.
Offstreet parking and a private entrance make this an ideal headquarters for touring Southern California. "Well-behaved" children acceptable. Many glowing testimonials from guests, including this one from a
couple celebrating their anniversary: "The breakfast was fantastic.
Thank you also for keeping our champagne cold. You have a beautiful
home. We enjoyed the patio, even the raccoon." (Top 100.)

■ *Author's tip:* Don't miss the Universal Studios Tour when you're staying
in this part of California. The "earthquake" in a subway station is
probably the most realistic adventure you would probably want to
experience. (Not for the faint of heart but many kids seem to love it.)

■ Ranch-style home in suburban Los Angeles, California. Has an
unobstructed view of the ocean. The hosts will share membership privileges with you in the private beach club right across the road. Breakfast
specialties include honey-baked ham, French toast, or quiche.

■ Home in Newport Beach, California. When you stay here, you'll be
near the tip of the Balboa Peninsula. Special decorative touches: used
brick and natural wood, stained-glass windows; and a raised-hearth

fireplace. Located about 40 minutes from Disneyland. Daily ferry service to Catalina Island (May to October).

COVERED BRIDGE BED & BREAKFAST
P.O. BOX 447, NORFOLK, CT 06058

Offers B&B Homes In: Cornwall, Kent, Sharon, Norfolk, New Hartford, Litchfield, Lakeville, and other towns in the northwest corner of Connecticut; the Berkshires—Lenox, Great Barrington, Sheffield, Stockbridge, Williamstown—in Massachusetts; Shaftesbury in Vermont; East Haddam, Old Mystic, North Stonington, Fairfield, and Norwalk in southern Connecticut; also New York and Rhode Island
Reservations Phone: 203/542-5944
Phone Hours: 10am to 7pm daily
Price Range of Homes: $50 to $150 single, $55 to $150 double
Breakfast Included in Price: Most offer full breakfast or Continental plus (cereals, homemade breads and muffins, juices, fruit, coffee, tea)
Brochure Available: Free; booklet available for $3
Reservations Should Be Made: Two weeks in advance (last-minute reservations accepted if possible)

Attractions Near the B&B Homes: Tanglewood Music Festival, Williamstown Theater, Jacob's Pillow, Sharon Playhouse, Norfolk Chamber Music Festival, Music Mountain, Appalachian Trail, whitewater canoeing, skiing, antiques, Lime Rock car racing, state parks, White Flower Farm
Major Schools, Universities Near the B&B Homes: Williams, Bennington, Simon's Rock at Bard, Hotchkiss, Kent, Salisbury, Berkshire, Indian Mountain Gunnery, Taft, Vassar, University of Connecticut, Connecticut College, Coast Guard Academy

Best B&Bs

■ Elegant 1898 Victorian Tudor estate in Norfolk, Connecticut, set on five landscaped acres. The grounds include extensive perennial gardens and a gazebo. Tiffany windows surround the library, living, and dining rooms. The antique-decorated guestrooms, several with fireplaces, canopies, and balconies, offer a romantic retreat. A full breakfast which includes herbs and berries from the owners' garden and honey from their beehives, is served in the dining room, in the gazebo, or guests can treat themselves to breakfast in bed **(Top 100.)**

■ 1861 Victorian home set in historic N. Stonington, Connecticut, close to Mystic. Fond memories of years spent traveling in England inspired the hosts to furnish their home in the Georgian manner with formal antique furniture and accessories, many of which are offered for sale. The four guestrooms have four-poster canopy beds. A full English breakfast is served in the elegant dining room. An 1820 Victorian house adjoins the main house by a landscaped courtyard. The whole house can be reserved, which includes two bedrooms, living room, and kitchen, or the bedrooms can be reserved individually.

■ 1800's Colonial home within walking distance of the village center of Lenox, Massachusetts. There are several common rooms for the guests including a living room with a wood-burning stove. The seven guestrooms are decorated with the owner's collection of antique quilts. A Continental breakfast is served in the pleasant dining room.

■ 1841 Georgian Colonial home in Hopewell Junction, New York. Built for a prominent Dutch silversmith, it is set on six acres which include lovely perennial gardens and a pool. The house has six fireplaces with double living rooms that are adorned with large imported crystal chandeliers and a fabulous sunroom which overlooks the grounds. The common rooms and the four guestrooms are all beautifully decorated with antiques, some of which the owners collected when they lived in France. A full country breakfast is served by the host who attended the Culinary Institute of America.

■ Early 1900s beach home in Haversham, Rhode Island, which the artist/architect owner has redone to create a spectacular home in a secluded setting overlooking a salt-water pond and with a view of the ocean. A private beach is a short bike ride away. There are two guestrooms in the main house, one with a balcony, which are decorated with antiques and paintings done by the owner. There are also two cottages on the grounds. A Continental plus breakfast is served in the dining room or on the terrace overlooking the water.

■ 1700s Colonial farmhouse set on forty magnificent acres in New Hartford, Connecticut. The grounds include a spring-fed pond for swimming and fishing, a barn for horses, chickens and pigs, and beautiful flower gardens. There are several old brick fireplaces for guests to enjoy, a large living room with a sunporch next to it, and a big, old country kitchen. A full breakfast is served in the dining room, on the terrace, or by the pond. The four guestrooms are antique decorated and include two canopy beds.

The Northeastern States

CONNECTICUT

―――――――― B&B Reservation Services ――――――――

NUTMEG BED & BREAKFAST
222 GIRARD AVE., HARTFORD, CT 06105

Offers B&B Homes In: Connecticut, Rhode Island, Berkshires of New York and Massachusetts (190 homes)
Reservations Phone: 203/236-6698
Phone Hours: 9:30am to 5pm Monday through Friday
Price Range of Homes: $40 to $70 single, $45 to $105 double
Breakfast Included in Price: Continental or full American; many homes serve full breakfast, often featuring their own specialties
Brochure Available: $5 for a complete directory
Reservations Should Be Made: Two weeks in advance (last-minute reservations accepted if possible). Credit Card number required to hold reservations: MasterCard, Visa, American Express

Attractions Near the B&B Homes: Mystic Seaport, Sturbridge Village, Tanglewood, Litchfield County, etc. (guests are advised of attractions in the area before arrival)
Major Schools, Universities Near the B&B Homes: Yale, Wesleyan, Trinity, Coast Guard Academy, Hotchkiss, Kent, Pomfret, Lakeville, Choate, Rosemary Hall, Wallingford and Miss Porter's Farmington prep schools

Best B&Bs
■ This new center-chimney Colonial home in Lyme, Connecticut, was built as your hosts' dream home. It's located on several acres of woods and has its own walking trail and horseshoe court. Your hosts are well traveled so their deluxe breakfast includes varied European dishes. The two comfortable guestrooms each have private bath with shower; one has a beautiful queensized canopy bed, and the second has antique twin beds. This hilltop B&B is convenient to the Old Lyme Art Center, all shoreline attractions, and many outstanding restaurants. (We designate this our best based on the wonderful written comments we have received from all of the guests) (Top 100.)

Inn-to-inn vacations in New England: Would you like to hopscotch across New England, staying in posh inns at every stop as you pursue your own personal interests? The Country Inn Collection is an association that can send you a free brochure that will help you plan such a vacation, e.g. an antique inn tour or a country inn tour. You can reserve all of the inns along the way with one phone call, and pay a package price for the whole vacation. You can charge the trip on major credit cards. For more information and a free brochure, call 1-800-852-INNS.

Would you like a comprehensive, four-color map of New England that shows the location of over 300 hotels, motels, resorts, country inns, and B&Bs? This map can be particularly handy when you're trying to navigate country roads. Send $3 to New England Innkeepers, P.O. Box 1089, North Hampton, NH 03862.

■ B&B in Essex, Connecticut, with the Connecticut River as its backyard. It's close to many area attractions—20 miles from Mystic Seaport, close to Hammonasset public beach in Madison, theaters, and fine restaurants. Two guestrooms, one with a double canopy bed and one with twin beds. Both rooms share a bath and a great view of the river. Your host is a boating enthusiast. If you share her passion for sailing, she loves to swap sea stories. The full breakfast is served on the glass-enclosed porch, with another river view.

■ Italianate Victorian house in Westport, Connecticut. In this artist/writer/ad folk community you might see Paul Newman shopping on the street. At this B&B you will see a formal garden, grape arbor, brook, terrace and sculpture studio. The guestroom looks out over all this lovely space and has a double bed and private bath. The hosts are well-known artists, and their work is beautifully interspersed with their furnishings. Breakfast is served in the formal dining room.

■ Log cabin in Stony Creek, Connecticut. You are hardly roughing it here in a large double-bedded guestroom, with the use of a pull-out queen-size sofabed in the living room. The kitchenette is fully stocked for an elegant breakfast. At night you can turn to such diversions as a stereo and TV, or warm yourself around a wood-burning stove. Ah, wilderness.

■ Restored Victorian home near downtown Hartford, Connecticut. Located on an attractive residential street, this B&B offers such surprises as a billiard room with a king-size bed. The pink room has a double bed with semi-private bath. Both rooms are air conditioned.

■ Vintage Colonial home in Salisbury, Connecticut. Your choice of two guestrooms or a suite. This is a handy place to stay if you have children attending some of the many private schools that dot beautiful Litchfield County, which is great photo country if you like to snap great old churches and magnificent giant trees. Breakfast includes fresh juice and homemade baked goods. It can be served on the screen porch overlooking the water.

BED & BREAKFAST LTD.
P.O. BOX 216, NEW HAVEN, CT 06513

Offers B&B Homes In: Connecticut; Providence and Newport, Rhode Island; and selected Massachusetts areas
Reservations Phone: 203/469-3260
Phone Hours: 5 to 9:30pm weekdays and 24 hours weekends during the academic year; in summer, 24 hours daily
Price Range of Homes: $40 to $50 single, $50 to $75 double
Breakfast Included in Price: Continental or full American; varies with individual home
Brochure Available: Free if you send a stamped, self-addressed no. 10 envelope; call to assure availability
Reservations Should Be Made: Prefer one week in advance (last-minute reservations accepted if possible)

Attractions Near the B&B Homes: New Haven Coliseum, Long Wharf Theater, Powder Ridge ski area, Shubert Theater, Connecticut shore, Mystic Seaport, Peabody and British art museums, antique shops, historic country villages
Major Schools, Universities Near the B&B Homes: Yale, Wesleyan, Southern Connecticut State, Albertus Magnus, Hopkins, Choate, Milford Academy, Hamden Hall, Coast Guard Academy, Taft

Best B&Bs
■ 1770 home near New Haven, Connecticut, on six acres. "This is a gorgeous home!" says the reservation service. "It is the most 'bed-and-breakfast' looking home we represent. Every room is filled with antiques." One suite available. Jacuzzi and private bath. (Top 100.)

■ Colonial home in Greenwich, Connecticut. If you've been to Greenwich, you know what a lovely (rich!) town this is. You can stay in a carefully restored home near the water which has three fireplaces and a formal garden.

_____ **B&B Inns** _____

COPPER BEECH INN
MAIN STREET, IVORYTON, CT 06442

Reservations Phone: 203/767-0330
Description: This is a gracious home in a woodland setting with
wonderful gardens. There are four guestrooms in the main house and
nine additional rooms in the old carriage house.
Amenities: Complimentary breakfast of fresh fruit, cold cereals, freshly
baked French breakfast pastries, juice, coffee or tea

Nearby Attractions: The village of Essex with charming old homes, the
Essex Steam Train, antiques shops, Gillette Castle, the Goodspeed
Opera House, Ivoryton Playhouse, local beaches
Special Services: Picnic lunches available. Jacuzzi baths in carriage
house rooms
Rates: $100 to $160 double in high season (May through October)

HOMESTEAD INN AND MOTEL
5 ELM ST., NEW MILFORD, CT 06776

Reservations Phone: 203/354-4080
Description: All the rooms in this 140-year-old Victorian inn have been
recently renovated. The front porch overlooks the town green. Rooms
in the motel are also available to guests.
Amenities: Expanded Continental breakfast, all private baths

Nearby Attractions: Lake Waramug, Indian Archeological Institute, two
wineries, art galleries, museums
Special Services: Innkeeper in residence 24 hours a day for your
convenience
Rates: $56 to $72 single, $65 to $85 double

MAINE

———— **B&B Reservation Services** ————

BED & BREAKFAST OF MAINE
32 COLONIAL VILLAGE, FALMOUTH, ME 04105

Offers B&B Homes In: Maine
Reservations Phone: 207/781-4528
Phone Hours: 6 to 11pm, plus 24 hours daily via an answering
  machine
Price Range of Homes: $35 to $70 single, $40 to $150 double
Breakfast Included in Price: Full American; "We encourage hosts to
  serve hearty breakfasts. At least fresh breads and real butter; blue-
  berry pancakes are popular and fresh fruit cups and jams."
Brochure Available: $1
Reservations Should Be Made: Two months in advance for July
  through mid-October

Attractions Near the B&B Homes: Daily cruise to Nova Scotia, clam
  bakes, lobster festivals, craft shows, foliage tours, art festivals, island
  cruises, coastal resort activities
Major Schools, Universities Near the B&B Homes: U. of Maine,
  Bates, Maine Maritime, Northeastern, Westbrook, Bowdoin, Colby
  College

Best B&Bs
■ If you love antiques, have we got a place for you—in
Kennebunkport. This is reputed to be the oldest home in Maine (built in
1737) that currently offers B&B lodging. Restoration has continued for
many years in this classic New England Colonial home. Your host has
used her stenciling skills throughout the home to great effect. Your other
host is a former *New York Times* journalist who has traveled worldwide.
He speaks French and German. You are close to village shopping and
the beaches. A full country breakfast is served in the dining room next
to the fireplace lit on cool mornings. *Insider's Tip:* Ask for the room with
its own balcony. (Top 100.)

■ Large Greek Revival home in Newcastle, Maine, built in 1850. Step
right out the door for a wonderful view of the Damariscotta River.
Several of the guestrooms also have river views. Your hosts, former
college librarians, have filled the home with Victorian Baroque period
antiques as well as Colonial and primitive pieces. You can take a short

walk to the center of town or drive to the end of the Pemaquid Pennisula for the sandy beaches and coastal views. Bring along your camera to photograph the lighthouse and old fort. *Insider's Tip:* A single traveler willing to share a bathroom can get a room for as little as $40!

■ Victorian brownstone in Portland, Maine. This B&B is located in one of the nicest residential areas of the town. You can walk to the museum and some good restaurants. It is also close to the Maine Medical Center. Your hosts are retired professionals. All guestrooms have private baths.

■ Old house on Deer Isle in Stonington, Maine. The house overlooks Penobscot Bay (wonderful place for viewing the windjammers that ply these coastal waters). You reach Deer Isle by a two-lane bridge. *Insider's Tip:* Ask for the largest guestroom. It has a water view.

■ Refurbished home in Bass Harbor, Maine. Would you like to stay in a sea captain's home right on a knoll overlooking the ocean? You just found it. This B&B is close to the Oceanarium and the Gilley Bird Museum. Interested in woodcarving? The host is a woodcarver.

■ Contemporary home on Mount Desert Island, Southwest Harbor, Maine. The reservation organization describes this as "one of the prettiest spots on Mount Desert Island." From the glassed-in family room and the several decks, you can enjoy a fabulous view. The property borders Acadia National Park. You can begin your hike, or jog through the woods right from the back door. *Insider's Tip:* You can rent bicycles and canoes in the village.

BED & BREAKFAST DOWN EAST, LTD.

BOX 547, MACOMBER MILL ROAD, EASTBROOK, ME 04634

Offers B&B Homes In: Maine, statewide; including Acadia National Park, Mount Desert Island area, coastal, inland, rural, western lakes, and mountains
Reservations Phone: 207/565-3517
Phone Hours: 9am to 6pm Monday through Friday, to 11am on Saturday
Price Range of Homes: $40 to $60 singles, $45 to $90 double
Breakfast Included in Price: Most hosts give guests a choice between Continental and full American; some specialties served are blueberry scones, popovers, and "toad-in-a-hole"
Brochure Available: $3 for 45-page directory
Reservations Should Be Made: At least 2 weeks in advance (last-minute reservations accepted if possible)

Attractions Near the B&B Homes: Acadia National Park, Jackson Laboratory, Bar Harbor, scenic coastal areas, historic sites, museums, hiking trails; ski areas

Major Schools, Universities Near the B&B Homes: U. of Southern Maine, Portland, Gorham, Colby, Waterville, Bates, Lewiston, Bowdoin

Best B&Bs

▪ Federal home in Kennebunkport, Maine. Close to beaches, town, and restaurants. You have a choice of five guestrooms, three with private bath. You can spend some time in the large yard and talk with your hosts, a friendly couple who moved here from New Jersey in 1984.

▪ A 1772 home in Freeport, Maine. This home was built by O. Israel Bagley right before the start of the American Revolution. You can choose from five bedrooms that have handmade quilts and rugs. One room has a working fireplace. Be sure to see the kitchen—it has a huge fireplace and a beehive oven. Six acres of woods surround this B&B.

▪ Colonial home for animal lovers in Otisfield, Maine. The host describes the place as a "James Herriot" farm, an accurate description when you meet some of the eight resident dogs, eight cats, plus assorted rabbits and geese. As you might expect, the hosts are strong environmentalists and animal welfare advocates. But no, you can't bring your own pet (full house!).

▪ A stagecoach B&B in Waterford, Maine. This home was built in the late 1700s to soothe the weary bones of stagecoach passengers who had bounced over dirt roads all day long. It's now listed on the National Register of Historic Places. All rooms have private baths and two have their own porch. You can walk across the road to take a swim in the lake.

▪ Lakeside home in Bridgton, Maine. This home was built at the beginning of the 20th century, amidst some wonderful old oak and pine trees. The Victorian dining room has a corner fireplace. At night you might want to congregate in the parlor, which also has a fireplace, a library, a grand piano, and an organ. *Insider's Tip:* A barbecue, picnic table, and a canoe are free to guests, on private frontage on Highland Lake just across the road.

_____ **B&B Inns** _____

BLACK FRIAR INN
10 SUMMER ST., BAR HARBOR, ME 04609

Reservations Phone: 207/288-5091

Description: Restored Victorian home offers six guestrooms with queen-size beds and private baths.

Amenities: Full cooked breakfasts with homemade breads and cinnamon rolls. Afternoon refreshments and rainy-day teas.

Nearby Attractions: Acadia National Park, hiking, biking, canoeing

Special Services: Can arrange for fly fishing day trips with a registered Maine Guide.

Rates: $70 to $90 single, $75 to $95 double. Pre-season discounts to June 15 and after Columbus Day. Two-night minimum most of the season.

Innkeeper's Tip: "You can walk to the waterfront from the inn," says Barbara Kelly. "During July and August the Bar Harbor and Music Festivals, antique shows and many boat excursions keep Bar Harbor a busy place."

TOWN MOTEL AND GUEST HOUSE
12 ATLANTIC AVE., BAR HARBOR, ME 04609

Reservations Phone: 207/288-5548

Description: Combining old-fashioned comfort with modern convenience, the guestrooms have pull-chain "johns," marble sinks, and period furniture. Some rooms feature working fireplaces and porches.

Nearby Attractions: Acadia National Park, fishing, swimming, golf, tennis, restaurants

Special Services: Color TV

Rates: $35 single, $66 to $95 double

NORSEMAN INN
HCR-61, BOX 50, BETHEL, ME 04217

Reservations Phone: 207/824-2002

Description: This newly renovated, 200-year-old building complex sits on four acres of land in the western foothills of Maine.

Amenities: Full breakfast with fruit of the season, as available

Nearby Attractions: Excellent hiking and camping facilities, downhill and cross-country skiing
Special Services: Activity room, living room with large fireplace, lounge with bar service
Rates: $60 single, $75 double, in winter; $40 single, $48 double, in summer

BLUEHILL FARM COUNTRY INN
P.O. BOX 437, BLUE HILL, ME 04614

Reservations Phone: 207/374-5126
Description: An old turn-of-the-century farm situated at the foot of Blue Hill Mountain, all its rooms overlooking 48 acres of field, pond, and woods. A barn was recently added to provide seven new guest-rooms.
Amenities: Squeezed orange juice, fruit of the season, local Camembert cheese on fruit plate, their own granola, cereals, fresh-baked muffins, breads, or popovers—all served with fresh-ground coffee

Nearby Attractions: Acadia National Park, Kneisel Music Camp, Blue Hill Fair
Special Services: Snowshoeing and cross-country skiing
Rates: double, $68 to $78

TOPSIDE
MCKOWN HILL, BOOTHBAY HARBOR, ME 04538

Reservations Phone: 207/633-5404
Description: A historic sea captain's house furnished with antiques—all rooms have a private bath and a refrigerator.

Nearby Attractions: Reid State Park, Carousel Music Theater, Boothbay Dinner Theater, golf, boat rides
Rates: $80 single, $90 double, in summer; $50 single, $75 double, in spring and fall

ELMS BED AND BREAKFAST
84 ELM ST., RTE. 1, CAMDEN, ME 04843

Reservations Phone: 207/236-6250
Description: Colonial B&B inn built in 1806. "A couple-oriented inn" with romantic candles in the windows, and antique furnishings.
Amenities: Full country breakfast made with fresh herbs from the garden, creative egg dishes, French toast stuffed with poached peaches and sour cream, apple walnut loaf, honey-cured ham steaks, and muffins. A well-stocked library.

Nearby Attractions: Great mountain views
Rates: $50 to $90 double. Rates change seasonally
Innkeeper's Tip: Fine restaurants are nearby offering French, Italian, and Cajun cuisine. Ask us for directions.

WHITEHALL INN
52 HIGH ST. (P.O. BOX 558), CAMDEN, ME 04843

Reservations Phone: 207/236-3391
Description: This 1834 building has operated as an inn since 1901. Edna St. Vincent Millay recited her poetry here. Whitehall guests helped her at Vassar with a full scholarship. Inn houses a collection of Millay memorabilia. The inn is furnished with antiques and Oriental rugs. The porches have rocking chairs for the guests.
Amenities: Full country breakfast and dinner included

Nearby Attractions: Camden state parks, many accessible islands
Special Services: Tennis court
Rates: $80 single, $130 double, in summer
Innkeeper's Tip: "The world's largest passenger windjammer fleet sails from the harbor just a short walk from the Inn," writes J. D. Dwing. "With a waterfall downtown, flowerboxes hanging from the lamp posts, the harbor park, and the numerous gardens, Camden has often been called 'the prettiest town in Maine.' We certainly think it is."

LINCOLN HOUSE COUNTRY INN
LINCOLN HOUSE, DENNYSVILLE, ME 04628

Reservations Phone: 207/726-3953
Description: Built in 1787, this four-square Colonial sits on 95 acres

overlooking the Dennys River. The building has been carefully restored and has earned a place on the National Register of Historic Places.
Amenities: Full country breakfast; dinner is included.

Nearby Attractions: Campobello Island, Roosevelt International Park, Moosehorn National Wildlife Refuge, Cobscook State Park, Reversing Falls
Special Services: Salmon fishing, whale watching, swimming, tennis
Rates: $65 single, $130 double

CRAB APPLE ACRES INN
RTE. 201, THE FORKS, ME 04985

Reservations Phone: 207/663-2218
Description: This 1835 farmhouse on the Kennebec River has seven guestrooms and two shared baths. The new log lodge has six additional guestrooms with private baths. There are quilts on all beds and a wood-burning stove in the kitchen.
Amenities: Complimentary Continental breakfast is served.

Nearby Attractions: White-water rafting on the Kennebec River, Fall Foliage Festival (package trips available), canoeing, hunting, fishing, cross-country skiing
Special Services: They will make full arrangements for your rafting trips.
Rates: $44 to $50 double with shared baths, $56 to $61 double with private baths.

COVESIDE
NORTH END ROAD, FIVE ISLANDS, GEORGETOWN, ME 04548

Reservations Phone: Toll free 800/326-2807
Description: Nestled on the shore of a quiet cove with herons and lobster boats, Coveside has three rooms comfortably furnished in New England antiques, all with a water view. There is a hot tub on the deck and a boat at the dock.
Amenities: Full three-course breakfast served on the deck in season, a coffee tray at the door when you awaken, terry robes and bedtime sweets in each room. Smoke-free.

Nearby Attractions: Boating and fishing, sailing charters, fine restaurants, 1½-mile-long beach at Reid State Park, cross-country skiing.

Special Services: Large, sunny deck, sitting room with books and games, winter/spring theme weekend special packages. Carriage house adjacent has two three-room suites available weekly in season. Brand new, completely furnished.

Rates: $89 per room; suites $600/week. Children under 12 in suites only. No pets.

COUNTRY AT HEART B&B

37 BOW STREET, FREEPORT, ME 04032

Reservations Phone: 207/865-0512

Description: This 1870 country home has been converted to a small B&B inn with three guest rooms, each with a unique decor. The "Teddy Bear Room" is decorated with stuffed animals. The "Shaker Room" has Shaker-reproduction furniture and Shaker-style wall pegs for clothes, and the "Quilt" room has antique quilts on the wall. There is also a gift shop especially for guests.

Amenities: A full breakfast is served, including specialties such as heart-shaped waffles, ham/cheese french toast.

Nearby Attractions: Outdoor attractions of Maine, plus all of the discount/factory outlet shops of Freeport. The L.L. Bean Factory Outlet and Retail Store is only two blocks away.

Special Services: One of the owners is also a veteran tour bus operator. He will help map out driving tours for guests.

Rates: $55 to $65 single; $65 to $75 double. Seasonal discount in the winter.

Innkeeper's Tip: Mrs. R. Dubay says, "Be sure to let us know if you're coming for a special occasion such as an anniversary. We'll have a chilled bottle of champagne waiting in the room to help you celebrate."

THE GREEN HERON INN

OCEAN AVENUE (P.O. BOX 2578), KENNEBUNKPORT, ME 04046

Reservations Phone: 207/967-3315

Description: Built in 1908 on an inlet of the Kennebunk River, 300 yards from the ocean, this inn has no two rooms alike. Each room has private bath and color TV.

Amenities: A hearty breakfast included in the room rate

Nearby Attractions: Colonial village with historic houses. Trolley Museum, beaches, shops, art galleries
Rates: $44 to $65 single, $60 to $85 double; special rates by the week or month

THE INN ON WINTER'S HILL
P.O. BOX 44, KINGFIELD, ME 04947

Reservations Phone: 207/265-5421
Description: This gracious old mansion sits above the three graceful curves of the Carrabassett River. The architect/owner restored this old Victorian mansion with care and furnished it in the proper style, right down to the stuffed armadillo over the fireplace in the parlor, mid-18th-century portraits, and Egyptian knickknacks.
Amenities: Continental breakfast

Nearby Attractions: Sugarloaf, Robert Trent Jones golf course, whitewater rafting, tennis court, Stanley Museum
Special Services: Swimming pool, outdoor hot tub
Rates: $95 to $139 double

PUFFIN INN BED & BREAKFAST
233 MAIN ST. (P.O. BOX 2232), OGUNQUIT, ME 03907

Reservations Phone: 207/646-5496
Description: This 150-year-old sea captain's home, tastefully decorated with period furniture, is set on landscaped grounds abounding with flowers.
Amenities: Continental breakfast. Occasional surprises include home-baked blueberry cornbread.

Nearby Attractions: Perkins Cove, Ogunquit Playhouse, Rachel Carson Wildlife Preserve, Marginal Way (a footpath along the rocky coast)
Special Services: Guidance in planning your day and a local map
Rates: $55 to $75 double

CRAIGNAIR INN
CLARK ISLAND ROAD, SPRUCEHEAD, ME 04859

Reservations Phone: 207/594-7644
Description: The inn is set in a tiny town of 100, formerly a boarding house for workers from the granite quarry, overlooking the ocean and Clark Cove.
Amenities: Full breakfast with fruit from the garden, eggs, bacon, sausage, muffins, cereal, coffee and tea; full-service restaurant featuring local seafood

Nearby Attractions: Lighthouse, ferry to offshore islands, Montpelier (Gen. H. Knox's home), Monhegan Island
Special Services: Pickup service, swimming in an old quarry
Rates: $40 single, $65 double, in summer; $36 single, $57 double, in winter; rates include breakfast

EAST WIND INN AND MEETING HOUSE
MECHANIC STREET (P.O. BOX 149), TENANTS HARBOR, ME 04860

Reservations Phone: 207/372-6366
Description: An authentic coastal inn, the three-story frame building, with a wrap-around porch, is located at the water's edge. It's furnished with period antiques, and singles, doubles, and suites are available.

Nearby Attractions: Farnsworth Art Museum, Owls Head Transportation, ferry to Monhegan Island, Vinalhaven, and Islesboro, antique shops, lighthouses, and movie theaters
Special Services: The French sloop *Surprise* leaves from the wharf daily
Rates: $68 to $130 double in summer, $80 to $100 double in winter

DOCKSIDE GUEST QUARTERS
HARRIS ISLAND ROAD (P.O. BOX 205), YORK, ME 03909

Reservations Phone: 207/363-2868
Description: On a peninsula jutting out into the harbor at York, the main lodge was an early seacoast homestead. Four contemporary multi-unit cottages and a dining room building complete the complex.

The furnishings of the public rooms include antiques, ship models, and choice marine paintings. Most bedrooms have their own bath and direct access to the porch or lawn.

Amenities: Buffet-style Continental breakfast served on the oceanside porch (not included in rate)

Nearby Attractions: The center of York Village is a National Historic District and the buildings are open to the public.

Special Services: Marina, boat rentals, special yachting excursions, spacious grounds, lawn games, river cruises

Rates: $48 to $85 double

MASSACHUSETTS

B&B Reservation Services

ABC: ACCOMMODATIONS OF BOSTON AND CAMBRIDGE

335 PEARL ST., CAMBRIDGE, MA 02139

Offers B&B Homes In: Boston, Cambridge, Brookline, Weston, and surrounding towns

Reservations Phone: 617/491-0274

Phone Hours: 9am to 5pm daily.

Price Range of Homes: $50 to $75 single, $60 to $95 double.

Breakfast Included in Price: Continental: juice, fresh fruit, cold cereal, muffins/croissants or similar, and coffee or tea. American breakfast includes the foregoing plus eggs, any style, and sometimes bacon/ham.

Brochure Available: Free

Reservations Should Be Made: As far in advance as possible for best choices.

Attractions Near the B&B Homes: All historic sites plus Constitution Hill, Quincy Market, Museum of Fine Arts, Isabella Gardner Stewart Museum and Fenway Park, Boston Garden and Boston Common.

Major Schools, Universities Near the B&B Homes: Brown and Nichols, Harvard, M.I.T., Boston University, Lesley College, Emerson.

Best B&Bs

■ An 1842 brick Federal-style town house in Beacon Hill, Boston, Massachusetts. Beacon Hill is one of the most attractive neighborhoods in Boston, shaded by linden trees and rimmed with cobblestone streets. The host has visited over 90 countries and brought back small treasures from many of them to decorate her home. You will find everything from primitive handicrafts to tiny sophisticated sculptures. Two guestrooms are available with a shared bath. A full breakfast is served on request, and children and pets are most welcome.

■ A country farmhouse just 20 minutes from Boston, Massachusetts. You can drift off in one of the five bedrooms, each designed differently by the host but all with a country flair. The house sits on two acres, surrounded by flowers. In nice weather the Continental breakfast is served outdoors on a screened porch.

■ Five-story town house near Copley Square in Boston, Massachusetts. This B&B is filled with antiques. Even breakfast is served with luxurious touches, on Lenox china. Fresh flowers are on display daily and—did you just hear a splash? Right in the center of the house is a fish pond.

■ A Back Bay, Boston, Massachusetts, turn-of-the-century town house with three large guestrooms, each with a private bath and air conditioning. The host serves a sumptuous full breakfast each morning. Only a few blocks from the Boston Public Garden and Copley Square.

■ A row house B&B near Copley Square, Boston, Massachusetts. Built in 1852, this home offers two rooms. One of these rooms has a formal garden where you can have your breakfast.

■ An 1840 granite building in Boston, Massachusetts. This building was once a warehouse and features many antique touches—exposed brick and heavy wooden beams. From your room you will have a view of the sailboats in Boston Harbor.

■ An 1881 Victorian town house in Boston, Massachusetts. Close to Copley Place and the Hynes Convention Center. You have a choice of three guestrooms. *Insider's Tip:* One is a garden apartment. The host serves a full gourmet breakfast.

■ Five-story home in Beacon Hill, Boston, Massachusetts. This B&B has a tree-lined roofdeck on a charming cobblestone private street. A Continental breakfast is served.

■ Boston, Massachusetts, brownstone in the historic South End area. Stay here and you will be close to all theaters as well as Copley Square. This Victorian home dates back before the Civil War and has been fully restored to its early glory. Host enjoys surprising guests with gourmet breakfasts.

▪ Renovated early Victorian town house in Boston, Massachusetts, with an ultra-modern interior. Queen-size beds and private baths. *Insider's Tip:* Go up to the roofdeck at sunset for a wonderful view of the Boston skyline.

A BED & BREAKFAST AGENCY OF BOSTON
44 COMMERCIAL WHARF, BOSTON, MA 02110

Offers B&B Homes In: The heart of historic downtown Boston
Reservations Phone: 617/720-3540 or toll free 800/248-9262
Phone Hours: 9am to 10pm daily
Price Range of Homes: $55 to $80 single, $70 to $100 double
Breakfast Included in Price: Continental or full American
Brochure Available: Free
Reservations Should Be Made: As soon as possible ("Rooms go quickly")

Attractions Near the B&B Homes: Historic Boston Harbor and Faneuil Hall, Paul Revere's House, Old North Church, Haymarket, the New England Aquarium
Major Schools, Universities Near the B&B Homes: Boston University, Harvard, MIT, Northeastern, Emerson

Best B&Bs
▪ Elegant 1828 Federal town house in historic Beacon Hill, Boston, Massachusetts, a block from Boston Common. You can sleep in any of three guestrooms, each with a private bath and a working fireplace. The home is filled with antiques. Breakfasts are served in a period dining room and consist of home-baked breads, tarts and muffins, followed by eggs, or French toast, or waffles, with coffee and tea. The dining room is "tea-papered." *Insider's Tip:* Two of the rooms overlook one of the famous hidden gardens of Beacon Hill. The other looks out on one of the truly beautiful streets in America. (Top 100.)

FOLKSTONE CENTRAL MASSACHUSETTS BED & BREAKFAST
DARLING ROAD, DUDLEY, MA 01570

Offers B&B Homes In: Worcester County
Reservations Phone: 508/943-7118 or 800/726-2751
Phone Hours: 9am to 5pm daily

Price Range of Homes: $50 to $65 single, $55 to $85 double, $85 suite

Breakfast Included in Price: Continental (juice, roll or toast, coffee) or full American with such specialties as beef or chicken hash, homemade English muffins, omelets to order, pancakes with seasonal fruits and berries

Brochure Available: Free

Reservations Should Be Made: In advance (last-minute reservations accepted when possible); MasterCard, VISA, and American Express accepted

Attractions Near the B&B Homes: Sturbridge Village, Worcester Science Center, Higgins Armor Museum, Horticultural Society, Wachusett Mountain Ski Area

Major Schools, Universities Near the B&B Homes: U. Mass. Medical Center, Clark U., Worcester Polytech, Anna Maria College, Atlantic Union College, Holy Cross, Assumption College

Best B&Bs

■ 18th-century Georgian farmhouse in Auburn, Massachusetts. Here's your chance to live for a weekend or a week in another time. You have a choice of four guestrooms with private baths on the second floor. Or you might select a two-room suite with bath on the third floor. Cozy fireplaced parlors and a keeping room with a large hearth add to the feeling of 18th-century time travel. The host serves a full country breakfast in the keeping room or in the sunroom overlooking the gardens. The pool is available to guests in warm weather. The hosts are knowledgeable about local history. (Top 100.)

■ 200-year-old converted barn in Boylston, Massachusetts. Two double-bedded guestrooms available with a shared bath. Full breakfast served on weekends only. In the evening you can enjoy the family room with a woodstove, overlooking the pool and tennis court. Close to cross-country skiing areas, and the Tower Hill Botanic Garden.

■ 1755 with eight—yes, eight—fireplaces in Holden, Massachusetts. In the morning you can take a stroll past a flock of Suffolk sheep. Close to downtown Worcester, museums, historic sites, and ski areas.

■ English Tudor home in Sturbridge, a little over a mile from Old Sturbridge Village. This is the perfect place if you plan to visit the restored village. Also close to factory outlets and antiques shops.

■ A B&B in a working apple orchard in Sterling, Massachusetts. This is a 1740 Colonial family homestead with two large bedrooms with private baths. Open March through December.

BED & BREAKFAST, BROOKLINE/BOSTON

P.O. BOX 732, BROOKLINE, MA 02146

Offers B&B Homes In: Boston proper (including Beacon Hill, Back Bay, Brookline, Cambridge), Cape Cod, Nantucket Island, Gloucester, Swampscott, Nahant, and other Massachusetts areas
Reservations Phone: 617/277-2292
Phone Hours: 10am to 4pm Monday through Friday
Price Range of Homes: $40 to $50 single, $50 to $65 double
Breakfast Included in Price: Continental breakfast can include homemade jams such as "Beach Plum" on Cape Cod, cranberry muffins, croissants, cereal, "Anadama bread"; several hosts serve full breakfasts.
Brochure Available: Free. For accommodations lists, send $1 and a stamped, self-addressed no. 10 envelope.
Reservations Should Be Made: Anytime—"first come, first served"

Attractions Near the B&B Homes: All of Boston's attractions are minutes away by subway; the Museum of Fine Arts, Gardner Museum, and Fenway Park are especially convenient to several of the host homes.
Major Schools, Universities Near the B&B Homes: Harvard, Boston U., Tufts, Simmons, Wheelock, plus centers for international visitors and studies

Best B&Bs

- English brick home in Brookline, Massachusetts. This home, actually three attached town houses joined by a balcony across the front, is listed in the National Registry of Historic Places. Many of the furnishings were collected by the host during her world travels (she speaks fluent Spanish). You're close to downtown Boston.

GREATER BOSTON HOSPITALITY

P.O. BOX 1142, BROOKLINE, MA 02146

Offers B&B Homes In: Boston, Brookline, Cambridge, Newton, Danvers, Needham, Wellesley, Winchester, Marblehead, Salem, Swampscott, Charlestown, Belmont, Brighton, Gloucester
Reservations Phone: 617/277-5430
Phone Hours: 24 hours daily
Price Range of Homes: $35 to $80 single, $40 to $90 double
Breakfast Included in Price: Full American, which may include homemade peach preserves and scones, hot chocolate, buttermilk pancakes, bagels with smoked salmon and cream cheese, croissants . . .

and a vegetarian/macrobiotic home serves fresh carrot juice, rice muffins with tofu cream cheese, hot oatmeal, apple-pear crunch, brown rice, tea or coffee.

Brochure Available: Free

Reservations Should Be Made: Two weeks in advance (last-minute reservations accepted if possible)

Attractions Near the B&B Homes: Boston Symphony, Boston Pops, Boston Ballet, Christian Science Church, Kennedy Library, Museum of Fine Arts, Isabella Stewart Gardner Museum, Faneuil Hall, Quincy Market, Freedom Trail, Chinatown, Beacon Hill, N.E. Aquarium

Major Schools, Universities Near the B&B Homes: Harvard, M.I.T., Boston U., Boston College, Emmanuel, Lesley, Pine Manor, Northeastern, Simmons, Wellesley, Massachusetts College of Art, New England Conservatory, Tufts, Babson, Brandeis

Best B&Bs

■ Converted Georgian carriage house in Boston (Brookline) Massachusetts. The RSO calls this an "unusual five-star B&B, formerly part of a larger estate located on a cul-de-sac in an outstanding neighborhood of gracious homes." You have a choice of a twin or queen-size bedded guestroom, both with private bath. In the summer you will breakfast on a tree-shaded patio. Your hosts are thoroughly familiar with Boston and will be happy to give you local advice. Parking is included. You can walk to an express carline to the center of Boston. **(Top 100)**

■ An 1847 Greek Revival home in Boston (Winthrop Square) Massachusetts. This B&B home puts you within 100 yards of the Freedom Trail and close to the second oldest park in Boston, where troops trained for the Revolutionary and Civil wars. Your bedroom has a double bed, a large deck that overlooks a garden courtyard, and a private bath. There is one cat, described as "unobtrusive." Plenty of onstreet parking. Full breakfast on weekends, and Continental during the week.

■ 1790 town house in Boston (Beacon Hill) Massachusetts. This home has a separate floor for B&B guests with a double-bedded room, dining room, kitchen, bathroom, and a living room with a connecting roofdeck filled with flowers.

■ Boston, Massachusetts, bargain at the foot of Beacon Hill. Rooms are modest but comfortable and the rates are a bargain by Boston standards. Bath is shared. There are kitchens on each floor. Your hosts will be happy to talk about food or medicine. They are, respectively, a former chef and a nurse. Children over five are welcome.

■ Classic 1890 brownstone in Boston (Back Bay), Massachusetts. Located in a beautiful and quiet residential area. The guestrooms have 18th-century mahogany furniture, and some have Oriental rugs. Each room has a private adjoining bathroom. If you're musically minded, you can play the grand piano. Smoking permitted (a growing rarity in many B&B homes).

■ Two renovated town houses in Boston, Massachusetts. These town houses were modeled after a small European inn. They are located in the heart of Boston's Back Bay area, minutes from the Prudential Center, Copley Square, and the Christian Science Center. Continental breakfast and, later in the day, refreshments and hors d'oeuvres are served on the outdoor deck (weather permitting).

BED & BREAKFAST CAMBRIDGE & GREATER BOSTON (INCLUDING BED & BREAKFAST IN MINUTEMAN COUNTRY)
P.O. BOX 665, CAMBRIDGE, MA 02140

Offers B&B Homes In: Downtown Boston, Brookline, Cambridge, Lexington, and surrounding towns. Most locations have easy access to public transportation—you do not need a car in Boston, Brookline, or Cambridge, nor is one needed from Logan Airport to the city.
Reservations Phone: 617/576-1492
Phone Hours: 9am to 6pm Monday through Friday, 10am to 3pm Saturday
Price Range of Homes: $45 to $80 single, $60 to $100 double
Breakfast Included in Price: Continental breakfast including coffee/tea, juices, breads/rolls/muffins, fresh fruit, cereals.
Brochure Available: Free
Reservations Should Be Made: As much as two months in advance during the period of May through October. "However, we are often able to accommodate last minute requests."

Attractions Near the B&B Homes: Boston's Freedom Trail, Faneuil Hall, Harvard Square, major art and historical museums, sites of the American Revolution, whale watches, the Charles River and Esplanade concerts, the Boston Symphony Orchestra, and all performing arts from ballet to theatre.
Major Schools, Universities Near the B&B Homes: Harvard, MIT, Tufts, Boston U.

Best B&Bs

■ **B&B on Beacon Hill, Boston, Massachusetts.** A lovely little room with an antique double bed and private bath, with sitting room adjacent. Walk to almost everything you want to see from this private hideaway. Coffee and juice are delivered to your sitting room in the morning. On the fourth floor—an excellent value. Ask for "Top of the Hill."

■ **1853 Greek Revival home in Cambridge/Harvard area of Massachusetts.** There are three guestrooms featuring New England antiques. Enjoy homemade breads and muffins in the morning. Relax by the fire when you come home. Subway nearby—you won't need a car. Ask for "Bunter's."

■ **Victorian home in Cambridge/Harvard area of Massachusetts.** Custom built in 1892, this gracious home has period furniture to match. Two double rooms share a bath together. Both have fireplaces, you are welcome to use the sitting room or enjoy the large patio. A third room has its own bath. Quiet private street, lovely trees and gardens. Parking available. Ask for "The Gambrel."

■ **1874 Italianate Victorian house in Cambridge, Massachusetts—near Harvard's Quad.** There are two large, sunny guestrooms, each with TV, desk, and easy chairs. Antique and contemporary furniture are combined in a cheerful atmosphere. The lovely quiet neighborhood invites walking. Just three blocks to the system. Ask for "Blackwell House."

■ **A country Victorian home in historic Lincoln, Massachusetts,** that is a paradise for nature lovers and cross-country skiers. Easy access to Boston by commuter train or Mass. Pike. Set among gardens and woodlands, this charming house has lovely antiques and is a showcase of the skills of your host, a noted interior designer. Double room with private bath, a second room is available for a third person. Ask for "Beechtree Cottage."

■ **Cape Ann Colonial on a country road in historic Bedford, Massachusetts,** is on two acres of formal and informal gardens. Take an easy chair by one of the four fireplaces or try your hand at the regulation pool table in the games room. Three guestrooms (one with a private bath). Enjoy this historic town as well as nearby Concord and Lexington. Boston is 30 minutes away. Ask for "Emma & Maude's"

HOST HOMES OF BOSTON
P.O. BOX 117, WABAN BRANCH, BOSTON, MA 02168

Offers B&B Homes In: Boston, Brookline, Cambridge, Newton, Concord, Lexington, Needham, Wellesley, Westwood, Weymouth, Cape Cod, and other areas
Reservations Phone: 617/244-1308; FAX: 617/244-5156
Phone Hours: 9am to noon and 1:30 to 4:30pm Monday through Friday; closed weekends and holidays (or an answering machine with same-day callback in winter)
Price Range of Homes: $45 to $85 single, $57 to $100 double
Breakfast Included in Price: "Hearty" Continental (may include home-baked muffins, scones or croissants, bran and yogurt, cheese, fresh fruit) or full American (depending on the host or day of the week)
Brochure Available: Free; free directory
Reservations Should Be Made: Two weeks in advance (late reservations accepted if possible)

Attractions Near the B&B Homes: "All of the cultural, recreational, and educational offerings of Boston." This includes the Fine Arts Museum, Museum of Science, Freedom Trail, Faneuil Hall and Quincy Market, Boston Symphony, Hynes Convention Center, Bayside Exposition Center, Lexington and Concord, and Old Sturbridge Village.
Major Schools, Universities Near the B&B Homes: Boston College, Boston U., Harvard, Simmons, Brandeis, Tufts, M.I.T., Wellesley College, Pine Manor, Babson, Northeastern, New England Conservatory

Best B&Bs

■ Rockledge, a stately Victorian home in Newton, Massachusetts. Built in 1882, this home is close to Back Bay and Copley Square in Boston. There are three second-floor guestrooms but only two are booked at any one time. The rooms are bright and spacious and furnished with antiques. Guests can use the special parlor on the second floor. The hosts are friendly and from the world of academia. The RSO selected this B&B as their "top" home primarily because of the glowing comments of guests. Here are a few:

"Our experience at Rockledge confirms our belief that B&Bs are the way to travel."

"Your whole host family was a welcome surprise—so friendly, so nice. Cloe, the cat, was an added joy."

"The breakfasts were fantastic—much more than 'full.' We would certainly stay there again." (Top 100.)

■ 1868 B&B in Beacon Hill, Boston, Massachusetts. This town house offers three guestrooms with private baths. Two of the rooms have river views.

■ Victorian Bows, an 1860 Victorian family town house in the historic district of Boston, Massachusetts. The second-floor twin room has a Jacuzzi bath, high ceilings, and a ceiling fan. The garden level has a queen-size bed and a den with sofabed and bath. The subway is three blocks away. Children are welcome.

■ Proper Bostonian, an 1872 town house close to Copley Square in Boston, Massachusetts, with authentic decor from the good old days. The third-floor guestroom is extra large. There's even a small, well-stocked kitchen where you can make your own breakfast.

■ Briarwood, a historic home in Brookline, Massachusetts. This B&B, built in 1875 and only a block from Boston College, is furnished with early American antiques and some modern amenities. The first-floor guest wing has its own private entrance, as well as a queen-size bed, two twin beds, skylights, and an alcove with a dining table and cooking facilities. This is ideal for a family traveling together.

BED & BREAKFAST ASSOCIATES BAY COLONY, LTD.
P.O. BOX 57166, BABSON PARK BRANCH, BOSTON, MA 02157-0166

Offers B&B Homes and B&B Inns In: Boston's Beacon Hill, Back Bay, Waterfront, Medical District, South End, Copley/Prudential area, as well as Cambridge, Brookline, Newton, Cape Cod, Marblehead, Gloucester, and seaside and suburban towns throughout eastern Massachusetts.

Reservations Phone: 617/449-5302; FAX: 617/449-5958

Phone Hours: 9:30am to 5pm Monday through Friday. After hours on answering machine ("in season").

Price Range of Homes: Singles $45 to $85 in Boston, $45 to $75 in the suburbs; doubles $75 to $130 in Boston, $55 to $75 in the suburbs.

Breakfast Included in Price: Coffee, tea, muffins, croissants, breakfast pastries, fruit juice, fresh fruits, and cereals. Some B&Bs offer a full American or gourmet Continental breakfast.

Brochure Available: Free; a full descriptive directory is available for $5.

Reservations Should Be Made: Well in advance for holiday periods, graduation time, and foliage season. A minimum of two weeks' notice is advisable at other times.

Attractions Near the B&B Homes: Historic Boston's Freedom Trail, Faneuil Hall/Quincy Market, art museums, Fenway Park, Christian Science Center, New England Aquarium.

Major Schools, Universities near the B&B Homes: Harvard, MIT, Boston U., Tufts, Wellesley, Simmons, Wheelock, Emerson, Brandeis

Best B&Bs

■ Restored 1863 town house in Boston, Massachusett's Copley Square area. The reservation service describes this as a showplace bed-and-breakfast with five gracious guestrooms, each with private bath and romantic furnishings, featuring armoires and Oriental rugs. A full breakfast is served in the dining room. **(Top 100.)**

■ Romantic early American farmhouse in Stowe, Massachusetts. Each of the three guestrooms is furnished with fine antiques and handmade quilts. Each has a working fireplace, full private bath, and cable TV.

■ A 20-room B&B inn on Boston, Massachusett's prestigious Beacon Hill. Guests can choose from several large rooms furnished with two double beds and accompanying private baths or smaller rooms with queen-size beds and private baths. You can walk to the famous swan boats in the Public Garden and to the historic Freedom Trail and waterfront area. The breakfast is self-serve in the "open kitchen."

■ Victorian home in Medford, Massachusetts, a mile from Tufts University and a block from the commuter train to Boston. Built in 1909 this B&B is carefully maintained. *Insider's Tip:* Choose the large double-bedded room with a bay window and private porch.

■ B&B in Brookline, Massachusetts. This home with three guestrooms is located on a street of large, Victorian homes, near Boston University and the Longwood Medical area. All rooms have private vanity sink and queen-size or double-size beds.

■ Large home in Cambridge, Massachusetts, in a quiet neighborhood right next to jogging paths. This home is close to Harvard Square and features skylights, sliding doors to a deck, and many plants.

NEW ENGLAND BED & BREAKFAST, INC.
1045 CENTRE ST., NEWTON CENTRE, MA 02159

Offers B&B Homes In: Boston and other special places in New England
Reservations Phone: 617/244-2112 or 617/498-9819
Phone Hours: 9am to 2pm daily (498-9819 is a 24-hour service)
Price Range of Homes: $30 to $45 single, $40 to $57 double
Breakfast Included in Price: Continental (juice, roll or toast, fruit, cereal, tea, coffee)
Brochure Available: Free
Reservations Should Be Made: Two weeks in advance (last-minute reservations accepted if possible)

Attractions Near the B&B Homes: All Boston attractions, sand and dunes of Cape Cod, mountains and streams of New Hampshire and Maine, rolling hills of Vermont, Freedom Trail, historic Concord and Lexington, theaters and museums
Major Schools, Universities Near the B&B Homes: Harvard, Boston College, Boston U., Berklee College of Music, Lesley, Northeastern, La Salle, Bentley, Brandeis

Best B&Bs

■ "Margaret's Room" in Newton Centre, Massachusetts. John and Margo own and operate the New England Bed & Breakfast guesthouse agency. John is also executive director of a private day-care agency, and Margo is a travel specialist and a writer. The room they offer guests used to be the quarters of their maid, Margaret, and has a private bath and a private entrance. A second room down the hall and connected to Margaret's room is a second bedroom also with a private bath, which makes it convenient for families or two couples traveling together. A gourmet cook, John's favorite pastime is sitting on the screened-in porch in summer or by the fireplace in winter and sharing tea or wine and stories with his guests. **(Top 100.)**

■ The nearest subway station is a one minute walk from Margaret's house in Newton Centre, Massachusetts, near Boston College, and you can get to downtown on the "T" in 15 minutes. Born in Nova Scotia, Margaret used to run a delicatessen in Newton, and of late she's been spending the better part of her free time doing work for the Catholic Church, when she isn't visiting with one of her 28 grandchildren or 7 great-grandchildren. Margaret bakes her own muffins and offers guests a room with twin beds and a shared bath.

■ Jennie's house, almost entirely obscured by evergreens, is a short drive from downtown Boston, Massachusetts, and a one-mile walk to the subway stop for a 20-minute ride to the tourist district of the city center. She has a delightful Austrian accent, and her taste in silver and crystal seems to reflect the Old World heritage her voice evokes. Jennie offers guests a suite of rooms with a balcony, where many of them like to eat breakfast. The living room is quite large, with big vases filled with dried flowers reflected by numerous mirrors in this tastefully decorated home.

■ A short walk from Harvard Square in Boston, Massachusetts, this guest home offers one room with a private bath and a separate entrance by the side of the house. The hosts are Jane, a nurse, and Bob, who is a school psychologist in the Cambridge school system. They have four adult children. Their home features an open back porch where they serve breakfast when the weather is nice.

PINEAPPLE HOSPITALITY, INC.

P.O. BOX F821, NEW BEDFORD, MA 02742

Offers B&B Homes In: Massachusetts, Rhode Island, Connecticut, Maine, New Hampshire, Vermont
Reservations Phone: 508/990-1696
Phone Hours: 9am to 7pm Monday through Friday, April to November; 11am to 7pm, November to April
Price Range of Homes: $45 to $65 single, $55 to $130 double
Breakfast Included in Price: Continental or full American
Brochure Available: "Directory of host homes and small inns for all New England" for sale at $5.95
Reservations Should Be Made: Two weeks in advance (24-hour last-minute surcharge)

Attractions Near the B&B Homes: Attractions throughout New England

Best B&Bs

■ Prouts Neck home in Scarborough, Maine. This 1779 home was built on the site of an Indian fort. Historic markers tell of the first Native American death here which started the Indian Wars. This B&B is right on the ocean and is adjacent to the Winslow home and studio and the sanctuary, which he willed to the state. Guests may roam and explore the grounds. The B&B suite consists of a large bedroom with a panoramic view and a double bed with a canopy, a large private bath with an adjoining dressing room, a living room with fireplace, and a glassed-in sunroom with kitchen facilities for the guests. The upstairs bedroom also has a wonderful view, and shares the living room and sunroom with the guest on the first floor. All of the amenities of Black Point Inn—including tennis, golf, and weekend entertainment—are available to B&B guests. (Top 100.)

■ An 1830s restored Victorian home in Harwich Port, Massachusetts. Only five minutes from Bank Street Beach and Nantucket Sound. The home has been restored with furnishings and linens from England. Three sleeping rooms. *Insider's Tip:* If you want to try something different for breakfast, ask for "soft-boiled eggs and soldiers" (an English favorite your host will explain).

■ Country house in Manchester, Vermont. This B&B dates back to 1880 (with many additions since then). You will find a fireplace in the living room and a woodstove in the dining room. *Insider's Tip:* Ask for bedroom 1 upstairs; it has a view of Mount Equinox. Breakfast specialty of the house is homemade scones (blueberry, raspberry, cranberry, and orange).

■ Victorian house in New Bedford, Massachusetts. Want to see the famous New Bedford Whaling Museum? It's only six blocks away. This home, built in the 1870s, is bright and cheerful. If you'd like some tips about downhill and cross-country skiing, ask your hosts. They're both avid skiers.

ORLEANS BED & BREAKFAST ASSOCIATES
P.O. BOX 1312, ORLEANS, MA 02653

Offers B&B Homes In: Cape Cod, from the Harwiches to Truro
Reservations Phone: 508/255-3824 or toll free 800/541-6220
Phone Hours: 8am to 8pm Monday through Friday (also accepts calls on weekends and holidays)
Price Range of Homes: $55 to $95 per room per night
Breakfast Included in Price: Expanded Continental (juice and fruit in season, home-baked breads); some hosts are gourmet cooks and do large omelets, French toast, etc.
Brochure Available: Free
Reservations Should Be Made: Three weeks in advance (last-minute reservations accepted when possible)

Attractions Near the B&B Homes: Cape Cod National Seashore, whale watch, beaches, bike trails, museums, art galleries, antique and crafts fairs

Best B&Bs

- "The Red Geranium" home in Orleans, Massachusetts. Located right on the main street, this country-style home offers easy access to village shopping and fine dining. The ocean and bay beaches are nearby. The home is completely furnished with antiques. Mary Chapman, executive director of Orleans Bed & Breakfast Associates, describes this B&B as "a little gem. It is most like a small pension (that you might find in Europe). Guests meet at breakfast to share delicious foods at tables set with beautiful antique china and unusual seasonal decor." A guest wing is now available. (Top 100.)

- "Winterwell" home in Orleans, Massachusetts. This is a restored 18th-century Cape Cod farmhouse almost right on top of Skater Beach. It is also close to town and a bird feeder. Guests are invited to share the living room for TV and reading.

BE OUR GUEST, BED & BREAKFAST

P.O. BOX 1333, PLYMOUTH, MA 02360

Offers B&B Homes In: Cape Cod, Plymouth, and the neighboring towns of Hingham, Scituate, Kingston, Duxbury, Marshfield, and Quincy

Reservations Phone: 617/837-9867

Phone Hours: 9am to 9pm daily

Price Range of Homes: $40 to $60 single, $55 to $65 double

Breakfast Included in Price: "Continental breakfast is required, but most hosts serve a good hearty, full breakfast . . . pancakes and blueberries, zucchini bread (homemade vegetables from garden), and croissants are the favorites."

Brochure Available: Free, enclose self-addressed, stamped envelope

Reservations Should Be Made: Two weeks in advance preferred, but will try to make reservations the same day as your arrival in town

Attractions Near the B&B Homes: Plimoth Plantation, the *Mayflower* ship, Plymouth Rock, Cranberry World, Commonwealth Winery, Edaville Railroad, Plymouth Wax Museum, Cape Cod, historic homes, beaches, state parks, whale watching, deep-sea fishing, sailing

Major Schools, Universities Near the B&B Homes: Bridgewater State College, and all major Boston schools, colleges, and universities within 30 to 60 miles

Best B&Bs

- Cape-style home in Falmouth, Massachusetts, located on the Vineyard Sound. Come see the town that successfully resisted two British invasions: during the Revolutionary War and the War of 1812. This B&B offers you a choice of two beautifully decorated rooms and a self-contained studio apartment with separate entrance (great for families). The hosts have been welcoming guests for over eight years. Falmouth is located on Cape Cod, 72 miles from Boston and 35 miles from Plymouth. If you're a history buff, don't miss the nearby Congregation Church with a bell cast by Paul Revere. (Top 100.)

- Antique Federal colonial home in Marshfield, Massachusetts, located less than one mile from the beach. Three beautifully decorated guestrooms with wicker, brass, and sleigh beds are available, with fireplaces and many antique furnishings throughout. Full breakfast is served in the dining room, which has a fireplace.

- Antique Colonial home in Sandwich, Massachusetts, located in the oldest town on Cape Cod. There is one guestroom with private bath and an adjoining bunk room is available for children.

- Antique Victorian home in Marshfield, Massachusetts, is situated in a quaint village setting, with one guestroom with twin beds and private bath. The beach is only two miles away.

- Farmhouse located in Hanover, Massachusetts. This 136-year-old home has one twin guestroom. Beautifully decorated, this cozy retreat has displays of the host's talent for flower arranging throughout.

- Colonial home located in Plymouth, Massachusetts, within walking distance to the historic Plymouth waterfront, is a short ride from Plimoth Plantation. There is a twin guestroom with private bath.

- Antique Federal colonial home in Kingston, Massachusetts. Located only five miles from historic Plymouth Center. Beautifully decorated adjoining guestrooms are available. Full breakfast is served in the dining room.

- Ranch-style home in Scituate, Massachusetts. In the Scituate Harbor area. Three guestrooms, each decorated with a mix of modern and antique furnishings. Decks allow guests to sit and relax in the cool ocean breeze. Within walking distance of Scituate Harbor, the marina, and all shops and restaurants.

BED & BREAKFAST CAPE COD
P.O. BOX 341, WEST HYANNISPORT, MA 02672

Offers B&B Homes In: Cape Cod, Nantucket, Martha's Vineyard, Gloucester, Cape Ann, and the Greater Boston area
Reservations Phone: 508/775-2772
Phone Hours: 8:30am to 6pm (answering machine off-hours)
Price Range of Homes: $38 to $50 single, $48 to $175 double
Breakfast Included in Price: Continental or full country; homebaked specialties such as native berry pancakes and preserves and home-made bread and muffins are often served.
Brochure Available: Free
Reservations Should Be Made: Two or three weeks in advance (last-minute reservations possible but choices are often limited)

Attractions Near the B&B Homes: Ferries to Martha's Vineyard and Nantucket, Heritage Plantation, Sandwich Glass Museum, Cape Cod National Seashore and Park, Audubon Sanctuary, Cape Playhouse, Melody Tent, Falmouth Playhouse, golf courses, deep-sea fishing, lake trout fishing, sandy beaches, bike paths, whale watch trips
Major Schools, Universities Near the B&B Homes: Woods Hole Oceanographic Institute, Cape Cod Community College, Cape Cod Conservatory of Music and Art, Boston universities and colleges (1½-hour drive)

Best B&Bs

■ Barn restoration in Barnstable, Massachusetts. This town achieved early American history fame in the King Phillips Wars, with several skirmishes occurring almost at the doorstep of this B&B. The whole village has now been declared a National Historic District. The barn itself was built in 1821. It was restored to a splendid home with 4,200 square feet of living space. The stairs to the second floor and a wet bar were lifted right from a Massachusetts courthouse. (Perhaps the old judges were secret tipplers.) Go up to the third-floor cupola for a great view of Cape Cod. There's another water view from the covered porch on the second floor. There are three bedrooms, each with double beds and private baths. All rooms have a Victorian decor. Breakfast is full Continental, and the host serves fresh fruit, juices, homebaked breads, and muffins. Said one guest, "Their home welcomes guests with a homey feeling, yet very private. Made us feel like a king and queen. I will go back and recommend them to everyone." (Top 100.)

■ Cape Cod Colonial home in Falmouth, Massachusetts. This is a great location to explore the Cape, with great little shops surrounding the village green, Woods Hole—the famous port for deep sea explorers, and Falmouth Harbor with a ferry to Martha's Vineyard all nearby.

"The home was built in 1793 and reflects the early American/primitive/country decor of its origin," says the RSO. The first- and second-floor suites have double four-poster canopy beds, fireplaces, and sitting areas, where the host will serve breakfast about 8:30am.

■ Cape Cod, Massachusetts, ranch-style home on Cape Cod Bay. This 18-year-old home, on top of a cliff, offers a great view of a nearby fresh water lake (well stocked with fish). The two guestrooms have views of this lake, and have private baths. On pleasant days the Continental breakfast is served outside on the patio. *Insider's Tip:* You can use a private beach right on the lake.

■ Cape Cod home in Sandwich, Massachusetts. Located on Academy Hill overlooking the first town on Cape Cod, the house was built over six years ago with a wing later added by famous architect Royal Barry Willis. The host is a retired personnel director for a major U.S. corporation, a good person to talk with about how to prepare an effective resumé. *Insider's Tip:* Be sure to sample the muffins and breads, often made with corn meal fresh from Sandwich's Dexter Grist Mill.

■ An 1898 cottage in Gloucester, Cape Ann, Massachusetts. This is the place to sit back on the 100-foot wrap-around porch and watch the ships sail by. This home has been completely restored and sits majestically on a hillside overlooking the Annisquam River. All guestrooms have a water view.

BED & BREAKFAST FOLKS
48 SPRINGS RD., BEDFORD, MA 01730

Offers B&B Homes In: Concord, Lexington, Westford, Groton, Chelmsford, Dunstable, Pepperell, Boxborough, Lowell, Burlington, Boxford, Newton, Brookline, Billerica, Tynesboro, Reading, and Bedford
Reservations Phone: 617/275-9025
Phone Hours: 8am to 10pm Monday through Friday; also on weekends and holidays
Price Range of Homes: $40 to $60 single, $50 to $70 double
Breakfast Included in Price: Continental plus
Brochure Available: Free
Reservations Should Be Made: In advance (also attempts to accept last-minute reservations)

Attractions Near the B&B Homes: Concord, Lexington, Walden Pond, ski areas, Boston, Cambridge

Best B&Bs

■ Restored 200-year-old colonial home in Pepperell. This is a huge rambling farmhouse chock-full of working fireplaces (six) and antiques, surrounded by a barn full of horses and sheep. Two of the guestrooms have fireplaces, and on chilly evenings the host will set you up with a warm fire. The morning specialty of the house is French toast, smothered in maple syrup made right on the farm. The host, being a retired school teacher, seems to know just what children like. "I give them a carrot to feed the horses, and some grain to give the ducks in the pond." She also will demonstrate to interested guests how homesteaders once spun yard, using an antique spinning wheel in the living room. Many of the guests staying here are professionals, some enrolling their children in some of the famous private schools nearby. (Top 100.)

■ Old Colonial home in Bedford, Massachusetts. This B&B has wide-board pine floors and exposed old brick. It's located in the historic district of Bedford, close to the town center. Cambridge, Lexington, Boston, and Concord are nearby.

■ 1775 restored colonial inn in Concord, Massachusetts. The rooms are charming. Guests can gather in the afternoon in the sitting room for tea or sherry. All rooms have private baths.

■ Pondside home in Chelmsford, Massachusetts. Guests can go swimming, fishing or boating, or use an indoor spa. You can have breakfast in your room or dine on the glassed-in patio.

BERKSHIRE BED & BREAKFAST HOMES

P.O. BOX 211, WILLIAMSBURG, MA 01096

Offers B&B Homes In: Sturbridge area; Pioneer Valley (Springfield, Northampton, Amherst); also in Berkshire County; eastern New York; northern Connecticut; and southern Vermont
Reservations Phone: 413/268-7244
Phone Hours: 9am to 7pm Monday through Friday, on Saturday 10am to 1pm
Price Range of Homes: $40 to $90 single, $45 to $150 double
Breakfast Included in Price: Continental or full American; some hosts will also prepare gourmet dinners
Brochure Available: Free; directory of hosts also available for $3
Reservations Should Be Made: Two weeks in advance; at least one month in advance for choice housing during the Tanglewood concert season

Attractions Near the B&B Homes: Basketball Hall of Fame, Sturbridge Village, Deerfield Village, Tanglewood, Jacob's Pillow, Mohawk Trail, downhill and cross-country ski trails

Major Schools, Universities Near the B&B Homes: Williams College, U. of Massachusetts, Amherst, Smith, Mount Holyoke, Hampshire, Western New England, North Adams State

Best B&Bs

■ An 1817 Mansard-style home on 12 acres, in Cheshire, Massachusetts. This B&B is furnished with Victorian and country antiques. Walk out the door for a view of the Berkshire Mountains. You have a choice of two guestrooms with queen-size beds and private baths. Also rooms with twin or single beds and semi-private bath. The parlor is for guest use. The price is very reasonable, and children of all ages are most welcome. (Top 100.)

■ 1850 Federal–Greek Revival home on 13 acres in Belchertown, Massachusetts. Choice of two guestrooms with double or twin beds. Shared bath.

■ 1928 Dutch Colonial on two acres in Wilbraham, Massachusetts. The home is furnished with antique and formal pieces, with wicker furniture in the sunroom. A parlor and den and an in-ground swimming pool are all available to guests.

■ 1987 contemporary post and beam home in Sturbridge, Massachusetts, with a pretty setting overlooking the lake. A Jacuzzi and a parlor are available to guests.

■ An 1870 country farmhouse on 127 acres. This home is furnished with country and natural wood items. You can choose from guestrooms, which include one with a queen-size bed, working fireplace, and private bath. There is an old-fashioned gazebo for summer reading.

HAMPSHIRE HILLS BED & BREAKFAST ASSOCIATION

P.O. BOX 553, WORTHINGTON, MA 01098

Offers B&B Homes In: The hills of western Massachusetts
Reservations Phone: 413/238-5914
Phone Hours: After 6pm; each home must be phoned directly; obtain numbers from the brochure or call the above number
Price Range of Homes: $35 to $45 single, $45 to $90 double
Breakfast Included in Price: Continental or full American, which can include such regional specialties as maple syrup, farm-fresh eggs, and homemade blueberry muffins

Brochure Available: Free if you send a stamped, self-addressed no. 10 envelope

Reservations Should Be Made: Two weeks in advance (last-minute reservations accepted if possible)

Attractions Near the B&B Homes: William Cullen Bryant Homestead, Historic Deerfield, DAR State Park, Chesterfield Gorge, Jacob's Pillow Dance Festival, Tanglewood Music Center, Williamstown Theater, Sterling Clark Museum, cross-country and downhill skiing, hiking trails, cycling, canoeing, tennis, golf

Major Schools, Universities Near the B&B Homes: Smith, Amherst, Hampshire, Mount Holyoke, U. Massachusetts, Williams, Deerfield Academy, Eaglebrook Prep

Best B&Bs

■ Cumworth Farm in Cummington, Massachusetts. Good family place. You can watch the activities of a working farm—gathering maple syrup, vegetables, and berries in season. This 200-year-old farmhouse offers six bedrooms and a choice of Continental or American breakfast. You're close to cross-country and downhill skiing. For reservations, call 413/634-5529.

■ The Hill Gallery home in Worthington, Massachusetts. The "gallery" in the name of the home is not an artifice; this spacious four-bedroom contemporary really *does* have an art gallery. You can relax on a spacious sundeck or patio. *Insider's Tip:* If you really want privacy, a separate cottage is available. For reservations, call 413/238-5914.

B&B Inns

DEERFIELD INN
THE STREET, DEERFIELD, MA 01342

Reservations Phone: 413/774-5587; FAX: 413/773-8712

Description: Located in the center of Historic Deerfield on The Street with 12 beautifully restored museum homes; the inn has 23 guestrooms with period furnishing, private baths, and air conditioning. The inn has been completely redecorated this year with Greeff fabrics that depict Deerfield Village scenes.

Nearby Attractions: Historic Deerfield with extensive collections of paintings, prints, furniture, silver, ceramics, textiles, and other decorative arts

Special Services: Private function rooms; full-service restaurant on the premises

Rates: $115 B&B, $177 MAP

NAUSET HOUSE INN

143 BEACH RD. (P.O. BOX 774), EAST ORLEANS, CAPE COD, MA 02643

Reservations Phone: 508/255-2195

Description: This old-fashioned country inn with fourteen guestrooms was originally built about 1810. The three-acre site includes a farm and apple orchard.

Amenities: Full breakfast with many selections. Complimentary wine and cranberry juice with hors d'oeuvres at 5:30pm daily.

Nearby Attractions: Nauset Beach

Rates: $55 to $95 double

THE OVERLOOK INN

P.O. BOX 771, RT. 6, EASTHAM, MA 02642

Reservations Phone: 508/255-1886

Description: This Victorian inn has 10 bedrooms furnished with antiques, a parlor, library, and Victorian billiard room.

Amenities: Full Scottish breakfast and afternoon tea with homemade scones and strawberry jam.

Nearby Attractions: Cape Cod National Seashore, hiking, biking, Audubon Wildlife Sanctuary, antiques shops.

Rates: $60 to $100 double

Innkeeper's Tip: "This is a nature lover's paradise with whale watching, windsurfing, sailing, fishing, and quiet walks on the seashore."

SHIPS KNEES INN

BEACH ROAD (P.O. BOX 756), EAST ORLEANS, MA 02643

Reservations Phone: 508/255-1312

Description: Built over 150 years ago, the inn is a restored sea

captain's house that gives you old-style New England lodging surrounded by the charm of yesterday while offering the convenience of
today. Many of the guestrooms have beamed ceilings, four-poster
beds, and authentic antiques. Several rooms have an ocean view and
the master suite has a working fireplace.
Amenities: Continental breakfast

Nearby Attractions: Nauset Beach, Cape Cod National Seashore
Special Services: Swimming pool, tennis
Rates: $40 to $100 double; open all year
Innkeeper's Tip: "Since Orleans is bordered on two sides by salt
water, boating and fishing are favorite pastimes in the area," says
Donna Anderson. "For many, the greatest pleasure is a leisurely stroll
along beautiful Nauset Beach with a sunset picnic or clambake to top
off the day."

MEETING HOUSE INN
40 MEETING HOUSE WAY, EDGARTOWN, MA 02539

Reservations Phone: 508/627-8626
Description: This 1750s farmhouse is attractively decorated and provides a living room and library for guests, as well as 58 acres for
walking.
Amenities: Full, home-cooked breakfast, greenhouse with hot tub, late
afternoon snack

Nearby Attractions: Historic Edgartown, beaches, fishing, tennis, golf,
horseback riding, bike trails, and hiking
Special Services: Available for small weddings
Rates: $85 to $95 double
Innkeeper's Tip: "Guests will enjoy many special summer theatre productions and concerts. September and October are beautiful and less
crowded with lower rates."

SEA BREEZE INN
397 SEA ST., HYANNIS, MA 02601

Reservations Phone: 508/771-7213
Description: A group of Cape Cod–style buildings with weathered
shingles, Sea Breeze has some rooms with an ocean view. All rooms
have private bath and color TV.
Amenities: Juice, cereal, fruit, bagels, muffins, toast, coffee.

Nearby Attractions: John F. Kennedy Memorial, boats for Martha's Vineyard or Nantucket, sightseeing boat around the harbor and the Kennedy Compound, three minutes' walk to the beach
Rates: $60 to $75 double in summer, $45 to $55 double in winter

CANDLELIGHT INN
53 WALKER ST., LENOX, MA 01240

Reservations Phone: 413/637-1555
Description: In the heart of historic Lenox Village, the inn has a turn-of-the-century elegance and is lit by candles and fireplaces.

Nearby Attractions: Tanglewood, Norman Rockwell Museum, Jacob's Pillow Dance Festival, Berkshire Playhouse, skiing, tennis, golf, swimming, boating
Rates: $120 to $155 double in summer and fall, $65 to $130 in winter and spring

GARDEN GABLES INN
P.O. BOX 52, 141 MAIN ST., LENOX, MA 01240

Reservations Phone: 413/637-0193
Description: An inn of many gables (as you might expect), on five well-treed acres in the middle of historic Lenox Village. There are a total of 12 guestrooms. Public rooms are furnished with English and American antiques.
Amenities: The buffet breakfast is bountiful: homemade bran and blueberry muffins, fresh cantaloupe and native berries, farm-fresh eggs, health cereals, cheese-filled crumb cakes, low-fat yogurts, and buttery croissants.

Nearby Attractions: The Berkshires, Tanglewood Festival (within walking distance of the inn), Jacob's Pillow Dance Festival, Berkshire and Williamstown Theatre Festival.
Special Services: Guest use of laundry facilities and refrigerator. Transportation to and from Tanglewood. A guest cookie jar.
Rates: $60 to $145 double. A single is $5 less than a double. Rates vary by season.
Innkeeper's Tip: "Several discount stores are within a comfortable driving distance and excellent restaurants are within a 10-minute walk."

WHISTLER'S INN
5 GREENWOOD ST., LENOX, MA 01240

Reservations Phone: 413/637-0975
Description: This is a French/English Tudor mansion built in 1820 in the heart of the Berkshires overlooking seven acres of gardens and woodlands. Central to the inn is its cozy library and elegant music room.
Amenities: A full breakfast featuring home-baked blueberry muffins and breads, eggs or cheeses, cereals, coffee, tea, and juice served on the sun porch and terrace.

Nearby Attractions: Miles of riding, hiking, and cross-country ski trails; Tanglewood; Norman Rockwell Museum; Chesterwood; many historical houses; Jacob's Pillow Dance Festival, a variety of sporting activities
Special Services: Complimentary sherry and afternoon tea
Rates: $70 to $180 double in summer, $50 to $150 double in winter

SEVEN SEA STREET INN
7 SEA ST., NANTUCKET, MA 02554

Reservations Phone: 508/228-3577
Description: This red oak post-and-beam guesthouse is furnished in Colonial decor. Each of the eight guestrooms and two suites has canopied beds. Two-minute walk to the beach.
Amenities: Continental breakfast, heated Jacuzzi whirlpool room, widow's walk deck overlooking Nantucket Harbor

Nearby Attractions: Beaches, museums, historic tours, golf, tennis, biking, sailing
Special Services: Library room, laundry service on premises, guest refrigerator
Rates: $95 to $165 double
Innkeeper's Tip: Try a Nantucket whalewatching cruise

MERRELL TAVERN INN
RTE. 102, MAIN STREET, SOUTH LEE, MA 01260

Reservations Phone: 413/423-1794
Description: Authentic brick Colonial stagecoach inn located in the tiny

New England village of South Lee, with two acres of grounds and gardens extending to a river bank below. Many of the furnishings date back to the period of the building's construction in the 18th century. Most of the 10 guestrooms have canopy beds, and some have wood-burning fireplaces.

Amenities: Full breakfast served in the breakfast room. A hammock stretched between two huge maples.

Nearby Attractions: Stockbridge and the Norman Rockwell Museum, Tanglewood Music Festival, and summer theatre

Rates: $65 to $95 double. Higher rates and two-night minimum stay on summer and fall weekends.

Innkeeper's Tip: "This area is very crowded on weekends in the summer and fall. Visit during the week when rates are lower and it's less crowded everywhere. Practically all the local entertainments have seats available on shorter notice. And the leaves in the fall are as beautiful on Wednesdays as they are on Saturdays."

UNDERLEDGE INN
76 CLIFFWOOD ST., LENOX, MA 01240

Reservations Phone: 413/637-0236
Description: This Victorian mansion has been completely restored and now has nine rooms, many with fireplaces, and all with private baths.
Amenities: Continental breakfast
Nearby Attractions: Tanglewood, Jacob's Pillow Dance Festival, Norman Rockwell Museum, Berkshire Theater
Special Services: Solarium
Rates: $110 to $150 double in summer, $60 to $95 double in winter

THE QUAKER HOUSE INN AND RESTAURANT
5 CHESTNUT ST., NANTUCKET, MA 02554

Reservations Phone: 508/228-0400
Description: This 1847 Quaker-style inn is located in the heart of Nantucket Island's historic district. Each of its eight guestrooms is appointed with antiques, queen-size beds, and private baths.

Nearby Attractions: Nantucket Whaling Museum, dozens of historic homes open for tours, art galleries, sandy beaches, sailing, golf, tennis

Rates: $95 double in summer, $75 double in spring and fall
Innkeeper's Tip: R. Taylor, owner of Quaker House Inn, suggests,
"Bring your cameras for a mid-June to mid-July Nantucket visit.
Climbing roses are everywhere. In the historic village of Siasconset
dozens of 17th- and 18th-century cottages are completely covered in
roses."

NEW HAMPSHIRE

B&B Reservation Services

NEW HAMPSHIRE BED & BREAKFAST
R.F.D. 4, BOX 88, MEREDITH, NH 03253

Offers B&B Homes In: 50 communities throughout New Hampshire
Reservations Phone: 603/279-8348
Phone Hours: 9am to 8pm Monday through Friday
Price Range of Homes: $35 to $85 single, $40 to $85 double
Breakfast Included in Price: Most homes serve full American break-
fasts, including organically grown foods, real maple sugar, home-
made cheese, and even pies and ice cream! Others serve a hearty
Continental breakfast.
Brochure Available: For $1
Reservations Should Be Made: Two weeks in advance (last-minute
reservations accepted if possible)

Attractions Near the B&B Homes: Lake Winnipesaukee, Lake
Sunapee, White Mountains, Merrimack Valley, ski areas, arts and
crafts show, historic sites, and museums
Major Schools, Universities Near the B&B Homes: Dartmouth, Plym-
outh State, Colby-Sawyer, Keene State, Tilton Academy, New
Hampton School, Holderness, Brewster Academy, St. Paul's, and
Concord schools

Best B&Bs
■ Contemporary home on Lake Winnisquam, Laconia, New Hampshire.
This home offers great mountain views and a beach area. *Insider's Tip:*
Stay upstairs if you want some lake views through your window. Stay
downstairs if you want to use the Jacuzzi. **(Top 100.)**

■ Hilltop home near North Conway, New Hampshire. You'll see why this whole area is called "the Switzerland of America" with its high mountains and rushing brooks. This B&B offers a view of Mount Chocorua. A tennis court and other outdoor yard games are near the large porch.

■ B&B in Jackson, New Hampshire, high on a birch-covered hill overlooking the famous Mt. Washington and the Presidential range. The three guestrooms are furnished with handmade quilts, equipped with ceiling fans, and offer great views of the mountains. *Insider's Tip:* Be sure to ride the railroad to the top of Mt. Washington for some good pictures (on a clear day). Don't take a hat unless it's really cold. The wind on Mt. Washington can sometimes seem like a small hurricane.

■ B&B in Meredith, New Hampshire, only two blocks from over 50 shops, galleries, and restaurants. This place is furnished with antiques and has stenciled walls and floors. A large brick fireplace in the guest parlor adds to the ambience.

■ Home on a 125-acre maple sugaring farm. You are surrounded by mountains, barns, and gardens, and have your choice of three guestrooms. There is an early American feeling throughout in the furnishings and decorations, and a full country breakfast is served.

■ B&B in Manchester, New Hampshire, close to all businesses in the Manchester–Concord region. Guests can share a spot around the fireplace in the living room, or dip into the in-ground swimming pool in the summer (lit for moonlight swims for the romantic).

NESTLENOOK FARM
P.O. BOX Q., DINSMORE ROAD, JACKSON, NH 03846

Reservations Phone: 603/383-9443

Description: New, lovely country inn near North Conway. The owners have tastefully redecorated a Victorian farmhouse. Every guestroom has a Jacuzzi, and many have fireplaces, 18th century stoves, and balconies with woodland views. Each room is named after a local artist and decorated with his or her paintings. The author feels this is one of the best new inns of the year in the New England area— wonderful!

Amenities: Horsedrawn sleigh rides and an ice skating pond in winter (after skating you warm up in a glassed-in gazebo with a fireplace). Trout fishing and horseback riding.

Nearby Attractions: Discount shops of North Conway.
Rates: On request.

THE BELLS BED & BREAKFAST
STRAWBERRY HILL STREET, BETHLEHEM, NH 03574

Reservations Phone: 603/869-2647
Description: A Victorian B&B high in the White Mountains, named
after the many bells that hang in its eaves. Two suites are available
with private sitting rooms, a room with a view cupola at the top of
the house, and a guest cottage with enclosed porch. All have private
baths and are furnished with antiques and Oriental rugs.
Amenities: Breakfast specials include blueberry oatmeal pancakes and
bacon, a sausage and wild rice dish with sour cream eggs, and
baked French toast.

Nearby Attractions: Mt. Washington, Franconia Notch State Park,
Bretton Woods, and Mt. Cannon ski areas.
Special Services: Assistance in planning day trips and making dinner
reservations.
Rates: $50 single, $60 to $70 double
Innkeeper's Tip: Says Louise Sims, "Bethlehem is a quaint New England town (the highest Main Street east of the Rockies) enjoying a
19th-century style of life—no fast-food restaurants, traffic tie-ups, or
water slides. Just good chefs, maple-lined streets, and wide verandas
with flower boxes. Nice place to come after skiing or a hectic day of
outlet shopping."

THE BRADFORD INN
MAIN STREET, BRADFORD, NH 03221

Reservations Phone: 603/938-5309, or toll free 800/669-5309
Description: This Federal-style building was opened in 1898 as a hotel.
It contains individually decorated rooms, a spacious parlor, a grand
staircase, and wide halls.
Amenities: Full breakfast, gourmet dinners

Nearby Attractions: Lake Sunapee; Sunapee, Winslow, and Rollins
state parks; Franklin Pierce's home; boat cruises

Special Services: Bus pickup in town, lake activities, golf, and skiing nearby
Rates: $59 to $79 double; multinight discount
Innkeeper's Tip: Mt. Kearsarge can be a fascinating excursion. The Penacook Indians knew it as a long hard climb but now, with Winslow and Rollins state parks dividing the north and south faces of the mountain, you can almost drive to the summit and the climbs are much easier. The views are still breathtaking with the White Mountains to the north, and the Green Mountains to the south.

MOUNTAIN LAKE INN
RTE. 114, BRADFORD, NH 03221

Reservations Phone: 603/938-2136, or toll free 800/662-6005
Description: Built by Bradford's first settler about 15 years before the American Revolution, the inn has country-casual furnishings with true period antiques. It's located on 167 acres with trout streams, waterfalls, and a quarter mile of beachfront on Lake Massasecum.
Amenities: Full country breakfast

Nearby Attractions: Boat and dinner cruises; three ski areas; golf; tennis; racquetball; horseback riding; hiking; fishing
Special Services: Private beach, cookout areas, swimming, bicycles for guests, snowshoeing, and cross-country skiing
Rates: $80 double with private bath

THE PASQUANEY INN
STAR RTE. 1, BOX 1066, BRIDGEWATER, NH 03222

Reservations Phone: 603/744-9111
Description: This turn-of-the-century inn on the edge of Newfound Lake has a long front porch facing the lake. Single and double rooms with shared or private bath are available.
Amenities: Features French/Belgian cuisine

Nearby Attractions: In the center of the state within range of most outdoor attractions
Special Services: Recreational barn, boats, bikes, sandy beach
Rates: From $84 double

FRANCONIA INN

RTE. 116, EASTON ROAD, FRANCONIA, NH 03580

Reservations Phone: 603/823-5542

Description: This resort offers quiet country life with mountain views from the Easton Valley. The 35 rooms have recently been redecorated and renovated.

Nearby Attractions: Mount Washington, Cannon Mountain Tramway, Tite Flume, the Old Man of the Mountains, White Mountain National Forest, ski areas

Special Services: Pool, hot tub, gliding, skiing, sleigh rides, ice skating, biking, tennis, horseback riding, and croquet all on the premises. Children welcome.

Rates: $65 to $125 double in summer and fall, $60 to $90 double in spring and winter

Innkeeper's Tip: Ask about a French picnic. "We know of some very secluded picnic areas—perfect for a red checkered tablecloth and a good bottle of wine. Order the night before."

FERRY POINT HOUSE

R-1 BOX 335, LACONIA, NH 03246

Reservations Phone: 603/524-0087

Description: A country Victorian home built in the early 1800s as a very wealthy family's summer retreat on Lake Winnisquam. The inn has a beach, a gazebo on the point overlooking the lake, and five guestrooms.

Amenities: Breakfast specials include stuffed French toast, cheese baked apples, breakfast crepes, stuffed poached pears, and other treats, plus breads and muffins baked fresh daily.

Nearby Attractions: Boating, hiking, swimming, golf, tennis. All the Lakes Region and White Mountains' attractions, including the Canterbury Shaker Village, the Flume, and Old Man in the Mountain.

Special Services: Use of VCR in the living room for rental movies.

Rates: $50 to $60 single, $55 to $65 double

Innkeeper's Tip: "We keep a basket of (restaurant) menus for browsing and we gladly make dinner reservations. Ask us about the many annual fairs in surrounding towns, and the demonstrations all summer by the League of New Hampshire craftspeople in Sandwich."

THE BUTTONWOOD INN

BOX 1817, MT. SURPRISE ROAD, NORTH CONWAY, NH 03860

Reservations Phone: 603/356-2625 or toll free 800/882-9928

Description: Located in the Mt. Washington Valley, this B&B inn was built in the 1820s. Nine guestrooms with private and semiprivate baths, all individually decorated with antiques.

Amenities: Full breakfast served with homemade breads and a choice of juices, maple syrup pancakes, eggs, sausage, bacon, and—following the trends—a low cholesterol breakfast.

Nearby Attractions: Alpine skiing one mile away. Also canoeing, tennis, golf, fishing, and rock climbing within 2½ miles of the inn. Drive up to the top of Mt. Washington, the tallest mountain in the Northeast. (Better yet, ride the scenic train to the top.)

Special Services: Two guest refrigerators and a games room with open fireplace and dry bar.

Rates: $35 to $40 single, $40 to $80 double.

Innkeeper's Tip: "Excellent restaurants are plentiful with discounts offered in the off season, i.e., April to June and November through December 23. Lodging rates are also lower during these periods. Remember—no sales tax in New Hampshire."

THE PEACOCK INN

P.O. BOX 1012, NORTH CONWAY, NH 03860

Reservations Phone: 603/356-9041 or toll free 800/328-9041

Description: This B&B inn is housed in one of the most historic buildings in the Mt. Washington Valley. Constructed in 1773, it has a guestbook that dates back to 1865. The 18 guestrooms are furnished with a blend of Colonial antiques and contemporary touches. There are brass beds, canopy beds, and rooms with skylights and antique rockers.

Amenities: Fresh flowers, fruit, chocolates, and special bath salts in your room. Breakfast includes fresh juices, fruit, cereals, egg dishes, bacon or sausage. Guests have access to Mt. Cranmore Racquet Club (indoor swimming, tennis, etc.).

Nearby Attractions: Near five major ski mountains, North Conway Scenic Railroad, and White Mountains National Forest.

Special Services: Inn guests can obtain 20% to 50% discount at nearby restaurants.

Rates: $39 to $59 per person, double occupancy

SUNNY SIDE INN
SEAVEY STREET, NORTH CONWAY, NH 03860

Reservations Phone: 603/356-6239
Description: This converted and expanded 1850s New England farm-house has casual and comfortable rooms private or shared bath, plus a living room with fireplace and TV
Amenities: Full breakfast

Nearby Attractions: White Mountains, four major downhill ski areas, three golf courses, museums
Special Services: Bus depot pickups
Rates: $25 to $50 single, $40 to $60 double

LAKE SHORE FARM
31 JENNESS POND RD., NORTHWOOD, NH 03261

Reservations Phone: 603/942-5521
Description: A family farmhouse expanded to accommodate guests, it has been under the same family management for 63 years.
Amenities: Full breakfast

Nearby Attractions: Shaker Village, Strawberry Banke Capitol Complex, a variety of outdoor sports
Special Services: Games room, tennis, volleyball, Ping-Pong, badminton, horseshoes
Rates: $55 double in summer, $38 double the rest of the year

THE CAMPTON INN
RTE. 175N (P.O. BOX 282), CAMPTON, NH 03223

Reservations Phone: 603/726-4449
Description: An 1835 New England farmhouse, the inn is at the foot of the White Mountains. All rooms are individually decorated with antiques. Private and shared baths available.
Amenities: Full breakfast includes the house specialty: baked apple pancake puff.

Nearby Attractions: White Mountain National Forest, Polar Caves, The Flume, Old Man of the Mountains, Lost River, Squam Lake (filming site of On Golden Pond)
Special Services: Guest refrigerator, evening snack

Rates: $34 to $40 single, $48 to $65 double

Maria Toscano Sleight writes, "We hope you will strongly consider this B&B as one of your 'bests'. We plan to return on our yearly vacations due to our wonderful treatment by hosts Dorothy and Ken Martin. Their New England hospitality and beautifully decorated home made for one very cozy and relaxing vacation. We have visited several inns in the New England area and not one compared to the Campton Inn—regardless of price. It is truly one of the best!"

HILLTOP INN

SUGAR HILL, NH 03585

Reservations Phone: 603/823-5695

Description: Victorian guesthouse built about 1895. All guestrooms are furnished with antiques, with shared or private bath.

Amenities: A deck that offers great sunset views. All rates include a full country breakfast.

Nearby attractions: Alpine and Nordic skiing; swimming, canoeing, and bicycling areas; the Old Man of the Mountain; and the Flume.

Rates: $40 single, $50 to $80 double. Two-night minimum during fall foliage season plus an additional $10 per room.

Innkeeper's Tip: "We are close to North Conway Outlet Stores, many great restaurants, two summer stock theaters, and chamber music concerts in July and August at the Sugar Hill Meeting House."

Author's Tip: If you're an L.L. Bean fan as I am, don't miss this outfitter's outlet store in North Conway. Really low prices.

NEW YORK

B&B Reservation Services

AAAH! BED & BREAKFAST #1 LTD.

P.O. BOX 200, NEW YORK, NY 10108

Offers B&B Homes In: New York City (also in London and Paris)

Reservations Phone: 212/246-4000, or toll free 800/776-4001; FAX (212)265-4346

Phone Hours: 9am to 5pm Monday through Friday and 10am to 2pm on Saturday (answering machine after hours and Sunday)
Price Range of Homes: $40 to $75 single, $50 to $100 double, and $250 luxury suites ($100 credit at first-class restaurant inclusive)
Breakfast Included in Price: Yes
Brochure Available: Free
Reservations Should Be Made: As soon as possible—early reservations ensure the best selection

Attractions Near the B&B Homes: All New York City attractions
Major Schools, Universities Near the B&B Homes: Columbia, Hunter, NYU, Adelphi

Best B&Bs

■ Penthouse studio apartment in Midtown Manhattan, breakfast included. Anyone who has paid a New York hotel bill recently knows what a bargain this is. And look what you get in the bargain—a "tastefully appointed studio penthouse apartment facing east with a panoramic view of Midtown Manhattan, which includes a view of the Empire State Building, World Trade Towers, the Statue of Liberty, and the Hudson River from the oversized terrace." The apartment is decorated with a Japanese motif with shoji screens and brand-new wall-to-wall carpeting. There are a queen size bed, a hideaway double sleigh bed, and a double futon couch. (Top 100.)

ABODE BED & BREAKFAST LTD.
P.O. BOX 20022, NEW YORK, NY 10028

Offers B&B Homes In: Manhattan; Park Slope, Brooklyn
Reservations Phone: 212/472-2000
Phone Hours: 9am to 5pm Monday through Friday and 10am to 2pm on Saturday; answering machine other hours
Price Range of Homes: $50 to $80 single, $65 to $95 double; plus $80 to $275 for unhosted studio to three-bedroom apartments; two-night minimum
Breakfast Included in Price: Most are Continental, consisting of juice, assorted rolls, muffins, condiments, and coffee or tea; some hosts serve a full breakfast.
Brochure Available: Free
Reservations Should Be Made: As soon as possible (last-minute reservations accepted if possible)

Attractions Near the B&B Homes: New York City's theaters, museums, parks, art galleries, architecture, etc.

Major Schools, Universities Near the B&B Homes: NYU, Columbia, Hunter, Baruch, Fordham, Marymount

Best B&Bs

■ 1884 Victorian brownstone on New York City's Upper West Side. The reservation service describes this as a "sumptuous brownstone." Guests enjoy a Continental breakfast at a suspended glass table in the lattice-framed breakfast nook. The guestroom has twin beds with a private bath adjacent to the room. The host enjoys helping newcomers who might become "disoriented in a big city." (Top 100.)

■ Modern apartment in Midtown Manhattan. This contemporary accommodation is located in a luxury building with a 24-hour doorman and features a private room large enough for a double bed and a sofabed with adjacent private bath.

■ Upper East Side, Manhattan apartment in a luxury building. Say hello to the mayor of New York if he happens to be out strolling; the mayor's residence—Gracie Mansion—is only a few blocks from this apartment. All amenities are in the carpeted, twin-bedded guestroom. The private breakfast nook has a great view of the city. The room and private bath are freshened daily. Two cats are in residence.

■ Showtime! This B&B penthouse with hanging art is located right in New York City's theatre district. You have a choice of two guestrooms, one with a queen-size four-poster bed, desk, and a rocking chair. A smaller room has a high blue Chinese-style double bed surrounded by airy gauze curtains. Shared bathroom (with the host). Both rooms have private phones.

■ B&B on Central Park West in the West 80s of Manhattan with a full view of that great park. This is a luxury building with a 24-hour doorman. The twin-bedded guest suite has a private sitting room and an adjacent private bath. A full breakfast is served in the room or in the dining room.

BED & BREAKFAST (& BOOKS)
35 WEST 92ND ST., NEW YORK, NY 10025

Offers B&B Homes In: New York City.
Reservations Phone: 212/865-8740
Phone Hours: 9:30am to 5pm, Monday through Friday
Price Range of Homes: $50 to $75 single, $60 to $95 double. $100 to $170 for two to four people in unhosted apartments.
Breakfast Included in Price: Fresh coffee, teas, fresh croissants, jams, cold cereals, juice, and bagels with cream cheese.

Brochure Available: Free (with stamped, self-addressed envelope)
Reservations Should Be Made: Best in advance, particularly in the busy fall and spring seasons. But last-minute reservations also can be available.

Attractions Near the B&B Homes: Metropolitan Museum of Art, Museum of Natural History, Guggenheim Museum, Museum of Modern Art. All of the many other attractions of New York.
Major Schools, Universities Near the B&B Homes: NYU, Parsons School of Design, City U. of New York, School of Visual Arts, The New School, and major New York medical schools.

Best B&Bs

■ Sunny, plant-filled apartment on New York's Upper West Side in Manhattan. You will stay in a twin bedroom with an adjacent bath. You can walk to Lincoln Center, Central Park, and the Museum of Natural History. You have the extra security of a doorman. Your host is an accountant and music lover. The rates are a genuine New York bargain. The host is away during the summer so you will have the place to yourself then.

■ Beautifully renovated town house on a quiet street on New York City's Upper West Side in Manhattan. A double-bedded room with a bath next door. You can also enjoy a quiet sitting area with TV and books. Another bargain.

■ Elegant pre—World War I building on the Upper West Side of Manhattan, with 24-hour elevator and doormen service. You can walk to Lincoln Center and—on nice nights—to Broadway theaters.

■ Rooms with a view on the 31st floor of a Manhattan apartment building. In fact, you have a view from almost every room of the skyline or the Hudson River. The host is an interesting world traveler. And the price is certainly right.

■ East Side, Manhattan apartment in pre—World War I building, with doorman and elevator. Attractively furnished bedroom with a kitchen. Guests can use the laundry room in the basement. They also can use the TV/VCR if they'd like to sample movies from New York's huge and numerous movie rental places.

BED & BREAKFAST NETWORK OF NEW YORK
134 WEST 32ND ST., SUITE 602, NEW YORK, NY 10001

Offers B&B Homes In: New York City
Reservations Phone: 212/645-8134

Phone Hours: 8am to 6pm Monday through Friday
Price Range of Homes: $50 to $60 single, $70 to $90 double,
  hosted; $80 to $300 unhosted. Weekly, monthly rates available.
Breakfast Included in Price: Yes, except for several unhosted homes
Brochure Available: Free
Reservations Should Be Made: Several weeks in advance

Attractions Near the B&B Homes: All New York City attractions
Major Schools, Universities Near the B&B Homes: NYU, Columbia

Best B&Bs

■ This reservation service organization has classified their best homes by the first names of the hosts. You can request these homes with that name.

■ "Robin"—a loft in Midtown Manhattan. New York apartments in movies always seem to be huge affairs with living rooms the size of South Texas. As anyone who has ever lived there knows, most apartments barely have room for postage stamps laid flat. That's why this B&B is such a surprise treat—it has 4,000 square feet. The master bedroom has a queen-size antique bed with down pillows and a private bath. As a guest, you will enjoy the walls filled with original artwork, a private telephone line, a pool table, and more. **(Top 100.)**

■ "Scott"—a beautifully furnished studio on the 34th floor of a luxury building, with 16 feet of windows overlooking Central Park in Manhattan. Unhosted—that is, you fix your own breakfast.

■ "Don"—a lovely duplex penthouse in Manhattan, with terrace and southern exposure, king-size bed, and queen sleep sofa. Only minutes from Broadway theaters, Lincoln Center, Central Park, and Carnegie Hall. Unhosted.

■ "Steven"—a doorman building on Central Park South in Manhattan. This B&B offers a lovely room with queen-size bed, cable TV, refrigerator, toaster oven, and air conditioning. Handsomely furnished.

■ "Guida"—a Victorian English town house on the Upper East Side of Manhattan, with gardens, four working fireplaces, and antique rugs.

■ "Nan"—five apartments in a 100-year-old brownstone in Manhattan, a half block from Central Park and a five-minute walk from Lincoln Center. Choose from two studios, two one-bedroom apartments, and a two-bedroom apartment with a garden.

■ "Bevy"—a duplex loft in the heart of Soho, Manhattan. This is the place to stay if you would like to be close to all of the Soho art galleries, shops, and restaurants. The exposed brick and original artwork add to the charm of this unusual getaway.

■ "Peter"—a luxury doorman building on the West Side of Manhattan. Located steps from Carnegie Hall, Lincoln Center, and the Broadway theaters. The apartment has good views, a balcony, and cable TV. Guest room has a queen-size bed, private bath, and powder room.

URBAN VENTURES, INC.
P.O. BOX 426, NEW YORK, NY 10024

Offers B&B Homes In: New York City (over 500 accommodations)
Reservations Phone: 212/594-5650; FAX: 212/947-9320
Phone Hours: 9am to 5pm Monday through Friday, on Saturday to 3pm
Price Range of Homes: $35 to $60 single, $45 to $85 double
Breakfast Included in Price: Continental (juice, roll or toast, coffee)
Brochure Available: Free
Reservations Should Be Made: 2 weeks in advance (last-minute reservations accepted if possible)

Attractions Near the B&B Homes: Broadway theaters, Central Park, skyscrapers, famous restaurants, and all the many other "Big Apple" attractions
Major Schools, Universities Near the B&B Homes: Columbia, NYU, Pace

Best B&Bs
■ Mississippi B&B in New York City. Sounds unlikely but its true. The host has brought the lushness of her southern state to Manhattan in her apartment. This B&B has two terraces and great views of New York City.

■ B&B on East 33rd Street, off Lexington Avenue in Manhattan. You're in the shopping heart of New York City and close to many publishing, public relations, and advertising firms that have been moving toward the lower part of Manhattan these past few years. Your host speaks Spanish and French and can communicate in basic German. The small room has a double bed, and the price is extra low for New York.

■ Apartment on 92nd Street, close to Central Park in Manhattan. The building has an elevator and doorman. The apartment has two cats.

■ B&B in a new building on East 76th Street and 1st Avenue in an interesting, quieter part of Manhattan. The apartment has a double bed and private bath.

■ Greenwich Village, Manhattan B&B. You can choose a room with a double bed or one with a twin bed.

CITY LIGHTS, BED & BREAKFAST, LTD.
P.O. BOX 20355, CHEROKEE STATION, NEW YORK CITY, NY 10028

Offers B&B Homes In: New York City (including Manhattan, Queens, and Brooklyn), and Westchester
Reservations Phone: 212/737-7049; FAX: 212/535-2755
Phone Hours: 9am to 5pm Monday through Friday; 9am to 12pm Saturday
Price Range of Homes: $40 to $75 single, $55 to $90 double
Breakfast Included in Price: Continental to full breakfast
Brochure Available: Free
Reservations Should Be Made: As soon as possible, especially for peak travel periods

Attractions Near the B&B Homes: Lincoln Center, Rockefeller Center, Metropolitan Museum of Art, theaters, Central Park, and all of the other many sights of New York City
Major Schools, Universities Near the B&B Homes: Hunter, NYU, Columbia, and others

Best B&Bs
■ Four-story Upper East Side (80s) town house in Manhattan. The host is an English lady of the theater. She and her Scottish housekeeper look after the needs of B&B guests. You can choose a suite or a "special" room and relax in a large living room decorated with rare Chinese antiques and silk sofas, with tall French windows flanked by two finely leafed palms. An intricately carved coffee table sits in front of a wood-burning fireplace. The suite on the floor above has two bedrooms, two baths, a living room with a convertible queen-size sofa, and kitchen facilities for light snacks. The front room is double bedded while the larger of the two rooms faces the garden. This room also has a wood-burning fireplace. *Insider's Tip:* The "special" room is just that: a king-size bed with a view of the fireplace, a huge dressing room, and bath. Think of Hollywood of the 1930s and you have some idea of the glamour of this room.

■ B&B in a luxury building on Madison Avenue at 90th Street in Manhattan. This apartment has it all—from a beautiful oak credenza and hutch in the oak-paneled dining room down to Oriental rugs. Rooms have private baths and a view of New York's skyline.

■ West End apartment (mid 80s) in Manhattan. This one-bedroom apartment is decorated in rich French traditional style. There is a queen-size four-poster bed and mahogany chests. This is an unhosted apartment so you fix your own breakfast in a fully equipped kitchen. You can also do practical things such as catching up on your laundry (a washer/dryer is in the kitchen). The apartment is furnished with antiques and a wonderful old étagère displaying a china collection. Compare all the space and freedom you get here with any other hotel suite in New York at twice the price. Small wonder we think B&Bs are a wonderful way to travel today.

■ Victorian brownstone in Manhattan, close to the Mayor's mansion on the East Side. You check into a room decorated with Liberty of London prints. The English decor continues with fine English antiques. You can retreat to an unusual balcony/library nook overlooking a rotunda-like dining area.

■ B&B on the West Side of Manhattan hosted by a lively woman who is an art collector and co-owner of an advertising agency. This single room with private bath is in an attractive older building in the west 80s.

■ A room with the sound of music, in the west 80s of Manhattan. The host is an actor/singer and choreographer. As you might expect, the apartment is decorated with art deco and theatrical posters.

■ Stay in a TV executive's apartment. There is an attractive oversized studio in a new highrise in the west 50s of Manhattan. The skyline view is wonderful—and you're within walking distance of Central Park, Lincoln Center, Carnegie Hall, and the Broadway theater district.

RAINBOW HOSPITALITY
466 AMHERST ST., BUFFALO, NY 14207

Offers B&B Homes In: Niagara Falls, Chautauqua, Lewistown, Youngstown, east to Rochester and Buffalo, and south to Pennsylvania
Reservations Phone: 716/874-8797 or 716/283-4794
Phone Hours: 9:30am to 5pm weekdays, on Saturday to noon
Price Range of Homes: Modest, $35 to $55; moderate, $55 to $65; luxury, $65 to $140
Breakfast Included in Price: Continental or full American, according to the individual home
Brochure Available: $1 if you send a stamped, self-addressed no. 10 envelope
Reservations Should Be Made: Two weeks in advance (last-minute reservations accepted if possible)

Attractions Near the B&B Homes: Niagara Falls, Canada, Lewistown Art Park, Fatima Shrine, Fort Niagara, Kleinhans Music Hall and Buffalo's theater district, Chautauqua Institute, four large amusement complexes, lakes, rivers, convention centers, antique and outlet shopping, museums and art galleries, winter sports

Major Schools, Universities Near the B&B Homes: Niagara U., SUNY at Buffalo, Buffalo State, Canisius

Best B&Bs

■ White Victorian home on the lower Niagara River, New York, just seven miles north of the falls. In pleasant weather you can have breakfast on the deck overlooking this river. *Insider's Tip:* Be sure to try some of the host's homemade orange marmalade on fresh-baked muffins, a house specialty. The host is an interior decorator. (Top 100.)

■ Dutch Colonial home on Chautauqua Lake, New York. Located on an 11-acre wooded estate. A private beach and dock are available. Other nearby attractions include local winery tours, Midway Amusement Park, and a sail on the Sea Lion. Winter sports include skiing, snowmobiling, and ice fishing.

BED & BREAKFAST OF LONG ISLAND
P.O. BOX 392, OLD WESTBURY, NY 11568

Offers B&B Homes In: Eastern Long Island Hamptons beaches, Miller Place, Amagansett, Southampton, Garden City, Glen Cove, Syosset, Peconic, Southold, Port Jefferson, Sayville, Westbury, Manhasset, East Islip, Roslyn, Oldfield, Long Beach, Massapequa, East Northport, Baldwin

Reservations Phone: 516/334-6231

Phone Hours: 9am to 12:30pm Monday through Friday; answering machine to 10pm weekdays, 10am to 9pm weekends

Price Range of Homes: $48 to $68 single, $58 to $125 double

Breakfast Included in Price: Continental or full American, plus regional specialties like homemade beach plum jam, sautéed mushrooms and eggs, blueberry muffins, waffles, buttery croissants, carrot cake, quiche

Brochure Available: Free if you send a stamped, self-addressed no. 10 envelope

Reservations Should Be Made: Two weeks in advance (last-minute reservations accepted if possible)

Attractions Near the B&B Homes: Sag Harbor Customs House, Whal-

ing Museum, John Drew Theater, Guild Hall Art Exhibits, Home
Sweet Home Museum, Parrish Museum, Nassau Coliseum, Shinnecock
Indian Reservation, Halsey Homestead, Montauk Hither Hills State
Park, sport fishing, Watermill Old Mill Museum & Windmill

Major Schools, Universities Near the B&B Homes: Hofstra, Adelphi,
SUNY at Stony Brook, Southampton College, Dowling College,
C. W. Post, Kings Point Marine Academy, Webb Institute, LaSalle
Academy

Best B&Bs

▪ Waterfront contemporary home in Sayville, Long Island, New York.
The outside may reflect 1990s taste but the interior is from another
era—antiques, brass beds, Tiffany lamps, oak pieces, and Oriental
rugs. Everything has been coordinated by an interior designer and
school teacher. You can play on two nearby golf courses or on free
tennis courts. The hosts are world travelers who like to sail. They often
take their guests on their boat to Fire Island, which is right across from
their home. Don't miss breakfast: homemade carrot cake, breads, and
gourmet omelets. Close to the beach and LaSalle Academy and
Dowling College. (Top 100.)

▪ Restored 1800 farmhouse in Setauket, Long Island, New York. The
house is furnished with period antiques (not too surprising since the
owner is an antiques dealer), and you have your choice of two bedrooms, one with a double bed, the other with two single beds. It is only
a half mile from a small private beach and close to Stony Brook with its
museums and university. The host brings coffee to your room before the
full breakfast is served buffet style.

▪ Palatial home in Long Beach, Long Island, New York. You can walk to
the beach and the Long Island Railroad from this home, which has
stained-glass windows and antiques from many different periods. Breakfast is wonderful—cheese platters, fruit, choice of breads, coffee, and
jam. Sundays are special with a full English breakfast served in the
formal wood-paneled dining room. Or you can choose to have breakfast in your room. *Insider's Tip:* Bikes are available to guests. The hosts
will provide beach passes.

▪ Rambling home in East Setauket, Long Island, New York, with a great
view of Long Island Sound. You can watch from a hammock or lounge
on this two-acre property close to Stony Brook and Port Jefferson.

▪ Victorian home in Glen Cove, Long Island, New York. You can
breakfast by an atrium with a view of landscaped gardens and a
swimming pool. There are two upstairs bedrooms. Depending on your
mood for the night, you can choose an antiques-filled room with a
Tiffany-style lamp and brass double bed, or the other bedroom with a

casual country feeling with scrubbed pine furniture and some pampering touches (bidet, heated towel racks, and a lighted mirror).

■ Second-oldest house in Manhasset, Long Island, New York. Built in 1840, to be exact, and completely restored. From the huge dining room with its three chandeliers and the original carved fireplace to the doors with original brass hinges, this home is a gem. There are several guestrooms, with sitting rooms nearby on separate landings with TV. You can walk to the Long Island Railroad for the trip to New York City, or drive to the beach.

A REASONABLE ALTERNATIVE, INC. AND THE HAMPTON REGISTRY BED AND BREAKFAST ON LONG ISLAND

117 SPRING ST., ROOM 6, PORT JEFFERSON, NY 11777

Offers B&B Homes In: Nassau and Suffolk counties of Long Island, New York, including all of the Hamptons
Reservations Phone: 516/928-4034 weekdays
Phone Hours: 11am to 5pm June thru August; 11am to 3pm September to May (Eastern Standard Time)
Price Range of Homes: $36 to $125 (single or double)
Breakfast Included in Price: Continental (juice, roll or toast, coffee); occasional extras and regional specialties provided in some homes.
Brochure Available: Free if you send a stamped, self-addressed no. 10 envelope
Reservations Should Be Made: Two weeks in advance (last-minute reservations accepted if possible, with a credit card)

Attractions Near the B&B Homes: Bethpage Recreation Village, Hargreaves Vineyards, Sag Harbor Whaling Museum, Sag Harbor Museum and Custom House, game farm and zoo, Fire Island National Seashore, Montauk Lighthouse, Jones Beach, Westbury Music Fair, Stony Brook museum complex, Sagamore Hill, Vanderbilt Planetarium, Sunken Meadow State Park
Major Schools, Universities Near the B&B Homes: Hofstra, Adelphi, C. W. Post, SUNY at Stony Brook

Best B&Bs

■ Colonial home in quaint North Shore, Long Island, New York, village. This 1817 B&B represents a great value for the money in pricey summer Long Island and is in a particularly attractive setting, overlooking a brook. Your host is a teacher. You can walk to the beach. There is a queen-size bed and private bath in your air-conditioned suite. Also available: a library/sitting room and an extended Continental breakfast. A pleasant headquarters for exploring all the restaurant and gallery charms of the North Shore. (Top 100.)

■ Large Victorian home on private grounds in North Shore, Long Island, New York. Choice of two rooms, each with a private bath. Breakfast is served in a sunny breakfast room. Afterward guests can use the inground swimming pool.

■ Contemporary salt-box summer home in the eastern dunes of Long Island, New York. The guestroom has a double bed with a private bath. You can walk just four short blocks to the ocean.

■ Restored Colonial farmhouse in the hub of the Hamptons, Long Island, New York. This home has some very unusual touches. Built originally in 1790, various residents over the years have added other rooms. Now the owner/architect has restored each of the rooms to its original period. That is why you will find a combination of styles in this B&B, from Colonial to Victorian to more modern periods. There is a queen-size bed in each guestroom, and you can hike (a mile) to the beach. Available only in summer months.

AMERICAN COUNTRY COLLECTION OF BED & BREAKFAST HOMES AND COUNTRY INNS
984 GLOUCESTER PL., SCHENECTADY, NY 12309

Offers B&B Homes In: Northeastern New York, Vermont, and western Massachusetts
Reservations Phone: 518/370-4948
Phone Hours: 10am to noon and 1 to 5pm Monday through Friday (answering machine always on)
Price Range of Homes: $30 to $80 single, $40 to $175 double (rates in and around Saratoga, NY, increase approximately 50% in August, the racing season)
Breakfast Included in Price: Breakfasts range from homemade Continental to traditional American. There are also elegant four-course gourmet breakfasts. Many Vermont and New York country breakfasts include maple syrup tapped right on the farm. Special treats include waffled French toast, hot fruit soufflé, and blueberry walnut pancakes.
Brochure Available: Free if you send a stamped, self-addressed no. 10 envelope; directory for $4

Reservations Should Be Made: Three weeks in advance (over a month in advance during the peak travel seasons)

Attractions Near the B&B Homes: Several in the Saratoga area, near the Saratoga Race Course, Empire State Plaza in Albany, Baseball Hall of Fame in Cooperstown, Bennington Museum and Battlefield, Hyde Park and the Roosevelt Estate, Shaker Museum, Catskill Game Farm, Tanglewood, and Lenox, Massachusetts

Major Schools, Universities Near the B&B Homes: Skidmore, SUNY at Albany and SUNY at Cobleskill, Williams, Smith, Bennington, Middlebury, U. of Vermont, Union College

Best B&Bs

■ Alpine-style home in the Worcester Mountain Range, six miles from Stowe, Vermont. "This is what Vermont living is all about," says the host as she surveys a domain that includes 10 acres of spruce and white pines, with about the only sound coming from a gurgling brook. The home itself is modern, with vaulted ceilings and large windows. She and her husband have furnished this B&B with antiques that complement modern furnishings. B&B guests have the entire second floor to themselves and window views of the gardens and the mountains. The guestrooms are decorated with original art as well as Vermont photographs. For breakfast you might have blueberry pancakes or Belgian waffles. Or Eggs à la Goldenrod and ham (if you're one of those lucky people who doesn't have to worry about cholesterol). The host is a retired mechanical engineer and his wife is a concert pianist. Don't be surprised if she treats you to an occasional concert on her Steinway Grand. **(Top 100.)**

■ Hilltop farm in Great Barrington, Massachusetts. Enjoy the view of the surrounding Berkshire Hills from the wrap-around porches. This is one of the original farms in the area (the barn dates back to the 1820s). Two dwellings create an eight bedroom B&B. You can stay in the restored barn or in the house. Don't opt too quickly for the house. The barn has two air-conditioned suites in the hayloft. *Insider's Tip:* If you're a tall traveler, request the "Library" in the main house (available March through November), which has one bed that is seven feet long.

■ B&B in Germantown, New York. Since it was first constructed in 1807, this home has had a colorful history as a roadside tavern, dance hall, and even a fox farm. Guests have access to the living room with TV and fireplace, a card room, and a screened porch. Closed in winter months.

■ Greek Revival home in Fair Haven, Vermont. The reservation service describes this as a "textbook Greek Revival." It is nicely situated on 3½ acres of mostly gardens and lawns. The five guestrooms are individually decorated in soft hues. Each has a window view of mountains and farms. The formal parlor, TV room, and breakfast room are open to guests.

■ Old farmhouse in Manchester, Vermont. In 1890 this building was home to a tenant farmer. Now it has been restored and furnished with eclectic old furnishings and antiques. The setting is perfect, at the foot of the Green Mountains, bordered by a brook.

ELAINE'S BED & BREAKFAST AND INN RESERVATION SERVICE

143 DIDAMA ST., SYRACUSE, NY 13224

Offers B&B Homes In: Apulia, Cazenovia, Fayetteville, Clay, De Witt, Geneva, Jamesville, Syracuse, Liverpool, Baldwinsville, Rome, Lafayette, Watertown, Vernon, Saranac Lake, Tully
Reservations Phone: 315/446-4199
Phone Hours: 10am to 8pm, daily
Price Range of Homes: Starts at $35 single, $45 double, with shared bath, to $75 for suites and studio apartments
Breakfast Included in Price: Each is different—some Continental, some more elaborate. Advance requests for special diets are honored. Includes such items as homemade muffins, cantaloupe, cereal, orange juice.
Brochure Available: Send a stamped, self-addressed envelope
Reservations Should Be Made: By phone at least two weeks in advance, and a deposit sent immediately

Attractions Near the B&B Homes: Everson Museum of Fine Art, Erie Canal Boat Cruises, Beaver Lake Nature Center
Major Schools, Universities Near the B&B Homes: Syracuse University, LeMoyne College

Best B&Bs

■ Hilltop colonial home in Baldwinsville, New York. Over 145 years old, this charming house is filled with antiques. You have a choice of four bedrooms. The master suite offers a king-size bed, a fireplace, and a private bath with dressing room. This home is located a short walk from the village and the Seneca River. (Top 100.)

■ Colonial home in Pompey, New York. This home has two bedrooms with fresh flowers and their own private entrance (which means you can come and go as you please). A full country breakfast is served; would you believe heart-shaped waffles topped with pure maple syrup? The home is close to Syracuse (25 minutes) and several major ski areas, including Toggenburg and Song Mountain. *Insider's Tip:* For a minimum of two nights, two couples could rent this place as their own private apartment with its own modern kitchen and living room.

■ White Colonial home in Cleveland, New York, on the north shore of Oneida Lake. Back in 1820 the richest man in town built this 6,000-square-foot home. All of the bedrooms have working fireplaces. This home is filled with surprises. The large playroom has a billiard table, jukebox, and many musical instruments. The family room has a bar and a leaded stained-glass window. The formal living room is filled with antiques and a player piano. (The owners have over 1,000 piano rolls.) *Insider's Tip:* On hot summer days, request one of the two bedrooms with air conditioning.

■ Tudor Colonial home in Syracuse, on a thoroughfare of gracious homes. A gourmet breakfast is served in a newly decorated formal dining room. The bedrooms share a vintage bath. *Insider's Tip:* If you don't want to miss Johnny Carson late at night, ask for the bedroom with its own sitting area and TV set.

■ Victorian farmhouse in Rome, New York (close to the Griffis Air Force Base). This 150-year-old house is owned by a descendant of one of the original settlers and offers a host of amenities on its 40 acres: inground swimming pool, hiking and cross-country ski trails, and gardens. History buffs will want to take sidetrips to nearby Fort Stanwix, an Erie Canal Village, and the Oriskany Battlefield.

■ Hill home near Syracuse, New York. From this hilltop perch you can see 35 miles and three lakes. Yet you are only 15 minutes from downtown Syracuse. *Insider's Tip:* Be sure to see the unique solarium full of plants.

BED & BREAKFAST CONNECTION
RD#1 P.O. BOX 325, VERNON, NY 13476

Offers B&B Homes In: Central New York State, from the Adirondacks to Binghamton and from Nelliston to Syracuse, including the Cooperstown area
Reservations Phone: 315/829-4888
Phone Hours: 9am to 9pm Monday through Saturday
Price Range of Homes: $30 to $65 single, $35 to $125 double plus a $5 reservation fee.
Breakfast Included in Price: Full or Continental (cereal, baked items, juice, and coffee).
Brochure: Free, with a self-addressed, stamped envelope

Reservations Should Be Made: One week in advance. For priority weekends, up to three months in advance.

Attractions Near the B&B Homes: Revolutionary War historical sites, Baseball Hall of Fame, Oneida silver outlet

Major Schools, Universities Near the B&B Homes: Hamilton College, Colgate University, Utica College, Syracuse University, SUNY Binghamton, SUNY Oneonta, Cazenovia College, and community colleges in the Mohawk Valley—Onondaga, Herkimer, and Broome County.

Best B&Bs

■ A 1799 Federal homestead in Vernon, New York. Now called Lavender Inn, it offers a guest dining room that includes a brick fireplace with a bread oven and stone hearth. There are many other early touches you will enjoy, such as the entry hall with nine-foot ceilings that opens into a parlor with a crackling fire. Your day here begins with a hearty country breakfast of eggs, bacon, waffles, French toast, hot cereal, and homemade granola. The home is furnished with antiques and the host's handmade quilts and weavings. **(Top 100.)**

■ An 1840 Colonial salt-box home in Rome, New York. There are two double bedrooms with a shared bath and a large studio bedroom with a private bath. A full country breakfast is served. *Insider's Tip:* Take a tour of the little schoolhouse (completely furnished) in the backyard.

■ A Victorian Italian village in the historic district of Oneida, New York. This home has many Victorian touches, from the crystal chandeliers and marble fireplaces to period antiques.

■ A Victorian mansion in Ilion, New York. The RSO reports, "The architecture combines Second Empire and late Victorian Italianate and is furnished in exquisite detail." Historic trivia: This B&B had the first indoor bathroom ever installed in Herkimer County.

■ Restored Victorian home in Richfield Springs, New York. This B&B is listed on the National Registry of Historic Places and is a good place to stay if you're planning to visit the Baseball Hall of Fame and Cooperstown (15 miles away). Relax on three acres of lawn and trees.

———————— **B&B Inns** ————————

THE HEDGES
BLUE MOUNTAIN LAKE, NY 12812

Reservations Phone: 518/352-7325
Description: In a historic Adirondack camp with unique architecture, the inn's rooms are furnished with antiques. There are 15 separate cottages set on secluded Blue Mountain Lake.
Amenities: Full breakfast cooked to order; complimentary bedtime snack

Nearby Attractions: The Adirondack Museum, Adirondack State Park with miles of hiking trails (many trails begin near the inn)
Special Services: Clay tennis court, canoes and rowboats, swimming
Rates: $114 to $134 double July to September; in June, September, and October deduct 10%.

THOUSAND ISLANDS INN
335 RIVERSIDE DR., CLAYTON, NY 13634

Reservations Phone: 315/686-3030
Description: Serving the public since 1897, the inn's 17 sleeping rooms were remodeled in 1980 with private bath and cable color TV. Most rooms have a view of the St. Lawrence River, and central fire and smoke-detector systems have been installed.
Amenities: Full breakfast with flapjacks, sourdough bread French toast, and broccoli-and-cheese omelet, among the specialties

Nearby Attractions: Shipyard Museum, Town Hall Museum, Thousand Island Craft School & Textile Museum, fishing and water sports
Special Services: Scenic boat and airplane tours of the Thousand Islands, fishing charters
Rates: $45 single, $60 double, in summer. Open May 17 to September 29.
Innkeeper's Tip: "Contact the Clayton Chamber of Commerce if you're planning a trip to the Thousand Islands for a free 32-page vacation guide, published annually. This includes information on area attractions and a schedule of major events throughout the year. Call toll free 800/252-9806.

"Take a boat tour of the islands. Uncle Sam Boat Tours, out of Clayton, is the most complete island tour available on the U.S. side of the river. Whereas tours from nearby Alexandria Bay are horse-shoe in direction, showing passengers half of the islands twice, the Clayton tour is circular, showing passengers all of the islands once. The cost and duration of both tours are the same."

BIG MOOSE INN
BIG MOOSE LAKE, EAGLE BAY, NY 13331

Reservations Phone: 315/357-2042
Description: Single and double rooms are available in this rustic lake-side lodge; up to 26 people may be accommodated.
Amenities: Continental breakfast

Nearby Attractions: Blue Mountain Museum, Old Forge, Enchanted Forest
Special Services: Cocktail lounge, a variety of summer and winter sports available
Rates: $43 double, with shared bath; $75 double, with private bath

SOUTH MEADOW FARM LODGE
CASCADE ROAD, LAKE PLACID, NY 12946

Reservations Phone: 518/523-9369
Description: There are beds for ten in these rooms, built around a living room with fireplace and a piano. The "Honeymoon Cottage" is a converted maple sugar house with a woodstove, where candles provide the only light.
Amenities: Large farm breakfast

Nearby Attractions: Winter Olympic site
Special Services: Cross-country skiing, farm chores to share in, camp rates available.
Rates: $45 to $50 single, $70 to $90 double

PINE HILL ARMS
MAIN STREET, PINE HILL, NY 12465

Reservations Phone: 914/254-9811 or 914/254-4012
Description: Established in 1882, the hotel lies between two ski cen-

ters. The 25 rooms have been completely remodeled and have private baths. The lounge has a large stone fireplace.

Nearby Attractions: Skiing, bicycling, golf, tennis, horseback riding, tubing, fly fishing
Special Services: Hot tub spa and sauna, exercise equipment, swimming pool
Rates: $35 to $57 single, $35 to $80 double. Seasonal rate changes, weekend packages available.

TIBBITTS HOUSE INN

100 COLUMBIA TURNPIKE, CLINTON HEIGHTS, RENSSELAER, NY 12144

Reservations Phone: 518/472-1348
Description: This 135-year-old farmhouse with an 84-foot enclosed porch has comfortably furnished rooms with shared bath, plus an apartment with an old keeping room with beamed ceiling and a corner, raised-hearth fireplace.

Nearby Attractions: The State Capitol and the Empire State Mall (two miles away), a 45-mile hiking and biking path along the Hudson and Mohawk rivers, public boat launch.
Special Services: Patio, picnic tables, spacious glass-enclosed porch, ample parking
Rates: $44 single, $46 double.
Tips: No gratuities

RHODE ISLAND

———————— B&B Reservation Services ————————

ANNA'S VICTORIAN CONNECTION

5 FOWLER AVE., NEWPORT, RI 02840

Offers B&B Homes In: Newport, Middletown, Jamestown, Portsmouth, Tiverton, Bristol

Reservations Phone: 401/849-2489
Phone Hours: The number above gives you an answering machine 24 hours. Your call will be returned from 8am to 11pm in summer, 10am to 2pm and evenings in winter, every day of the week.
Price Range of Homes: $35 to $150 per room, with surcharge for third person.
Breakfast Included in Price: Juice, fresh fruit, home-baked goods, coffee or tea.
Brochure Available: Free
Reservations Should Be Made: In advance, with full first night's deposit; VISA, MasterCard, American Express, En Route, Diners Club, Carte Blanche accepted

Attractions Near the B&B Homes: Newport beaches, mansions, boat shows, jazz, folk festival, international jumping derby, music festival, Virginia Slims and Volvo tournaments, sailing, navy base, Newport Yachting Center
Major Schools, Universities Near the B&B Homes: Portsmouth Abbey, St. Georges, Salve Regina, U. of Rhode Island, Brown U., Bryant College, Roger Williams College, Providence College

Best B&Bs

■ An 1850 home in Newport, Rhode Island. Located in Newport's historic Point Section, a neighborhood of 18th- and 19th-century houses, two blocks from the harbor and only a five-minute walk from the center of town. A brick walk banked with ivy and a colorful flower bed welcome you into this cheerful home. Great effort has obviously gone even into small details. Breakfast is served on china with stemware and fresh flowers. The host serves fresh fruits (peaches, strawberries, blueberries, melon, kiwi), homemade banana breads, German pancakes with fresh apples, blueberry pancakes (always on Sunday), and a variety of other delights. Guests are invited to use the piano and to relax in the glider in the yard. You'll find the fixings for tea, coffee, and bouillon as well as an electric coffee pot in your room. One attractively decorated room has two wing chairs, a writing desk, and plenty of natural light. Another has a loveseat and a bookcase filled with antique books, and a private bath. The host is a local florist. (Top 100.)

■ 1751 Georgian Colonial home in Newport, Rhode Island. One of Newport's wealthiest merchants spared no dollars in building this handsome home. But he may have overdone it. British General Prescott liked it so much he commandeered it as his headquarters during the Revolutionary War. The house is currently featured in the books *Architectural Heritage of Newport* and *Newport Restored*. You can check into a room with lovely period pieces, a working fireplace, and private bathroom. Some rooms have four-poster or canopy beds. *Insider's Tip:* If you want space, ask for the "ballroom." This room formerly was a ballroom and has a baby grand piano and Oriental carpets on wide-plank floors. Breakfast for the whole B&B is served beside a large fireplace on a 1750 table.

■ 100-year-old Victorian home in Newport, Rhode Island. This home has been carefully restored, preserving the original moldings, the fireplace mantel, and the stained-glass windows. Suites are located on the third floor. Both have ceiling fans, sky lights, cable TV, telephone, small refrigerators, and microwave ovens. Your host is a Captain in the U.S. Navy so former sailors particularly should feel right at home here. Your other host is a former English teacher.

■ Greek Revival home in Somerset, Massachusetts. Sea captain Daniel Brady once called this lovely old place his home. It was built in 1845 on gardens that date back to the 1700s. *Insider's Tip:* Ask for the suite with a balcony and fireplace overlooking the Tauton River. Your hosts speak fluent Spanish.

■ 1915 gabled home in Middletown, Rhode Island. You never know for sure what pleasant surprise you may encounter in this home—needlework decorations, railroad memorabilia, dollhouse miniatures. You're only five minutes by foot from an ocean beach. Newport is 1½ miles away.

■ Restored 1812 B&B in Providence, Rhode Island. Says the reservation service, "The host is a historic preservation consultant who puts her expertise to work in her own home. She has created a showplace of the Federal Period (1790–1820) with authentic antiques in every room." Close to Brown University and Rhode Island School of Design.

■ Turn-of-the-century home in Newport, Rhode Island. Susan, the host, is an RN with an empty nest. She has used some creative ideas in preparing special rooms—"Wicker," "Brass Bed," and "Lace." Each name denotes the main feature of the antique decor of that room. Susan serves a hearty Continental breakfast in the Eastlake sitting room.

■ Commodore Perry Victorian cottage in Newport, Rhode Island. Ten years ago the hosts, Sondra and Jim, celebrated their marriage with the purchase of a large cottage two blocks from the center of town. In the last decade they have carefully restored their home and offices (they practice psychology together). The entire third floor is devoted to B&B guests. Breakfast may consist of waffles, muffins, and fruit. Two children in the family, Kate and Dan, have made the painful but generous decision to share their toys with the children of visiting B&B guests.

BED & BREAKFAST OF RHODE ISLAND
P.O. BOX 3291, NEWPORT, RI 02840

Offers B&B Homes In: Rhode Island and bordering Massachusetts
Reservations Phone: 401/849-1298
Phone Hours: 9am to 5pm Monday through Friday (9am to 8pm Monday through Friday and 10am to 2pm on Saturday during summer)
Price Range of Homes: $40 to $80 single, $45 to $170 double
Breakfast Included in Price: Juice, fresh fruit, home-baked goods, tea and coffee. About 30% of the hosts serve a full breakfast, many of which are gourmet (Belgian waffles, quiche, fruited specialties, oven pancakes).
Brochure Available: Free; a host directory is also available for $4. Includes itineraries, information on each town, B&B descriptions
Reservations Should Be Made: Two weeks in advance (last-minute reservations accepted when possible, but guests may not always stay in the desired area)

Attractions Near the B&B Homes: Newport mansions and historic homes, yachting and sailing center, Colt State Park (Bristol), lighthouses and windmills, Slater Mill (Pawtucket), Providence's historic East Side, ocean beaches, country villages
Major Schools, Universities Near the B&B Homes: Brown, Rhode Island College, Providence College, Rhode Island School of Design, Johnson & Wales, U. of Rhode Island, Bryant, Salve Regina, St. George's School, Portsmouth Abbey

Best B&Bs

■ The King House in Newport, Rhode Island. This is another "cottage" Newport-style. That means it is an elegant Greek Revival mansion right in downtown Newport on a quiet neighborhood street. The reservation service says, "This B&B is truly elegant in both decoration and hosting, while still retaining fine pricing for private rooms and baths in often over-priced Newport." The furnishings are elegant—from an 1880 English Chippendale table in the living room to a 19th-century silk Oriental rug. Fresh flowers appear throughout this B&B. If you are an antiques buff, this is definitely the place for you. (Top 100.)

■ Country Goose Victorian farmhouse. This unusual house, only two miles from the heart of Newport, Rhode Island, is decorated seasonally —with scarecrows and pumpkins at Halloween, sleighs and toys at Christmas.

■ Emma's Front Porch. That's what the host calls this Newport B&B. She is an actress, dancer, and choreographer who enjoys meeting people. She welcomes you with some lovely Victorian rooms. Breakfast is served on the sun porch. You may have a surprise treat: If you go to the local Shakespeare Theater or the Island Moving Company, you may see your host performing on stage.

■ Brigham's, a B&B in the heart of a Newport yachting village. If you are interested in sailing, stay here. The home frequently hosts the crews of sailing yachts from around the world—including some Italians vying for the world championships for Flying Dutchman, a BOC singlehanded race, or some Americans competing in the Volvo regatta.

B&B REGISTRY AT NEWPORT
44 EVERETT ST., NEWPORT, RI 02840

Offers B&B Homes In: Newport, Middletown, and Portsmouth
Reservations Phone: 401/846-0362
Phone Hours: 9am to 7pm daily (except Wednesday); 1 to 5pm Saturday
Price Range of Homes: $50 to $75 single, $75 to $95 double
Breakfast Included in Price: Continental to full American, and various special dishes, at the hosts' discretion
Brochure Available: Free
Reservations Should Be Made: Two weeks in advance, three weeks in summer (last-minute reservations accepted if possible)

Attractions Near the B&B Homes: Naval War College, Topiary Gardens, at least five major boat shows a year, and the summer "cottages" of the rich and famous of yesteryear, yours to explore on fabulous Bellevue Avenue
Major Schools, Universities Near the B&B Homes: St. George's, Portsmouth Abbey prep schools, Salve Regina, Roger Williams

Best B&Bs

■ Smith Cottage in Newport, Rhode Island. A summer "cottage" in this town would be a glorious mansion anywhere else. Come to this unique B&B and live like the rich and famous in this stone and brick Colonial Revival home built in 1885. You can walk to the ocean (five minutes away) or stroll down historic Bellevue Avenue. (Top 100)

■ Meagher Newport Cottage in the historic Point Section of Newport, Rhode Island. This 100-year-old cottage is only three doors away from the bay and close to town.

■ Henderson Cottage in Newport, Rhode Island. This B&B is quite a bargain and it's located two blocks from the harbor at King's Park Beach.

■ Tarlton Carriage House in Middletown, Rhode Island. This home has been fully restored from the days when it was built back some 130 years ago and is located on a quiet suburban street close to the beaches and sightseeing areas. A full breakfast is served.

■ Trout Guest House in Portsmouth, Rhode Island. This is another retreat back to the Victorian era, where you can sit on the sprawling front porch in white wicker furniture and forget about the 20th century for a few minutes.

GUEST HOUSE ASSOCIATION OF NEWPORT
P.O. BOX 981, NEWPORT, RI 02840

Offers B&B Homes In: Newport only
Reservations Phone: Each home on their list must be called directly for reservations; call 401/846-ROOM (846-7666) for other information. Individual homes/inns take turns answering this phone number.
Price Range of Homes: $35 to $120 single, $35 to $120 double
Breakfast Included in Price: Continental (juice, roll or toast, coffee)
Brochure Available: Free
Reservations Should Be Made: Two weeks in advance in winter, a month or more in summer or fall (last-minute reservations accepted if possible)

Attractions Near the B&B Homes: National Historic Landmarks, Victorian "gilded age" mansions, Touro Synagogue (first in America), Cliff Walk, beaches, wharf dining, and shopping areas
Major Schools, Universities Near the B&B Homes: Naval War College, Salve Regina, St. George's Prep, St. Michael's, Portsmouth Abbey

_____ **B&B Inns** _____

POLLY'S PLACE
349 VALLEY ROAD, MIDDLETOWN, RI 02840

Reservations Phone: 401/847-2160

Description: A large home inn with five guest rooms plus a complete separate apartment with kitchen and patio (ideal for families). The property is surrounded by weeping willows and bordered by a lively brook.

Amenities: The Continental breakfast is definitely health-oriented with whole-grain muffins, cereals and fresh fruit.

Nearby Attractions: All of the famous mansion "cottages" of Newport are close by.

Special Services: The hostess, Polly, can provide expert guidance to local attractions, via back roads. "I also try to direct guests to the best restaurants and help them avoid others. I can help them visit the Newport mansions at the least crowded times. I usually have discount coupons for local attractions that I share with guests." _Insider's Tip:_ Save some time to talk with Polly, a fascinating, well-traveled real estate broker. She helped set up the real estate accommodations in Newport and Australia for the America's Cup teams.

Rates: $65 to $125 double. Some discounts are available to single travelers, based on the season and length of stay.

THE INN AT OLD BEACH
19 OLD BEACH RD., NEWPORT, RI 02840

Reservations Phone: 401/849-3479

Description: This 1879 Victorian inn is listed on the Rhode Island Historic Register and is decorated with touches of romance and whimsy.

Amenities: Fresh flowers, chocolates.

Nearby Attractions: International Tennis Hall of Fame, historic mansions, beaches, cliff walk.

Special Services: Games, cooks, guest pantry with refrigerator, and coffee and tea.

Rates: $95 to $115 in season, $65 to $85 off season

Innkeeper's Tip: "Don't miss the Newport Folk Festival and the Newport Jazz Festival."

=====

WILLIAM FLUDDER HOUSE
30 BELLEVUE AVE., NEWPORT, RI 02840

Reservations Phone: 401/849-4220 or 401/846-2229
Description: With four rooms on the "Walking Tour of Newport," the
guesthouse is a short walk to the waterfront for shopping and some
of Newport's finest restaurants. Note that breakfast is not served.

Nearby Attractions: Million Dollar Drive and the stately "cottages" of
Newport, the Newport Folk Festival, the Tennis Museum
Rates: $55 in summer

=====

VERMONT

———————— **B&B Reservation Services** ————————

VERMONT BED & BREAKFAST
P.O. BOX 1, EAST FAIRFIELD, VT 05448

Offers B&B Homes In: Vermont
Reservations Phone: 802/827-3827
Phone Hours: 9am to 5pm Monday through Friday
Price Range of Homes: $50 to $150
Breakfast Included in Price: Full or Continental plus
Brochure Available: Free with stamped, self-addressed envelope
Reservations Should Be Made: Telephone reservations are highly
recommended

Attractions Near the B&B Homes: Green Mountain National Forest,
Mount Independence, Stephen A. Douglas Birthplace
Major Schools, Universities Near the B&B Homes: U.V.M.,
Middlebury College, Green Mountain College, St. Michaels, Johnson
State College

Best B&Bs

- Colonial "cottage" in Barton, Vermont. Yes, this is a "cottage" in the hugely understated Newport sense of the word. That is, this is a large restored mansion located right on the shore of 400-foot-deep Lake Willoughby. This is a "gorgeous, gorgeous location," says the reservation service. It was once a summer camp for teenagers from very rich families. In fact, if you walk around the pavilion in back of the home you will find a number of carved names in the wood, including names as intriguing as "Rockefeller." Guests have full use of the facilities, which include swimming, windsurfing, canoeing, paddleboats, volleyball, and croquet. Full breakfast served. **(Top 100.)**

- Victorian home in Bennington, Vermont. This turn-of-the-century home has ten-foot ceilings and raised-plaster moldings. A special treat in winter is the massive mahogany fireplace in the library. The library is decorated in Italianate style.

- An 18th-century home in Brandon, Vermont. This white Colonial offers five guestrooms, all with private baths. You are only minutes from the Green Mountain National Forest.

- Farmhouse in Waterbury, Vermont. Relax in an 1830s farmhouse with a two-section common room. Each of the guestrooms is air-conditioned with individual temperature controls. *Insider's Tip:* Come home in the afternoon and the host will serve wine and cheese.

B&B Inns

THE EVERGREEN
SANDGATE ROAD, ARLINGTON, VT 05250

Reservations Phone: 802/375-2272
Description: Set in the Green Mountains, the inn can accommodate 30 guests in comfortable rooms surrounded by spacious lawns.
Amenities: Full breakfast served to guests

Nearby Attractions: Bennington Museum, Southern Vermont Art Center, Dorset Playhouse, Skyline Drive, discount shopping, Rockwell Museum

Special Services: Bus pickups, kitchen open in the evening for cookies and cakes, coffee or tea
Rates: $28 to $32 single, $56 to $64 double. Open May 20 to October 20

GREENHURST INN
R.D. 2, BOX 60, BETHEL, VT 05032

Reservations Phone: 802/234-9474
Description: This 1890 inn, listed on the National Register of Historic Places, is located in the geographic center of Vermont. It has eight fireplaces, a library of 3,000 volumes, and a Victrola and piano in the parlor.
Amenities: Choice of juice, hot muffins, quick bread, fresh fruit, and Colombian coffee

Nearby Attractions: Mountains, ski areas, outdoor sports
Special Services: Perrier in every room, mints on your pillow, game cupboard, electric blankets
Rates: $50 to $95 double
Innkeeper's Tip: Lyle Wolf says, "We offer five self-guided tours of the local countryside. Country auctions and flea markets abound. The White River, 100 yards away, is great for canoeing, rafting, and fishing."

THE BLACK BEAR INN
MOUNTAIN ROAD, BOLTON, VT 05477

Reservations Phone: 802/434-2126 or 802/434-2920
Description: In a unique mountaintop setting, many of the inn's rooms enjoy mountain views from balconies, and all rooms have private bath and color TV. Guests are welcome to enjoy all the sports and recreation facilities of the Bolton Valley Resort.

Nearby Attractions: Shelburne Museum, many ski areas
Special Services: Outdoor heated pool
Rates: On request

VILLAGE INN OF BRADFORD
MAIN STREET (U.S. 5), BRADFORD, VT 05033

Reservations Phone: 802/222-9303
Description: Built in 1826, this inn is a mix of several styles, Federal/
Victorian outside, colonial/Victorian inside. Rooms and a suite with
private or shared bath are available.
Amenities: Continental breakfast during the week, full breakfast on
Sunday

Nearby Attractions: Connecticut River, golf course, historic restored
mill, waterfall, horses, canoeing
Rates: $35 single, $40 to $65 double

TULIP TREE INN
CHITTENDEN DAM ROAD, CHITTENDEN, VT 05737

Reservations Phone: 802/483-6213
Description: In this gracious, rambling country house, a variety of
antiques furnishes the eight guestrooms. The paneled den has a stone
fireplace.
Amenities: Full breakfast served

Nearby Attractions: Green Mountain Forest, hiking trails, Killington
(for skiing), canoeing, fishing, golf
Special Services: Hot tub
Rates: $75 to $100 per person double occupancy with breakfast and
dinner

ECHO LEDGE FARM INN
RTE. 2 (P.O. BOX 77), EAST ST. JOHNSBURY, VT 05838

Reservations Phone: 802/748-4750; FAX: 802/748-1640
Description: "The Dwelling House of Phineas Page" was built in 1793.
Rooms have been freshly papered or stenciled, and have private
baths. (Sorry, no smoking, pets, or small children.)

Nearby Attractions: Maple Grove Museum and Factory, Fairbanks
Museum and Planetarium, most outdoor sports
Rates: $45 to $67 double

MOUNTAIN MEADOWS LODGE
R.R.1, BOX 4080, KILLINGTON, VT 05751

Reservations Phone: 802/775-1010
Description: This converted 130-year-old farmhouse and barn can accommodate 40 guests in summer. Most of the large rooms have private baths. The lodge is set on a 110-acre lake in a country setting.
Amenities: Full Vermont home-style breakfast

Nearby Attractions: Summer theater, Alpine slide, and Killington Gondola
Special Services: TV, games room, and pool; tennis, golf, and health clubs nearby
Rates: $50 single, $80 double, April to October; $83 single, $106 double, November to May (dinner and breakfast included)

THE ANDRIE ROSE INN
13 PLEASANT ST., LUDLOW, VT 05149

Reservations Phone: 802/228-4846
Description: This elegant country inn, built in 1829, has eight guestrooms with private baths and antique furnishings. Each room is unique and some have whirlpool baths.
Amenities: Country breakfast buffet. Candlelight dinners available.

Nearby Attractions: Skiing at Okemo Mountain or Killington, sleigh and carriage rides, swimming, boating, hiking, picnicking
Special Services: Picnic lunches available, shuttle service to ski areas
Rates: $95 w/breakfast, double, $80 single; $140 w/breakfast & dinner, double, $125 single
Innkeeper's Tip: "Autumn is a feast for the eyes and riding the Killington Gondola is a wonderful way to appreciate the brilliant Vermont foliage."

NORDIC INN
RTE. 11, LANDGROVE, VT 05148

Reservations Phone: 802/824-6444
Description: The inn is surrounded by the Green Mountain National Forest. It features five individual guestrooms and three dining rooms, two with fireplaces
Amenities: Juices, home-baked biscuits and sweet breads, fresh fruits,

coffee, tea, and hot chocolate are served in summer; a full breakfast with Swedish pancakes and Vermont products is served in winter

Nearby Attractions: Hapgood Pond; Bromley Alpine Slide; Hildene, Bromley, Magic, and Stratton Mountain ski areas; Dorset and Weston summer theaters; ice skating and horsedrawn sleigh rides
Special Services: Cross-country skiing over 15 miles of groomed trails, rentals and instruction available. Ideal for summer hikes, too.
Rates: $135 double, Modified American Plan (breakfast and dinner included), December through March; $53 double, European Plan (B&B), May to December
Author's Tip: The level trails right by this inn are ideal for "beginner" cross-country skiers.

THE WILDFLOWER INN
DARLING HILL RD., LYNDONVILLE, VT 05851

Reservations Phone: 802/626-8310
Description: This 1796 property is situated on 500 acres in Vermont's Northeast Kingdom. Rooms and suites feature hand-stenciled walls, country quilts, and four-poster beds.
Amenities: Hearty Vermont country breakfast, pool, sauna/spa; ice-skating pond, special playroom and activities for children.

Nearby Attractions: Burke Mountain, downhill and cross-country skiing, biking, hiking, fishing, canoeing.
Special Services: Library/games room, afternoon snacks at fireside, sleigh and hay rides, baby-sitting, restaurant
Rates: $64 to $125 double
Innkeeper's Tip: "This is real country living. There is never a lift line at Burke Ski Resort and if you want more restful activities, you'll find antique auctions, country fairs, and wildflower excursions. You can cross-country ski right outside the doors of the inn or get lost on our scenic back roads. We welcome your children and their special playroom comes with dress-up clothes for old-fashioned fun."

MIDDLEBURY INN
14 COURTHOUSE SQUARE, MIDDLEBURY, VT 05753

Reservations Phone: Toll free 800/842-4666
Description: This 1827 village inn has 75 rooms and has welcomed

guests since 1827. The property is on the National Register of Historic Places and is within walking distance of 155 other historic buildings.

Amenities: A hearty Vermont breakfast and an elegant afternoon tea

Nearby Attractions: Historic buildings, museums, Middlebury College, Fort Ticonderoga, festivals, skiing, skating, hiking, fishing, boating, golf

Special Services: Crafts and antiques shop, library, games, meals

Rates: $80 to $122 (without meals)

Innkeeper's Tip: "Don't miss the unique experience of maple sugaring. It's a delicious part of New England life."

BLACK LANTERN INN

RTE. 118, MONTGOMERY, VT 05470

Reservations Phone: 802/326-4507, or toll free 800/255-8661

Description: This restored Colonial building was built in 1803 as a stagecoach inn. The old brick building is less than ten miles from the Canadian border. The rooms are decorated with antiques, and the three-bedroom suite has a Jacuzzi and a fireplace. Four additional suites with fireplaces are available.

Nearby Attractions: Jay Peak ski area, Hazen's Notch Cross-Country Ski Center, covered bridges

Special Services: Swimming, tennis

Rates: $60 to $80 double

NORTH HERO HOUSE

CHAMPLAIN ISLANDS, NORTH HERO, VT 05474

Reservations Phone: 802/372-8237

Description: This is a small country inn overlooking Lake Champlain. All rooms have private bath, and lakeview accommodations have screened porches to view Mount Mansfield across the lake.

Nearby Attractions: Burlington, Shelburne Museum, Stowe, Trapp Family Lodge, fishing, sailing, waterskiing, tennis, skiing

Special Services: Sauna, games room

Rates: On request

NORWICH INN
225 MAIN ST. (P.O. BOX 908), NORWICH, VT 05055

Reservations Phone: 802/649-1143
Description: The building, an inn since 1779, has 22 guestrooms each
with private bath, telephone, and cable TV. Some of the rooms have
canopied, rice-carved four-poster beds, while others are furnished
with brass bedsteads.

Nearby Attractions: Swimming, hiking, fishing, canoeing, antiquing,
downhill and cross-country skiing
Rates: $60 to $96 double

VALLEY HOUSE INN
4 MEMORIAL SQUARE, ORLEANS, VT 05860

Reservations Phone: 802/754-6665
Description: Built in the 1800s, the inn has a large porch going
halfway around the building. There are 20 rooms in the inn, with a
cocktail lounge facing the common.
Amenities: Hearty Vermont breakfast served; lunch and dinner also
available.

Nearby Attractions: Old Stone House Museum, three lakes within a
three-mile radius, 18-hole golf course
Special Services: Live entertainment every Friday night
Rates: $26 to $40 single, $35 to $60 double; breakfast included with
some rooms
Insider's Tip: "The Valley House Inn is located in the center of
Vermont's Northeast Kingdom's lakes region. You can swim in Lake
Willoughby, a glacial lake of cool spring water that is protected
from development. Many people enjoy hiking on nearby Mt. Piscah.
In winter, you can drive to skiing at Jay Peak and Burke Mountain,
30 minutes away. You can access well-groomed snowmobile trails
near the inn."

CASTLE INN
P.O. BOX 157, PROCTORSVILLE, VT 05153

Reservations Phone: 802/226-7222
Description: This large stone castle built in 1904 contains elaborate

public rooms like the Great Hall, with the family coat-of-arms carved into the woodwork, or the library, where cocktails are served. The guestrooms are done up in the style of the period.
Amenities: Rates include a full breakfast from the menu and dinner

Nearby Attractions: Black River Museum; Calvin Coolidge's Birthplace; Woodstock and Queechee Gorge; Robert Todd Lincoln's home, "Hildene"; major ski areas
Special Services: Swimming pool, tennis court, hot tub, and sauna
Rates: $150 to $180 double, June to October and December to April

THE INN AT PITTSFIELD
P.O. BOX 675, PITTSFIELD, VT 05762

Reservations Phone: 802/746-8943
Description: This classic three-story Colonial inn was built in 1830 and overlooks the village green in a tiny valley hamlet. Each of the nine comfortable guestrooms, with private bath, has its own personality accented with handmade quilts and antiques.
Amenities: Full country breakfast. Dinner available.

Nearby Attractions: Downhill (Killington) and cross-country skiing, mountain biking and hiking from the inn. Horseback riding, golf, fishing
Special services: Books, games
Rates: $65 to $100 single or double
Innkeeper's Tip: "Our inn features floral design seminars once a month with instruction and practice on both fresh and dried flowers."

HARVEY MOUNTAIN VIEW FARM AND INN
ROCHESTER NORTH HOLLOW, ROCHESTER, VT 05767

Reservations Phone: 802/767-4273
Description: The inn was the subject of a full-page article by Noel Perrin in the *New York Times* describing living on a farm and petting and feeding the animals as a unique kind of vacation. Besides accommodations in the inn there is a two-bedroom chalet rented from Saturday to Saturday.
Amenities: Besides a full farm breakfast, dinner is included in the rates

Nearby Attractions: Lake Dunmore, ski areas with gondola and Alpine slide, tennis courts, Texas Falls with nature walk

Special Services: Bus pickup, swimming pool, a pond for fishing, animals to interact with, a pony to ride, lawn games
Rates: $38 to $45 single or double

GREEN MOUNTAIN TEA ROOM AND GUEST HOUSE
RTE. 7 (R.R. 1, BOX 400), SOUTH WALLINGFORD, VT 05773

Reservations Phone: 802/446-2611
Description: This former stagecoach stop was built in 1792. There are five guestrooms. The Colonial house is on eight acres of land bordering Otter Creek.

Nearby Attractions: Green Mountain National Park, Appalachian Trail, ski areas, fishing, canoeing
Rates: $45 single, $55 double; $15 per extra person

INN AT THE BRASS LANTERN
R.R. 2, P.O. BOX 2610, STOWE, VT 05672

Reservations Phone: 802/253-2229, or toll free 800/729-2980
Description: A traditional B&B country inn, a restoration of an early 1800s farmhouse and carriage barn. Nine guestrooms, furnished with antiques and handmade quilts. Some have fireplaces.
Amenities: Full Vermont country breakfast served

Nearby Attractions: Almost all winter and summer sports plus art galleries, craft shops, and theaters.
Rates: $65 to $95 double in summer; $5 to $10 higher in the winter and fall foliage seasons
Innkeeper's Tip: "We can package any activity—for example, skiing or theater—with our lodging and can book air and car rental. A gourmet package is available with a different dining experience each night—with no restaurant more than 10 minutes from the inn."

KEDRON VALLEY INN
RTE. 106, SOUTH WOODSTOCK, VT 05071

Reservations Phone: 802/457-1473
Description: The building has been operating as an inn for over 150 years. The guestrooms have canopied beds, Franklin stoves, fire-

places, private baths, and antique quilts. It's on a large lake with a beach.

Amenities: Full country breakfast (al fresco dining)

Nearby Attractions: Horseback riding, skiing, Silver Lake State Park, Vermont Institute of Natural Science, summer walking tours of historic Woodstock

Rates: $75 to $131 single, $80 to $136 double; midweek discounts available

Innkeeper's Tip: "Come in June and July. Our gardens are in full bloom and our room rates are reduced 25% to 30%."

WILD BERRY INN

RTE. 100, HCR65 #23, STOCKBRIDGE, VT 05772

Reservations Phone: 802/746-8141

Description: This restored 1780 farmhouse is full of Chippendale, Sheraton, and other antiques, pewter, and Haviland china.

Amenities: Full country breakfast

Nearby Attractions: Long Trail, Killington, and Pico ski areas nine miles away

Rates: $45 to $65 per person, double occupancy

FIDDLERS GREEN INN

MOUNTAIN ROAD (RTE. 108), STOWE, VT 05672

Reservations Phone: 802/253-8124

Description: This country inn in the Green Mountains was built in 1820 and is situated well off the highway next to a babbling brook.

Amenities: Breakfast specialties include home-grown blueberry and juneberry pancakes; Grand Marnier French toast; and cheese, mushroom, and herb omelets

Nearby Attractions: Mount Mansfield, Alpine slide, gondola ride, tennis, golf, balloon and glider rides

Special Services: Picnic grove

Rates: $40 to $60 double

Innkeeper's Tip: "A hiking and recreation path begins at our back door."

TIMBERHOLM INN
COTTAGE CLUB ROAD (R.R. 1, BOX 810), STOWE, VT 05672

Reservations Phone: 802/253-7603 (8am to 8pm)
Description: Inn located off a mountain road in a wooded setting. Ten individually decorated guestrooms.
Amenities: Breakfast includes granola, fruit, and quiche

Nearby Attractions: Mount Mansfield ski area and State Park, Stowe Village, Trapp Family Lodge, biking, hiking, tennis, golf
Special Services: Après-ski soup/afternoon tea, games room, cable TV, fieldstone fireplace
Rates: $35 to $50 single, $50 to $80 double
Innkeeper's Tip: "Stowe is well known as the home of Mt. Mansfield, Vermont's highest peak. There are also over 100 miles of cross-country trails. Summer activities include horse and dog shows, antique car rallies, concerts in a meadow, and summer theater. In January the winter carnival features ski races, casino night, snow golf, ice sculptures, and street night."

MAD RIVER BARN LODGE
RTE. 17, WAITSFIELD, VT 05673

Reservations Phone: 802/496-3310
Description: This is a traditional Vermont lodge with the charm of country living. Rooms are furnished in simple but comfortable style.
Amenities: Full breakfast. TV in rooms.

Nearby Attractions: Shelburne Museum, Lake Champlain, Audubon Society Nature Center, Rock of Ages quarries, Alpine slide
Special Services: Pool, golf, tennis, fishing, soaring, biking
Rates: $46 double with private bath, December to April; $28 double with private bath, May to November; children under 10 free in their parents' room

MILLBROOK LODGE
R.F.D. BOX 62, WAITSFIELD, VT 05673

Reservations Phone: 802/496-2405
Description: This Cape-style farmhouse dates to the 1850s. The seven guestrooms are decorated with hand-stenciling, antique bedsteads, and handmade quilts. There's a view of the Green Mountains.

Amenities: Full country breakfast including pancakes with fruit, French toast made with anadama bread, real Vermont maple syrup

Nearby Attractions: Some of the finest skiing in the East five minutes away, Sugarbush and Mad River Glen, 60 miles of groomed trails for the cross-country skier, golfing, canoeing, soaring, tennis, horseback riding, windsurfing

Rates: $60 to $90 single (MAP) $84 to $130 double (MAP) winter/fall; $35 to $60 single, $50 to $100 double summer

MOUNTAIN VIEW INN
R.F.D. BOX 69, WAITSFIELD, VT 05673

Reservations Phone: 802/496-2426

Description: Though built in 1826, the house has been an inn only for the last 40 years. The seven rooms, each with bath, are decorated in the Colonial style with antiques, quilts, and braided rugs.

Amenities: Breakfast begins with fruit and coffee or tea, and continues with bacon, eggs, and toast, or blueberry pancakes, or waffles, with bacon.

Nearby Attractions: Ski areas at Sugarbush, Mad River Glen, and the Long Trail; soaring, tennis, golf, horseback riding; Shelburne Museum; a Morgan horse farm

Rates: $130 double in winter, $120 double in summer

TUCKER HILL LODGE
RTE. 17 (R.D.1, BOX 147), WAITSFIELD, VT 05673

Reservations Phone: 802/496-3983, or toll free 800/543-7841

Description: Country inn on a wooded hillside, ringed by stone walls and flower gardens.

Amenities: Breakfast includes homemade bread and muffins, local berries, homemade jams, and maple syrup from the innkeeper's trees.

Nearby Attractions: Mad River for fishing and canoeing, Sugarbush and Mad River Glen ski areas, museums, craft galleries, Shelburne Museum

Special Services: Pool, two clay tennis courts, airport pickup, fresh flowers in guestrooms, handmade quilts

Rates: $96 double with breakfast

VALLEY INN
RTE. 100 (BOX 8), WAITSFIELD, VT 05673

Reservations Phone: 802/496-3450
Description: The first inn built in the Mad River Valley, the all-wood structure is made of native timbers. The parlor has a large stone fireplace.
Amenities: Full breakfast with fresh berries and Vermont maple syrup

Nearby Attractions: Sugarbush Ski Resort, Historic Waitsfield Village, covered bridges
Special Services: Tennis, golf, soaring, ski packages, private airport
Rates: On request

GRUNBERG HAUS BED & BREAKFAST
SCENIC ROUTE 100, R.R. 2, BOX 1595, WATERBURY, VT 05676

Reservations Phone: 802/244-7726
Description: Austrian chalet built by hand on 40 secluded acres. Features ten homey antiques-filled guestrooms with balconies overlooking the Green Mountains.
Amenities: Full Vermont breakfast of breads, muffins, fresh fruit creations, and main dish specialties.

Nearby Attractions: Stowe and Sugarbush ski resorts, Ben & Jerry's Ice Cream factory, and a "great swimming hole."
Special Services: Sauna, spa, library, tennis court, BYOB rathskeller.
Rates: $25 to $35 per person. Ask about special discounts.
Innkeeper's Tips: "Tour Ben and Jerry's Ice Cream Factory early in the day. Fall foliage peak varies with mountain altitude between September 15 and October 15. Five days of fireworks around the 4th of July."

WINDHAM HILL INN
R.R.1, BOX 44, WEST TOWNSHEND, VT 05359

Reservations Phone: 802/874-4080 or 802/874-4976
Description: This restored 1825 farmhouse and barn has 15 antiques-filled guestrooms and private baths set on 165 acres.
Amenities: Full breakfast and six-course gourmet dinner included in the rates

Nearby Attractions: Townshend State Park; Jamaica State Park; Marlboro Music Festival; Stratton, Bromley, and Magic Mountain ski areas
Special Services: Sherry in room on arrival, chamber music, nightly turn-down
Rates: $165 to $175 double occupancy

THE WHITE HOUSE OF WILMINGTON
RTE. 9, WILMINGTON, VT 05363

Reservations Phone: 802/464-2135
Description: This turn-of-the-century mansion set high on a hill has 12 distinctive rooms with private bath.
Amenities: Full breakfast and dinner included in the rates

Nearby Attractions: The Historic Molly Stark Trail, Bennington, lakes, horseback riding
Special Services: Pool, sauna, whirlpool, cross-country skiing
Rates: $190 to $220 double

The Middle Atlantic States

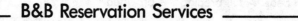

B&B Reservation Services

BED & BREAKFAST OF DELAWARE
3650 SILVERSIDE RD., BOX 177, WILMINGTON, DE 19810

Offers B&B Homes In: City and suburbs of Wilmington, Newark, Dover, Bridgeville, Milford, Selbyville, Odessa, Lewes, in Delaware; Chadds Ford, Landenberg, and Oxford and other towns in nearby Pennsylvania; and in Elkton, Fairhill and Ocean City, Maryland.
Reservations Phone: 302/479-9500, or toll free 800/233-4689
Phone Hours: 9am to 9pm daily (any hour on answering service)
Price Range of Homes: $35 to $45 single, $65 to $95 double (beach homes to $80 in summer)
Breakfast Included in Price: Full American (juice, eggs, bacon, toast, coffee)
Brochure Available: Free
Reservations Should Be Made: Two weeks in advance (last-minute reservations accepted if possible)

Attractions Near the B&B Homes: Winterthur, Longwood Gardens, Brandywine River Museum, Hagley Museum, Nemours, Old New Castle, beach resorts, Philadelphia attractions
Major Schools, Universities Near the B&B Homes: U. of Delaware, Delaware Law School, West Chester U., Goldey-Beacom College, Wilmington College

Best B&Bs

■ **Historic B&B in New Castle, Delaware.** Many travelers have yet to discover this tiny town right on the river, but its buildings faithfully reflect life of centuries ago as you walk down the cobblestone streets past an extraordinary number of homes and stores from another time. In the midst of all this charm is a B&B with four lovely rooms, all with queen-size beds and private baths, Laura Ashley linens, and Oriental rugs. A gourmet Continental breakfast is served in the morning. **(Top 100.)**

- Carriage house in Chadds Ford, Pennsylvania. Accommodations are in a 100-year-old barn converted to a cozy carriage house, located on the site of Hedgerow, a historic Victorian house (circa 1908) in the heart of southern Chester County. The carriage house provides a suite of rooms to accommodate up to four adults with two bedrooms and a single bath. A full kitchen, dining room, sitting room, and screened porch are available for your meals and relaxation. Queen room and twin beds. A full breakfast is provided.

- 18th-century home just over the Delaware state line in Pennsylvania. This is a charming country residence restored and furnished with period pieces. There are five spacious bedrooms with antiques, modern bathrooms, and two with fireplaces. Full breakfast is served on the sun porch or in the kitchen. Close to museums.

- 18th-century country manor listed in the National Register of Historic Places in Laurel. This home has four spacious rooms and one suite with authentic period furnishings and fireplaces. Bicycles and picnic lunches are available to explore the many pleasures of the Eastern Shore.

- Cottage in Lewes. This home is approximately 150 years old. All rooms enjoy the presence of many period pieces from the 17th, 18th, and 19th centuries. The bathrooms are totally modern; a large L-shaped screened porch comfortably furnished in rattan and old pine is available to guests. One mile from Delaware bay and five minutes by car from the Atlantic Ocean. Continental breakfast is served. The host is the director of music at a local church.

- Lovely Cape Cod home in a quiet suburban neighborhood, five minutes north of downtown Wilmington, Delaware, 27 miles south of center city Philadelphia, and minutes to Brandywine Valley museums, colleges, and industry. There are beautiful award-winning landscaped grounds, which are filled with blossoms from 1,000 annuals (germinated under lights) as well as perennials. In the winter, the mature hedges and unusual shrubs are decorated for the holidays. The three bedrooms have queen-size, king-size or twin beds and private bath. Full breakfast is served.

DISTRICT OF COLUMBIA

B&B Reservation Service

BED 'N' BREAKFAST LTD. OF WASHINGTON, D.C.

P.O. BOX 12011, WASHINGTON, DC 20005

Offers B&B Homes In: Washington, DC, and nearby Maryland and Virginia
Reservations Phone: 202/328-3510
Phone Hours: 10am to 5pm Monday through Friday, to 1pm on Saturday
Price Range of Homes: $40 to $90 single, $50 to $100 double
Breakfast Included in Price: Continental breakfast included in B&B rooms; no breakfast included in one-bedroom apartments
Brochure Available: Free
Reservations Should Be Made: One month in advance if possible (will make last-minute reservations, subject to availability)

Attractions Near the B&B Homes: All major Washington, DC, attractions
Major Schools, Universities Near the B&B Homes: Georgetown U., George Washington U., American U., Catholic U., Trinity College, Mount Vernon College, Johns Hopkins School of Economic and International Studies

Best B&Bs

■ A Victorian mansion in Washington, DC. This home was built on Logan Circle over 100 years ago. Its present owner has added landscaping, gardens, a terrace, and fountains to the original town house. Each guestroom has a color TV. Laundry facilities are available. *Insider's Tip:* You will certainly enjoy talking with your host. He is a former Fulbright Fellow and law clerk to Supreme Court Justice Tom Clark. He is now a senior partner of a prominent Washington law firm. **(Top 100.)**

■ Georgian-style home in Washington, DC. Right on Tenley Circle, this home is located on a tree-lined avenue in a residential neighborhood. You have a choice of two large guestrooms with color TV, and private bathrooms with tile showers. *Insider's Tip:* For romantic evenings, ask for the guestroom with a fireplace.

■ The host of this Washington, DC, B&B is a producer of the MacNeil-Lehrer Newshour, and the second host is a computer programmer analyst. The house this agreeable couple owns was built in 1899 and restored to much of its original character, an image burnished with antiques. There are books in abundance, a piano, and a you-know-what-news-program on TV

■ Washington, DC, town house in the tree-lined Capitol Hill area. This 13-room residence is a good example of Colonial Revival architecture and interior design (built in 1891). The Colonial feeling continues with Oriental carpets (the early marks of a luxurious Colonial home were exports from China), a library, and period chandeliers. The host is a corporate and government management consultant, originally from Montana.

■ Edwardian town house in the Adams Morgan/Mount Pleasant area of Washington, DC. The B&B is furnished with an engaging mix of modern and antique pieces. The rooms are large and the touches of the owner, a noted interior designer, who once had his own art gallery, are everywhere. Put all these facts together and you have a very appealing home in the capital. The White House is 28 blocks north.

B&B Inns

CAPITOL HILL GUEST HOUSE
101 FIFTH ST, NE WASHINGTON, DC 20002

Reservations Phone: 202/547-1050

Description: This narrow town house is nothing fancy, yet it has its own charm, with a magnificent fireplace and surprises (the names written into some of the desks and closets are those of young U.S. Senate pages who once lived here). And the location is fabulous. You can walk to the Capitol and Union Station in minutes. Parking is on the street and a spot can be hard to find later in the day in this residential neighborhood so arrive early in the afternoon. Also, baths now are "down the hall" but the owners are planning to install private baths. Ask when you call.

Amenities: Continental breakfast (usually muffins, orange juice, and coffee) served near that great old fireplace in the parlor.

Nearby Attractions: Many of the major sights of Washington, DC.
Rates: $35 to $75 single or double.

MARYLAND

B&B Reservation Services

THE TRAVELLER IN MARYLAND, INC.
P.O. BOX 2277, ANNAPOLIS, MD 21404

Offers B&B Homes In: Annapolis, Baltimore, and 45 other cities and towns throughout Maryland
Reservations Phone: 301/269-6232
Phone Hours: 9am to 3pm Monday through Thursday
Price Range of Homes: $55 to $75 single, $60 to $80 and up double (yachts, $100 and up)
Breakfast Included in Price: Continental
Brochure Available: No; please reserve by phone only
Reservations Should Be Made: As far in advance as possible; not less than 24 hours

Attractions Near the B&B Homes: Historic Annapolis, Baltimore Inner Harbor, Chesapeake Bay, U.S. Naval Academy, hiking and biking, major-league sports, horse racing, historic homes
Major Schools, Universities Near the B&B Homes: Johns Hopkins, Goucher, U.S. Naval Academy, St. John's, Washington College, U. of Maryland

Best B&Bs
■ **The House of Burgess.** Don't expect a wild night on the town in Queenstown, Maryland—a town that practically invented the words "quaint" and "sleepy." But Annapolis is only about 45 minutes away and you're right on top of the growing Chesapeake Pottery Shopping

Complex. The House of Burgess, however, defies such easy description. It's an amazing hodge-podge of a converted 1920s telephone exchange merged with a private residence. Surprisingly, it works—providing guests with a great room lined with antique tools and a huge bar (set-ups free). Each of the four guestrooms has a theme. Ask about the family suite upstairs with its own dollhouse and an extra bedroom for children (or two couples traveling together). All rooms have private baths. However, we must confess the real reason we have included this as one of the "Top 100" is the laid-back charm of the owners, Pete and Helen Burgess. They love to greet guests in the afternoon with wine and cheese. And Helen enjoys surprising guests at breakfast with orange/pecan bread and butter muffins. If you're a sailor, Pete will swap yarns with you about transatlantic voyages he has made (complete with pictures in the album on the bar.) (Top 100.)

AMANDA'S BED & BREAKFAST RESERVATION SERVICE

1428 PARK AVE., BALTIMORE, MD 21217

Offers B&B Homes In: Greater Baltimore, throughout Maryland, also Pennsylvania, Washington, DC, West Virginia, New Jersey
Reservations Phone: 301/225-0001; FAX: 301/728-8951
Phone Hours: 8:30am to 6:30pm Monday through Friday, Saturday 8:30am to noon
Price Range of Homes: $40 to $120 double
Breakfast Included in Price: Continental or full American; regional specialties sometimes served include shoo-fly pie and sausage bread
Brochure Available: Free
Reservations Should Be Made: Two weeks in advance (last-minute reservations accepted when possible)

Scenic Attractions Near the B&B Homes: Baltimore Inner Harbor, the Aquarium, Science Center, Baltimore Museum of Art, Zoo, historic neighborhoods, beaches
Major Schools, Universities Near the B&B Homes: Johns Hopkins, Peabody, Loyola, U. of Maryland–Baltimore

Best B&Bs

■ Victorian home in Lutherville, Maryland—right next to Baltimore. You can enjoy the best of both worlds—a quiet historic village followed by a 20-minute ride into the Inner Harbor of Baltimore with all of its excitement and attractions. Come during the welcome hour (5 to 6pm) and the hosts will greet you with a good local wine and cheese. Each of the rooms is decorated with various themes reflecting the owners' favorite places. Two suites are available with private baths. **(Top 100.)**

■ Historic row house in downtown Baltimore, Maryland. This B&B is located just seven minutes from the Inner Harbor. You really will get a sense of how early residents of Baltimore lived as you mount the white marble steps and walk through rooms with 12-foot ceilings.

■ Renovated 150-year-old barn on the water at Annapolis, Maryland. This is a wonderful walking town, with great old restaurants. This B&B is only five minutes from the center of town.

■ Victorian home in Easton, Maryland—near St. Michael's. Spend lazy summer and fall days on a great old wrap-around porch. This B&B is close to most of Maryland's shore events.

■ Working farm in Hagerstown, Maryland. The RSO says, "Great location for touring historic sites, and antiques and crafts shops. *Insider's Tip:* Ask for the room with the whirlpool bath."

B&B Inns

THE PAULUS GASTHAUS
2406 KENTUCKY AVE., BALTIMORE, MD 21213

Reservations Phone: 301/467-1688
Description: European Tudor-style home. Rooms are furnished with either twin beds or a queen-size bed. The home is in a residential neighborhood bordered by two parks. A full breakfast is served.

Nearby Attractions: Baltimore's Inner Harbor.
Special Services: Fluent German spoken.
Rates: $55 single, $60 double.
Innkeeper's Tip: Ask for directions to Baltimore's best crab house nearby.

MIDDLE PLANTATION INN
9549 LIBERTY ROAD, FREDERICK, MD 21701

Reservations Phone: 301/898-7128
Description: Rustic stone and log B&B inn several miles east of Freder-

ick on 26 acres. The large public room has a fireplace and stained glass. Each guestroom is air conditioned and has a private bath and a TV.

Amenities: Continental breakfast consists of seasonal fruits, fresh baked breads and pastries, fresh-brewed coffee or tea, and orange juice.

Nearby Attractions: There is a 33-block historic district in downtown Frederick—antiques and specialty shops, restaurants, museums, and art galleries, as well as New Mark—the antiques capital of the state. Civil War buffs can also tour Gettysburg, Sharpsburg (battle of Antietam), and Harper's Ferry in West Virginia; each location is only 40 minutes from this B&B.

Special Services: Woods and stream on the property can be used as a setting for bird-watching and hiking. Books and magazines available.

Rates: $85 double. (Reduced rates for stays of two to four nights.)

Innkeeper's Tip: Ask about the many annual events nearby, including the "Taste of Frederick" sampling of many restaurants, Bell and History Days (featuring Frederick's Civil War history), and the Battle of Moncacy (a living history encampment).

THE ROSEBUD INN

4 N. MAIN ST., WOODSBORO, MD 21798

Reservations Phone: 301/845-2221

Description: Opened as an inn in 1981, it was once the home of the founder of the Rosebud Perfume Co., which is still in operation next door to the inn. A rose motif is carried throughout the interior, reflected in the rosebud designs in the leaded-glass doors. There are large air-conditioned rooms, five with private bath. Marble mantels decorate the parlor and living room fireplaces. There is a German antiques gift shop on the premises.

Amenities: Continental breakfast

Nearby Attractions: Tennis, ice skating, bicycling, fishing, hiking, antiques shops

Rates: $50 single, $85 double

NEW JERSEY

―――――――― B&B Reservation Services ――――――――

NORTHERN NEW JERSEY BED & BREAKFAST
11 SUNSET TRAIL, DENVILLE, NJ 07854

Offers B&B Homes In: Northern New Jersey
Reservations Phone: 201/625-5129
Phone Hours: 9am to noon and 4 to 6pm Monday through Friday
Price Range of Homes: $35 to $75 single, $40 to $75 double
Breakfast Included in Price: Continental or full American (depending on the host)
Brochure Available: Free
Reservations Should Be Made: Two weeks in advance

Attractions Near the B&B Homes: Washington's Headquarters, Waterloo Village, Meadowlands Sports Complex
Major Schools, Universities Near the B&B Homes: Drew, Fairleigh Dickinson, Montclair State

Best B&Bs

■ Home on Indian Lake, Denville, New Jersey. Offers private guest quarters on the first floor. Guests can obtain free beach passes. Take some time to enjoy the view of the bay from the outside deck. Wine and cheese are served in the afternoon.

■ Comfortable Cape Cod in East Brunswick, New Jersey, less than an hour from New York City. You have a choice of three large rooms, each with a sitting area, TV, and air conditioning. Continental breakfast is served during the week, and a full breakfast on weekends.

■ New home on rural 3½ acres in Andover, New Jersey. The guestroom has a double bed. Horseback riding is available nearby.

■ 1844 historic B&B in Morristown, New Jersey. There are three air conditioned guestrooms, all with double beds and shared bath. A swimming pool is available for guests. This is a good headquarters for touring nearby Revolutionary War sites. Continental breakfast is served and special dietary needs are accommodated.

■ English-style manor house in Readington, New Jersey, close to all that discount shopping in Flemington. There are two guestrooms with private baths, a billiard room, wet bar, cable TV, and an outdoor pool in warm weather.

BED & BREAKFAST ADVENTURES
103 GODWIN AVE., SUITE 132, MIDLAND PARK, NJ 07432

Offers B&B Homes In: New Jersey (also in Pennsylvania, New York, Connecticut, and Florida); also reserves B&B inns.
Reservations Phone: 201/444-7409, or toll free 800/992-2632
Phone Hours: 9:30am to 3:30pm Monday through Friday (Eastern time)
Price Range of Homes: $50 to $95 single, $60 to $160 double
Breakfast Included in Price: Continental to full American
Brochure Available: Free; complete directory for $5
Reservations Should Be Made: As soon as travel dates are firm—two weeks preferred, but will attempt to handle last-minute requests

Attractions Near the B&B homes: New Jersey offers beautiful natural terrain, from the Ramapo Mountains to the Palisades, as well as easy access to New York City.

Best B&Bs

■ **Renovated country barn in Readington, New Jersey.** A semicircular balcony provides an architectural delight as you surround yourself with history in this unusual accommodation. It's a barn transformed into an elegant country manor home. The guest wing offers two tastefully decorated bedrooms—one with a queen-size bed and another with twin beds and each with a private bath. An exercise room with whirlpool, a billiard room with a wet bar, and a lovely swimming pool outdoors are also provided for your comfort. Don't forget to ask your hosts about their extensive antiques collection throughout the home. A gourmet or dietetic Continental breakfast is served each morning in the room near the fireplace. The setting is very rural, but there are many fine restaurants and great shopping in the area. Public transportation is only five minutes away. (Top 100.)

■ **Federal-style home in Columbus–Mount Holly, New Jersey.** This home is famous, having been featured in many country magazines. It is located in a country setting of 12 acres. The three guestrooms on the third floor are furnished with period antiques and country decor. *Insider's Tip:* The third bedroom has a working fireplace. Animal lovers will enjoy meeting the dog, two cats, six Suffolk sheep, an Arabian horse, and a Welsh pony on the grounds.

BED & BREAKFAST OF PRINCETON

P.O. BOX 571, PRINCETON, NJ 08540

Offers B&B Homes In: Princeton
Reservations Phone: 609/924-3189
Phone Hours: 24 hours
Price Range of Homes: $40 to $60 single, $50 to $70 and up double
Breakfast Included in Price: Mostly Continental, but some serve full breakfast
Brochure Available: Free with stamped, self-addressed no. 10 envelope
Reservations Should Be Made: As early as possible, but last-minute reservations accepted if possible

Attractions Near the B&B Homes: Historic homes, buildings, parks, downtown shopping and dining
Major Schools, Universities Near the B&B Homes: Princeton, Institute for Advanced Study, Princeton Theological Seminary, Rider College, Westminster Choir College

Best B&Bs

■ Large Victorian home in Princeton, New Jersey. You can choose from three double guestrooms. This home will be particularly convenient if you're visiting your children at school or attending a football game; it's only a few minutes walk from Princeton University and the center of town. But the main reason the RSO chose this as their "best" is the owner of the home! "The host, a long-time Princeton resident, will go out of her way to assure her guests' comfort, and to help them with problems of any nature." A Continental to Continental-plus breakfast is provided. "Staying in this home is like visiting Grandmother." (**Top 100.**)

■ Large town house about one mile from Princeton, New Jersey. This home may be perfect for a large family because of the variety of sleeping arrangements possible. *Insider's Tip:* There are reduced rates for long-term guests.

■ Ranch home about one mile from Princeton, New Jersey. One guestroom is available with twin beds and a private bath.

■ California contemporary home on two acres on the outskirts of Princeton. One double room is available.

■ Elegant home in Princeton, New Jersey, in a neighborhood of stately homes. It is close to the Princeton graduate school, golf course, and the Institute for Advanced Study.

_____ B&B Inns _____

HOLLY HOUSE
20 JACKSON ST., CAPE MAY, NJ 08204

Reservations Phone: 609/884-7365
Description: The house (c. 1890) is one of seven Victorian cottages
   that are famous as Cape May's Seven Sisters. Renaissance Revival in
   style, it's the work of Stephen Decatur Button. It has six guestrooms
   with two shared baths, plus an oceanview front porch with swing and
   rockers. The inn has achieved National Historic Landmark status.

Nearby Attractions: Physick House Victorian Museum, the Cold Spring
   Village restoration, a bird sanctuary and wildlife preserve, beach,
   shopping mall
Special Services: Parking permits and beach tags are supplied.
Rates: $60 to $65 double.

THE PRINCE EDWARD VICTORIAN SUITES
38 JACKSON ST., CAPE MAY, NJ 08204

Reservations Phone: 609/884-2131
Description: A restored Queen Anne cottage built near the sea in
   1896. One- and two-bedroom suites, each with a parlor, kitchen,
   and full bath and furnished with 19th-century antiques, are available.
   Decorated with crocheted bedspreads, quilts, lace curtains, stained-
   glass windows, and fresh flowers.
Amenities: Private entrance, color TV, and complimentary in-room
   coffee, tea, and juices.

Nearby Attractions: Located in the heart of the historic district, just a
   half block from the beach and Victorian walking mall.
Special Services: Offstreet parking, laundry facilities.
Rates: $65 to $95 one-bedroom suite (2 persons); $80 to $135 two-
   bedroom suite (4 persons).
Innkeeper's Tip: "Let us make reservations for you at some of Cape
May's finest restaurants."

NORTH CAROLINA

―――――――――― **B&B Reservation Services** ――――――――――

BED AND BREAKFAST IN THE ALBEMARLE
CAMPUS BOX 962, ELIZABETH STATE U., ELIZABETH CITY, NC 27909

Offers B&B Homes In: Northeastern North Carolina
Reservations Phone: 919/794-4776
Phone Hours: Answering machine available
Price Range of Homes: $30 to $50 single, $35 to $100 double
Breakfast Included in Price: Continental (juice, roll or toast, coffee); some hosts also serve Carolina country ham, and most homes serve country biscuits.
Brochure Available: Free; a host listing is also available for $5
Reservations Should Be Made: Two weeks in advance (can accept last-minute reservations for some locations)

Attractions Near the B&B Homes: Hope Plantation, Historic Edenton, Historic Bath, Museum of the Albemarle, Elizabeth City Historic District, Fort Branch Confederate Earthworks, Jockey's Ridge State Park, Outer Banks beaches, National Seashore Recreational Area, Merchants Mill Pond State Park, Sommerset Place State Historic Site
Major Schools, Universities Near the B&B Homes: East Carolina U., Chowan, Roanoke Bible College, College of the Albemarle

―――――――――――――― **B&B Inns** ――――――――――――――

RICHMOND HILL INN
87 RICHMOND HILL DRIVE, ASHEVILLE, NC 28806

Reservations Phone: Toll free 800/545-9238
Description: A historic inn that is listed on the National Register of Historic Places. Twelve guestrooms.
Amenities: All rooms include antiques, fresh flowers, down pillows, Caswell-Massey toiletries, TV, clock/radio, and telephone. Some even have Oriental rugs, fireplaces, and window seats. Breakfast may include a house specialty—poached eggs Florentine, apple raisin pancakes, and a petite biscuit basket with preserves at each table.

Nearby Attractions: The Biltmore Estate, the Thomas Wolfe Memorial, Flatrock Playhouse, whitewater rafting, and skiing.

Special Services: The inn's library has over 200 books that belonged to the original Pearson estate and an extensive collection of books about Western North Carolina as well as books by North Carolina authors. (Some of the inn's rooms are named after the authors.)

Rates: $90 to $200 single or double.

WOMBLE INN

301 W. MAIN ST. (P.O. BOX 1441), BREVARD, NC 28712

Reservations Phone: 704/884-4770

Description: Furnished with 18th- and 19th-century antiques, all rooms have private baths. The seven guestrooms are air-conditioned.

Amenities: Breakfast is served on a silver tray in your room, or in the dining room

Nearby Attractions: Pisgah National Forest, Biltmore House, North Carolina State Theater, the Brevard Music Center

Special Services: Swimming pool, tennis, shuttle to the music center

Rates: $40 single, $48 double, in summer; $36 single, $45 double, in winter

NANTAHALA VILLAGE

P.O. DRAWER J, BRYSON CITY, NC 28713

Reservations Phone: Toll free 800/438-1507

Description: Built of stone and wormy chestnut, the inn dates back to 1949. The cottages and log cabins are earlier. They offer simple but comfortable rustic accommodations.

Amenities: Full service restaurant on premises

Nearby Attractions: Great Smoky Mountain National Park, Cherokee Indian Reservation, white-water rafting, swimming, horseback riding, tennis, shuffleboard

Rates: $60 double in summer, $35 double off-season

ARROWHEAD INN
106 MASON RD., DURHAM, NC 27712

Reservations Phone: 919/477-8430
Reader Recommendation: Reader Angela Fisher says, "Not only was the home immaculate, the hospitality was friendly and relaxed. The food was wonderful and generous. The hosts made the extra effort to sense and provide for each guest's special needs. Truly a home away from home on a long and (otherwise) tiresome, seven-week business trip.

THE COLONIAL INN
153 W. KING ST., HILLSBOROUGH, NC 27278

Reservations Phone: 919/732-2461
Description: One of the ten oldest inns in the country, the Colonial has been in continuous operation since 1759. Lord Cornwallis and Aaron Burr stayed here. The eight bedrooms all have private or semi-private baths and are air-conditioned.
Amenities: Country breakfast

Nearby Attractions: Historic museum, 100 historic buildings within walking distance, near Durham and Chapel Hill Research Triangle Park
Rates: $48 to $65 double
Innkeeper's Tip: Sara McKee suggests exploring Hillsborough. "This is a charming, historic town with tree-lined streets and antebellum homes. Antiques buffs will enjoy the many antiques shops."

THE GREYSTONE INN
P.O. BOX 6, LAKE TOXAWAY, NC 28747

Reservations Phone: 704/966-4700, or toll free 800/824-5766 outside North Carolina
Description: Built in 1915, the Greystone offers complete resort facilities: Five soft-surface and one all-weather tennis courts; waterskiing (boat, skis, and driver provided); and sunset cruises on a party boat, *Mountain Lily II*
Amenities: High-country breakfast

Nearby Attractions: Blue Ridge Mountains; Biltmore House; waterfalls; Brevard Music Festival; 18-hole, par-72 championship golf course on North Carolina's largest lake

Special Services: White wicker sun porch, afternoon tea, library
Rates: $98 to $198 per person

THE TRANQUIL HOUSE INN
QUEEN ELIZABETH STREET, MANTEO, NC 27954

Reservations Phone: 919/473-1404, or toll free 800/458-7069
Description: A well-known waterfront inn with 28 individually decorated rooms. The inn has a library with fireplace, wrap-around
porches with rockers, and a lookout room with a great view of the
waterfront.
Amenities: Breakfast included, wine on arrival.

Nearby Attractions: *The Lost Colony* outdoor drama, the North Caro-
lina Aquarium, the Elizabethan Gardens, sportfishing, and the Wright
Brothers Memorial.
Special Services: Library stocked with books and games. Bicycles and
a gas grill for cookouts are available.
Rates: $65 to $125 double (seasonal changes)
Innkeeper's Tip: "Four hundred years of history come alive on Manteo,
renowned as the 'Birthplace of English America.' Walk aboard the
Elizabeth II, a 16th-century representative sailing ship."

OSCAR'S HOUSE
RTE. 12 (P.O. BOX 206), OCRACOKE ISLAND, NC 27960

Reservations Phone: 919/928-1311
Description: This island, to which Europeans first came in the 1500s,
was later the home of Blackbeard the Pirate and retains the feeling
of its historical beginnings. Oscar's House, built in 1940 by the
lighthouse keeper, now provides accommodations for island visitors.
Single or double rooms are available with shared baths.
Amenities: Breakfast is likely to include fresh fruit, garden tomatoes,
omelets, grits, cooked apples, French toast, muffins or breads

Nearby Attractions: The Lighthouse, British Cemetery, Pamlico Sound,
Silver Lake Harbor, Coast Guard Station
Rates: $40 to $45 single, $50 to $55 double, in summer; $35 single,
$45 double, in spring and fall, with full breakfast included; closed in
winter

THE PINES COUNTRY INN

719 HART RD., PISGAH FOREST, NC 28768

Reservations Phone: 704/877-3131
Description: Accommodations in this 1883 inn include seven double
   rooms with private bath, and five cabins and cottages. A family
   room with cable TV is available to all guests.
Amenities: A full breakfast with eggs any way you'd like them

Nearby Attractions: Pisgah National Forest, Holmes State Park,
   Brevard Music Center, Biltmore House, Carl Sandburg's House,
   Flatrock Playhouse
Special Services: Airport pickup upon request; rates include full
   breakfast.
Rates: $48 single, $58 double

BLUE BOAR LODGE

200 SANTEELAH RD., ROBBINSVILLE, NC 28771

Reservations Phone: 704/479-8126
Description: The lodge is a mountain hideaway in the Nantahala
   Forest. The accommodations are rustic but comfortable. The lodge is
   within walking distance of a lake.
Amenities: Breakfast with country sausage and ham, grits, gravy, and
   homemade biscuits

Nearby Attractions: Nantahala National Forest, Great Smokies,
   white-water rafting, fishing, Joyce Kilmer Memorial Forest
Special Services: Breakfast and supper are included in the room rate.
   Picnic lunches can be arranged.
Rates: $45 single, $80 double

PINE CREST INN

200 PINE CREST LANE, TRYON, NC 28782

Reservations Phone: 704/859-9135, or toll free 800/633-3001
Description: The inn's ten buildings on a wooded knoll contain a
   variety of accommodations—rooms, suites, and cottages. A full-
   service restaurant is on the premises.

Nearby Attractions: Blue Ridge Parkway, waterfalls, Biltmore House

Special Services: Fox hunting in season, nearby tennis, golf, swimming pool
Rates: $50 to $130 double

STONE HEDGE INN
P.O. BOX 366, TRYON, NC 28782

Reservations Phone: 704/859-9114
Description: Set at the base of Mount Tryon, the inn offers a cottage complete with fireplace next to the pool and three beautiful and spacious rooms in the main house. All rooms have private bath, color TV, air conditioning, and mountain views. One is a two-room suite.
Amenities: Full breakfast included

Nearby Attractions: Swimming pool, tennis, golf, hiking
Rates: $56 to $75 double occupancy

PENNSYLVANIA

B&B Reservation Services

BED & BREAKFAST OF SOUTHEAST PENNSYLVANIA
146 W. PHILADELPHIA AVE., BOYERTOWN, PA 19512

Offers B&B Homes In: Reading area, Lehigh Valley, Lancaster and Montgomery counties
Reservations Phone: 215/367-4688
Phone Hours: 24 hours daily
Price Range of Homes: $40 to $85 single, $55 to $150 double
Breakfast included in Price: Continental or full American (one host serves a vegetarian or macrobiotic breakfast)
Brochure Available: For $2
Reservations Should Be Made: Two weeks in advance (last-minute reservations accepted if possible)

Attractions Near the B&B Homes: Pennsylvania Dutch Country, historic Bethlehem, Dorney Park, Lehigh County Velodrome, Hopewell

Village, Kutztown Folk Festival, Reading shopping outlets, Hawk Mountain, Maplegrove Raceway
Major Schools, Universities Near the B&B Homes: Lehigh, Lafayette, Moravian, Allentown, Cedar Crest, Muhlenberg, Albright, and Alvernia colleges; Kutztown U.; Perkiomen School

Best B&Bs

- **"Wildernest" B&B in Springtown, Bucks County, Pennsylvania.** You will stay in a house surrounded by 12 acres of meadow, deer-filled woods, and a trout stream. This home is a cedar contemporary with country ambience and unique features: an orchid solarium with a Jacuzzi, a wrap-around deck, regional art and artifacts, and country Victorian antiques. You can stay in any of three double rooms, one with a private bath in the suite. All rooms are insulated against sound, and have high brass beds. You are only five minutes away from the Delaware River and Canal and Lake Nockamixon, where you can go tubing, boating, and hiking. Fascinating New Hope with all of its restaurants and art galleries is only 15 minutes away. *Insider's Tip:* For a special occasion, your hosts can arrange for a candlelight gourmet dinner or an early morning nature "stalk" with camera to catch wildlife in the act of being themselves. (Top 100.)

- **The Foreman House in Churchtown, Pennsylvania.** This solid stone house was built before 1920. It is surrounded by tall trees. Two guestrooms are available at the front of the second floor, with a bath shared by the two rooms. This B&B is a good base for exploring the discount factory outlets of Lancaster County and Reading.

- **Log house in Womelsdorf, Pennsylvania.** The home is new but the ambience is centuries old. Your host loves to garden, and it shows around the house. Two guestrooms are available, each with a king-size bed and private bath. Located only 20 miles from Hershey.

- **"The house on the old Canal" in Reading, Pennsylvania.** When you slip into your bed, you can be lulled to sleep by the sound of a waterfall on the nearby Schuylkill River. You will be staying in a 180-year-old stone farmhouse with a river view. For breakfast you can expect to sample some of your host's homemade breads, relishes, and jellies. *Insider's Tip:* You can borrow a boat for fishing or a bike for exploring.

- **Cottage at the Quiltery in Landis Store, Pennsylvania.** Staying here is like a trip to the English countryside. You're surrounded by woodland. The house has been decorated with antiques, handmade furniture, and quilts. You'll find one in the living room here. Good antiques shopping nearby.

BED & BREAKFAST OF PHILADELPHIA

P.O. BOX 252, GRADYVILLE, PA 19039

Offers B&B Homes In: Center City Philadelphia, all five surrounding counties of Bucks, Chester, Montgomery, Lancaster, and Delaware, including Main Line, New Hope, Doylestown, Valley Forge, West Chester, Chadds Ford, and Chestnut Hill

Reservations Phone: 215/358-4747, or toll free 800/733-4747

Phone Hours: 9am to 5pm Monday through Friday and 10am to 4pm on Saturday

Price Range of Homes: $25 to $35 single, $40 to $190 double (family rates in some specific homes)

Breakfast Included in Price: "Gourmet" Continental or full breakfasts, which may include quiches, Philadelphia sticky buns, scrapple, other host specialties, and regional fare

Brochure Available: $3 for "Sample of B&Bs"

Reservations Should Be Made: One week in advance or sooner (last-minute reservations accepted, according to availability)

Attractions Near the B&B Homes: Valley Forge National Park, Independence Hall and National Park, Philadelphia Museum of Art, Franklin Institute, Rodin Museum, Longwood Gardens, Winterthur Museum and Gardens, Hagley Museum, Brandywine River Museum (Wyeth paintings), Skippack Village, Mennonite and Amish country, Sesame Place, New Hope

Major Schools, Universities Near the B&B Homes: U. of Pennsylvania, Drexel, Temple, Haverford, Bryn Mawr, Villanova, Swarthmore, Eastern, Beaver, Cabrini, St. Josephs, La Salle, Rosemont, Philadelphia Textile College, Jefferson Medical School, Wills Eye Hospital, American College of Physicians, Presbyterian Hospital, Dufreye Medical Center

Best B&Bs

■ **The Inn at Centre Park in Reading, Pennsylvania.** The RSO enthusiastically describes this B&B as the "best of the best." And small wonder. It's a beautifully preserved mansion filled with classic Victorian architectural details: wood paneling, stained glass, carved plaster ceilings, marble fireplaces. Listed on the National Historic Register, the mansion offers two elegant suites and a room with a queen-size bed. All have private baths. The sitting room of the Blue Suite can also accommodate two additional guests. The home is located on a quiet street surrounded by the mansions of Reading's most elegant neighborhood. Centre Park is convenient for visits to the Amish Country and antiquing in Lancaster County. (Top 100.)

- John Hayes House, a late 1700 B&B set on a working dairy farm in Chester County, Pennsylvania. The farm is surrounded by Amish neighbors. You have a choice of three comfortable bedrooms on the second floor.

- Gilded Victorian B&B in West Chester, Pennsylvania. This mansion came to life in 1850. Today it has been completely restored and offers seven guest bedrooms. French window/doors lead out to a wrap-around porch. (Weddings are often held here.) It is close to all of the attractions of the Brandywine Valley.

- An 1819 farmhouse in Bucks County, Pennsylvania. For many decades New York and Philadelphia artists, writers, and ex-stockbrokers have scoured the gentle hills of Bucks County in search of "finds" such as this. This home shows its age charmingly—with a Franklin stove, wide-plank floors and trestle tables, and five fireplaces. Breakfast surprises may include shoo-fly pie (don't ask—you'll love it) and homemade scrapple.

- Colonial garden B&B near Philadelphia, Pennsylvania's historic area. In 1750 it was an urban inn created by joining two Colonial homes together. Nine guestrooms are available, many with antique furnishings. Weather permitting, the large walled herb-and-rose garden is the perfect spot for breakfast and the afternoon ritual: tea, or wine and cheese.

- Rittenhouse town house in the center of Philadelphia, Pennsylvania. Yes, on Philadelphia's elegant Rittenhouse Square. The four-story home conveys a European feeling in decor and in the hospitality of its widely traveled and multilingual host. A suite on the second floor has twin beds and a comfortable sitting room. The third floor is large with its twin beds, sofa, desk, and TV.

BED & BREAKFAST CONNECTIONS
P.O. BOX 21, DEVON, PA 19333

Offers B&B Homes In: Philadelphia, Chestnut Hill, Mount Airy, Germantown, Valley Forge, King of Prussia, Main Line communities
Reservations Phone: 215/687-3565 or toll free 800/448-3619 (outside of Pennsylvania)
Phone Hours: 9am to 9pm Monday through Saturday and 1 to 9pm on Sunday
Price Range of Homes: $25 to $145
Breakfast Included in Price: Continental or full American
Brochure Available: Free directory

Reservations Should Be Made: By phone only, preferably two weeks in advance

Attractions Near the B&B Homes: Historic Philadelphia, Independence National Park, Valley Forge National Historical Park, Brandywine Valley, Longwood Gardens, Winterthur

Major Schools, Universities Near the B&B Homes: U. of Pennsylvania, Swarthmore College, Drexel U., Bryn Mawr, Temple U., Villanova, Haverford College, Valley Forge Military Academy

Best B&Bs

■ Suburban home in Newtown Square, Pennsylvania. Centrally located to historic Philadelphia, the Brandywine Valley, and Valley Forge Park, this lovely home overlooks five acres of rolling hunt country. You may want to talk history with the host, who is a buff. The host will also serve a full breakfast either in the garden room or on the terrace overlooking the Pennsylvania countryside. This home is equipped for handicapped guests, with a chair lift to the second floor.

■ Fantasy cottage in Huntingdon, Pennsylvania. Only a half-hour from Philadelphia, yet light years away in atmosphere—a combination greenhouse and potting shed converted into a unique B&B. Inside you will find an interior decorated with a light touch, a fireplace; a refrigerator stocked with wine, cheese, and soft drinks; and a bath protected from public view by a grape arbor.

■ A Society Hill town house in Philadelphia, Pennsylvania, dating back to 1791. This could be the ideal headquarters for exploring the historic attractions of the city. You have a choice of three rooms. If you're interested in coin or stamp collecting, talk with your host. Your other host enjoys talking about ballet. *Insider's Tip:* A smaller room with a four-poster bed is perfect for the single business traveler, and the price is hard to beat in Philadelphia.

■ Historic registered row house in Philadelphia, Pennsylvania, very close to the University of Pennsylvania, Drexel University, the Civic Center, and Children's Hospital. Good spot for a family traveling together. The third-floor bedroom has two twin beds and a double bed. A sitting room at the opposite end of the hall is a nice place to relax by the TV or read a good book about the early history of Philadelphia. Another bargain.

■ Farmhouse in Chester Springs, Pennsylvania. Built before the Civil War, this B&B offers two spacious guestrooms. The "Blue Room" has an antique double bed, with a private phone. "Grandmother's Room" has a converted rope bed. You're surrounded by 10 rural acres with a stream. If you ever wanted to know about beekeeping, talk with your host. It's his hobby.

■ Six-room guesthouse in Brogue, Pennsylvania. The land bordering the Susquehanna River was once owned by Ben Franklin's grandson. You can fish in the river or swim in an old-fashioned swim hole. Or walk to an old grist mill now being restored. This is a good, private location for a family—or even for a small business meeting. Phone and FAX are available. Breakfast is included for all.

■ A 200-year-old "Bankhouse" in West Chester, Pennsylvania. This was once a working farm and sawmill. One guestroom is decorated with country mauves and pinks. The second is a twin-bedded room which reflects the simplicity of its Amish motif. A sitting room adjoins the two. Help yourself to reading materials and games. A full country breakfast is served, with muffins being the specialty of the house.

HERSHEY BED & BREAKFAST RESERVATION SERVICE
P.O. BOX 208, HERSHEY, PA 17033

Offers B&B Homes In: Lancaster County (Lancaster, Manheim, Elizabethtown, Lititz); Dauphin County (Hershey, Harrisburg); Lebanon County (Annville, Palmyra); southeastern Pennsylvania
Reservations Phone: 717/533-2928
Phone Hours: 7am to 10pm daily
Price Range of Homes: $45 to $50 single, $45 to $75 double
Breakfast Included in Price: Continental or full American; many Lancaster-area farm homes provide Pennsylvania Dutch country breakfasts, with their own cured hams and sausages, and breads and rolls baked early in the same morning; special gourmet breakfasts are served at a historic home in Annville and Elizabethtown.
Brochure Available: Free if you send a stamped, self-addressed no. 10 envelope
Reservations Should be Made: Two weeks in advance preferred, one week accepted (last-minute reservations accepted)

Attractions Near the B&B Homes: Pennsylvania Farm Museum, Amish Homestead, Strasburg Railroad, Dutch Wonderland, Hershey Park, Hershey Museum of American Life, Hershey Rose Gardens, William Penn Museum, Antique Automobile Club of America, Zoo America, Chocolate World, many shopping outlets
Major Schools, Universities Near the B&B Homes: Franklin and Marshall, Millersville, Elizabethtown College, Lebanon Valley College,

Capitol Campus of Penn State, M.S. Hershey Medical Center of Penn State, Harrisburg Area Community College

Best B&Bs

■ West Ridge Guest House in Elizabethtown, Pennsylvania. You have a choice of seven guestrooms. Each room is decorated in a different style: Victorian, Williamsburg, wicker, country, and "anniversary" where you can celebrate your anniversary. Each room has its own TV, telephone, and air conditioning. You can join other travelers in the special social room with a TV, work out in an exercise room and pop into the hot tub, or walk through the hobby farm and fish in one of two ponds. Only 20 minutes from Hershey Park and Chocolate World. (Top 100.)

■ Farm Fortune, an 11-room limestone farmhouse in New Cumberland, Pennsylvania (right across the Susquehanna River from Harrisburg, the state capitol). According to one legend, this home was part of the famous Civil War "underground railroad." You will certainly feel as if you've retreated to another century as you tread the wide floorboards and sit in front of a huge walk-in fireplace. You can use this home as a base for skiing (Ski Roundtop is 10 miles away) or for summer antiquing and fishing—right from the banks of Farm Fortune.

■ Victorian mansion in Annville, Pennsylvania. This home was built in 1860 and borders the Swatara Creek on four acres. Every room is different, with period furnishings, including canopy beds. A full Pennsylvania Dutch breakfast is served in the family dining room.

■ Large brick home (Country Pines Farm) in Manheim, Pennsylvania. Built in 1817, this home offers a front porch for warm summer evenings or a walk-in fireplace for cold winter nights. This is a working dairy farm on 100 acres. You're close to the attractions of Hershey and Lancaster when you stay here.

■ An 1800 log cabin in Hershey, Pennsylvania. Located on Stonelock Farm, this cabin offers you country charm. On cold winter evenings you can warm up with some hot cider by a pot-belly stove. Close to Hershey Park.

BED AND BREAKFAST OF CHESTER COUNTY
P.O. BOX 825, KENNETT SQUARE, PA 19348

Offers B&B Homes In: Brandywine Valley, from the Philadelphia suburbs and Wilmington, Delaware, to Pennsylvania Dutch country
Reservations Phone: 215/444-1367

Phone Hours: Anytime daily
Price Range of Homes: $40 and up single, $50 to $125 double
Breakfast Included in Price: Continental or full American, depending on individual home; many feature gourmet cooking with homemade specialties.
Brochure Available: For $3
Reservations Should Be Made: At least one week in advance preferred—"We try to accommodate immediately, or as soon as possible."

Attractions Near the B&B Homes: Longwood Gardens, Winterthur, Brandywine River Museum (Wyeth paintings), Delaware Natural History Museum, Valley Forge, Brandywine Battlefield, Phillips Mushroom Museum, Pennsylvania Dutch country
Major Schools, Universities Near the B&B Homes: West Chester U., Lincoln, Widener, U. of Delaware, Penn State at Lima

Best B&Bs _____

■ An 18th-century home near Longwood Gardens, Pennsylvania. The owner is an antiques dealer, as you can quickly tell as you walk through this B&B. A swimming pool is available to guests.

BED & BREAKFAST OF LANCASTER COUNTY
P.O. BOX 19, MOUNTVILLE, PA 17554

Offers B&B Homes In: Lancaster County, Gettysburg, Harrisburg, York, Hershey, Reading
Reservations Phone: 717/285-7200
Phone Hours: 9am to 2pm and 4 to 9pm every day
Price Range of Homes: $35 to $100 single, $55 to $100 double
Breakfast Included in Price: Continental to full American
Brochure Available: Free with stamped, self-addressed no. 10 envelope
Reservations Should Be Made: One week in advance recommended (last-minute reservations accepted if possible)

Attractions Near the B&B Homes: Pennsylvania Dutch country, Hershey, Gettysburg, state parks
Major Schools, Universities Near the B&B Homes: Franklin & Marshall, Millersville U., Lititz School for Girls, St. Anne School for Girls, Stevens Trade School

Best B&Bs

■ Grand Victorian house overlooking the Conestoga River in Lancaster, Pennsylvania. Imagine the life of an early iron baron, with millions to spend at a time when the dollar seemed to go forever. You might have built a house surrounded by magnificent gardens—filled with 50 varieties of natural wildflowers and wooded trails. You don't have to imagine. Come as a guest to the former iron baron's home, now a great B&B. You have a choice of a comfortable bedroom in the main house or (for extra privacy) an adjoining guesthouse, formerly a summer kitchen where the cook smoked huge hams. (Top 100.)

■ 1783 farmhouse inn in Lancaster, Pennsylvania. Consider such distinctive features as fanlights adorning the main entrance, six working fireplaces, and the original pine floors. *Insider's Tip:* Several couples or a family traveling together should consider the guesthouse right next to the farmhouse. Built in 1826, it features such surprises as a unique winding stairway to a second-floor room with old stenciled walls. Sleeps from two to seven people and has an efficiency kitchen and private bath.

■ B&B in Lancaster, Pennsylvania, over an antiques shop. You can go to sleep dreaming about antiques and then go shopping for them right downstairs. In fact, breakfast is served in the shop on a large mahogany table lighted by a Waterford crystal chandelier. Lemon herb bread is one of the specialties.

CENTER CITY BED & BREAKFAST
1804 PINE ST., PHILADELPHIA, PA 19103

Offers B&B Homes In: Center City Philadelphia, plus some outside the city
Reservations Phone: 215/735-1137
Phone Hours: 9am to 5pm Monday through Saturday, except holidays
Price Range of Homes: $35 to $59 single, $45 to $75 double
Breakfast Included in Price: Continental or full American (juice, eggs, bacon, toast, coffee); full breakfast served at certain homes
Brochure Available: Free
Reservations Should Be Made: Two weeks in advance (last-minute reservations accepted if possible)

Attractions Near the B&B Homes: Independence Hall, Betsy Ross House, Liberty Bell, Fairmount Park, Carpenters' Hall, Rodin Museum, Franklin Museum, Amish Country, Philadelphia Art Museum, Philadelphia Zoo

Major Schools, Universities Near the B&B Homes: U. of Pennsylvania, Temple, Drexel Institute, Moore College of Art, largest number of medical schools in mid-Atlantic area

REST & REPAST BED & BREAKFAST SERVICE
P.O. BOX 126, PINE GROVE MILLS, PA 16868

Offers B&B Homes In: Central Pennsylvania
Reservations Phone: 814/238-1484
Phone Hours: 10am to noon on Monday, Wednesday, and Saturday; 7 to 10pm on Monday, Tuesday, Wednesday, and Friday; other hours, answering machine
Price Range of Homes: $26 to $35 single, $35 to $55 double (on football weekends, $40 to $70 double, and a $7 surcharge for one-night stays; two-night minimum on Homecoming and Parents weekends)
Breakfast Included in Price: Continental or full American; almost half the hosts serve full breakfasts, including Pennsylvania Dutch specialties, fresh-gathered eggs, and homemade jams
Brochure Available: Free; directory available for $3.50
Reservations Should Be Made: Two weeks in advance (last-minute reservations accepted if possible); three to six months in advance for football weekends, and especially Homecoming Weekend

Attractions Near the B&B Homes: Penns Cave, Indian Caverns, Woodward Cave, 28th Division Military Shrine and Museum, Governor Curtin Mansion Village, four wineries, Belleville Amish Market, Baalsburg (home of Memorial Day)
Major Schools, Universities Near the B&B Homes: Penn State, Bucknell, Juniata College, Greer Girls School

Best B&Bs

■ Modern, unique home in Port Matilda, Pennsylvania. Imagine stepping into an octagonal house with skylight windows, a woodstove, with a deck overlooking acres of woodland. This is a great spot for privacy. There are a number of trails into the woods. Breakfast includes home-baked muffins and fresh fruit. *Insider's Tip:* Tell the host the night before that you like pancakes and you'll get them in the morning.

ALL ABOUT TOWN—B&B IN PHILADELPHIA AND SUBSIDIARIES
BED & BREAKFAST OF VALLEY FORGE
ALL ABOUT THE BRANDYWINE VALLEY B&B

P.O. BOX 562, VALLEY FORGE, PA 19481

Offers B&B Homes In: Philadelphia, Valley Forge, Brandywine Valley, Chestnut Hill, Phoenixville, Skippack, Newtown Square, Malvern, Bucks County, Lancaster County (all in Southeastern Pennsylvania)
Reservations Phone: 215/783-7838; **FAX:** 215/783-7783
Phone Hours: 9am to 9pm daily
Price Range of Homes: $25 to $65 single, $35 to $80 double
Breakfast Included in Price: Continental, full or gourmet (dependent on location)
Brochure Available: Free
Reservations Should Be Made: At your convenience; last-minute reservations accepted.

Attractions Near the B&B Homes: Independence National Historical Park, Liberty Bell, Penn's Landing, Art Museum, Valley Forge National Historical Park, Longwood Gardens, Winterthur, Reading Outlets, King of Prussia Court & Plaza, Hopewell Village, Devon Horse Show, Audubon Bird Sanctuary.
Major Schools, Universities Near the B&B Homes: Villanova U., U. of Pennsylvania, Bryn Mawr, Eastern, Rosemont, Haverford, Valley Forge Military Academy, Ursinus College, West Chester U., Immaculata College

■ Victorian 22-room charmer just west of Valley Forge, Pennsylvania, located about 45 minutes from Philadelphia. You can see the handiwork of craftspeople from Italy, England, and the U.S. who built this home almost 100 years ago. Each of the six bedrooms is a step back to a quieter era. The armoires are made of beautiful woods such as birds eye maple, tiger maple, cherry, and mahogany. The bathroom sinks are marble and stained-glass windows and fireplaces complete your sense of another century. *Insider's Tip:* Take some pictures of the front of this house. It's a classic. (Top 100.)

■ The Amsterdam, a B&B in a former general store near Pennsylvania Dutch country. The structure is hard to describe because the building has been remodeled so many times from the time it was built back in 1860. It made the transition from an all-purpose store that served the nearby farmers to a farmhouse. Now it has become a comfortable, unusual guesthouse. Your host is from Holland, something you will quickly detect in the decor and in the Dutch breakfast.

■ Rittenhouse Square highrise B&B in the most fashionable section of Philadelphia, Pennsylvania. The suite with a king-size bed is huge, 18 feet by 25 feet, with an adjoining bath. You're on the 20th floor with a great view of the city. You can walk to top shops, restaurants, and points of interest.

■ Country farm in Brandywine, Pennsylvania. This is a very old structure, dating back to 1704. In those days, before central heating, the fireplace was king—and this B&B has six of them. You have a choice of five bedrooms, with surprises in each such as a spool bed, a rope bed, hand-stenciled walls, rockers, and antique dolls. But lest you think everything is old, step into the hot tub, dip into the swimming pool, and relax in the air conditioning. The farm is close to Longwood Gardens, Winterthur, and only 12 miles from Philadelphia.

■ Squirrel Hill farmhouse, seven miles from Valley Forge, Pennsylvania. This can be your rural retreat, in five acres of woods, fields, and a pond. There are three guestrooms, all with private baths. The breakfast is big and gourmet. The handicapped are accommodated with a stairlift to the second floor. *Insider's Tip:* The business person can go right to work here. A computer and FAX are available.

■ B&B on Washington Square right in the center of Philadelphia, Pennsylvania, just a six-block walk to Independence Hall. It was constructed in 1790 and decorated with many collectibles and old-world antiques by a host who loves to travel. Three bedrooms are available, and each has a color cable TV and private phone. A full breakfast is served before a hearth fire in winter months.

GUESTHOUSES
P.O. BOX 2137, WEST CHESTER, PA 19380

Offers B&B Homes In: Pennsylvania, Delaware, New Jersey, Maryland
Reservations Phone: 215/692-4575 or toll free 800/950-9130; FAX 215/692-4451
Phone Hours: Noon to 4pm Monday through Friday
Price Range of Homes: $35 to $150 per night, double occupancy
Breakfast Included in Price: Yes
Brochure Available: Descriptive sampling and "package" brochures
Reservations Should Be Made: Last-minute reservations accepted; American Express, Visa, and MasterCard.

Attractions Near the B&B Homes: Winterthur, Longwood Gardens,

Hagley Museum, Brandywine River Museum (Wyeth), Brandywine Battlefield, Valley Forge

Major Schools, Universities Near the B&B Homes: U. of Delaware, Swarthmore, Villanova, Bryn Mawr, Hoverford, U. of Pennsylvania

Best B&Bs

■ "Lenni," a B&B located between West Chester and Wilmington, Delaware. Built on a landmark site, this is an Italianate serpentine stone country manor house built in the mid 1800s. You will experience how people lived during the Civil War as you relax with period pieces from the Buchanan and Lincoln eras. All of the guestrooms have fireplaces and there are spacious corner rooms on the second floor. For special occasions choose the suite that has a large central hall, master bedroom, second bedroom, nursery, living room with wood stove, bath, and kitchen. (Top 100.)

■ River house on the banks of the Conewago River, near Hershey, Harrisburg, and Gettysburg, Pennsylvania. The house has been newly restored by a prominent architect and offers three guestrooms with private baths. Or you could choose the newly converted carriage house, facing the front lawns and pool. You can roam over a half mile of river frontage and enjoy a swimming pool and the National Historic Register Adirondack gazebo (great for pictures). You're close to skiing and "Chocolate Town USA" as well as the battlefields of Gettysburg.

■ Yellow Breeches Manors in the Gettysburg/Harrisburg, Pennsylvania area. You'll sleep in a house on the banks of the swift Yellow Breeches Creek. A separate wing of the main house provides two floors of guest quarters, all with fireplaces. An old-fashioned "wash house" has been restored as a guestroom. The grounds include lawns, gardens, a natural pool, dam, waterfall, and islands. *Insider's Tip:* If you're a fisherman, bring your gear. The Yellow Breeches is famous for trout fishing.

B&B Inns

ACADEMY STREET BED & BREAKFAST

528 ACADEMY ST., HAWLEY, PA 18428

Reservations Phone: 717/226-3430
Description: This Civil War Victorian home was built in 1863, and is furnished with antiques and artifacts of the period.
Amenities: Gourmet buffet breakfast, high tea, homemade pastries.

Nearby Attractions: Lake and recreational activities, excellent restaurants close by.
Rates: $65 to $75 double; open May to October

THE TOWN HOUSE
S. FAIRFIELD AT LOYALHANNA, LIGONIER, PA 15658

Reservations Phone: 412/238-5451
Description: Primarily a pleasant restaurant that also happens to offer B&B accommodations.
Amenities: Continental breakfast buffet with fresh homemade breads and pastries, preserves, cereals, fresh fruits, juices, and other seasonal items. Guests may also choose a full breakfast of bacon, or ham and eggs, waffles, and pancakes.

Nearby Attractions: Fort Ligonier—a pre–Revolutionary War fort, Falling Water—the famous Frank Lloyd Wright–designed estate, the Johnstown Flood Museum
Rates: $55 to $65, single or double
Innkeeper's Tip: "Our guests are within a few steps of Ligonier's town square, which is typical turn-of-the-century Americana with band concerts on Sunday afternoons, antiques shops, and other attractions. In our common room coffee brews from seven in the morning."

THE INN AT PHILLIPS MILL
NORTH RIVER ROAD, NEW HOPE, PA 18938

Reservations Phone: 215/862-2984
Description: Aaron Phillips built a grist mill here in 1756. Over the years an art colony formed around the mill and organized art exhibitions, concerts, dances, and theatrical productions, and it's still a cultural center. There are now five comfortable bedrooms with private bath and three dining rooms. Each bedroom is furnished with antiques, quilts on four-poster beds, and embroidered cloths.

Nearby Attractions: Swimming pool, craft shows, an annual play production
Rates: $68 to $78 double—plus tax
Innkeeper's Tip: "You can visit many historical sites (Washington was quartered nearby and crossed the Delaware below New Hope). There is a marvelous museum nearby containing the largest collection of

pre-industrial American objects in the world. The art colony has produced many fine painters, now known as the New Hope Impressionists. There are many antiques shops, flea markets, summer theaters, art galleries, passenger mule barges on the canal, and canoeing on the canal." Ask at the Inn for more local tips and vacation ideas.

SOUTH CAROLINA

B&B Reservation Services

CHARLESTON SOCIETY BED & BREAKFAST

84 MURRAY BLVD., CHARLESTON, SC 29401

Offers B&B Homes In: The historic area of Charleston
Reservations Phone: 803/723-4948
Phone Hours: 9am to 5pm daily
Price Range of Homes: $60 to $70 single, $70 to $100 double
Breakfast Included in Price: Continental (juice, roll or toast, coffee)
Brochure Available: Free
Reservations Should Be Made: Two or three weeks in advance (last-minute reservations accepted if possible)
Attractions Near the B&B Homes: All the historic district homes and other historic points of interest are within easy walking distance
Major Schools, Universities Near the B&B Homes: The Citadel, the College at Charleston, Baptist College

Best B&Bs

■ Carriage house in Charleston, South Carolina. You'll have your own private entrance to this attractive home which has a living room with fireplace. Located in Charleston's Historic District.

■ Historic home on Battery, Charleston, South Carolina. This home offers a beautiful view of Charleston Harbor and a swimming pool. The two bedrooms have double beds.

■ One bedroom in the heart of the Old Market area in Charleston, South Carolina. The room has a fireplace, double bed, private bath, and has been recently decorated in reproduction, period furniture. A private entrance lets you come and go as you please.

■ Carriage house on Meeting Street in Charleston, South Carolina. This home can accommodate up to four people in two bedrooms—one with a double bed and the other with twin beds. There is also a private entrance and a living room with fireplace and a full kitchen upstairs.

■ Carriage house on Legare Street in Charleston, South Carolina. The house has a private entrance and a living room and is equipped with a toaster oven and a refrigerator for snacks. The bedroom has twin beds, and a bath (shower only).

HISTORIC CHARLESTON BED AND BREAKFAST
43 LEGARE ST., CHARLESTON, SC 29401

Offers B&B Homes In: The historic district of Charleston
Reservations Phone: 803/722-6606
Phone Hours: 24 hours daily
Price Range of Homes: $65 to $115 single, $65 to $125 double
Breakfast Included in Price: Continental (juice, roll or toast, coffee)
Brochure Available: Free
Reservations Should Be Made: Two weeks in advance; for the period March to June, two to three months in advance (last-minute reservations accepted if possible)

Attractions Near the B&B Homes: Historic homes, museums, harbor tours, famous gardens, beaches
Major Schools, Universities Near the B&B Homes: The Citadel, College of Charleston, Medical University of South Carolina

Best B&Bs

■ 1759 carriage house in Charleston, South Carolina. You step inside a walled garden to find this two-bedroom, two-bath carriage house that pre-dates the Revolutionary War. Your host greets you with complimentary wine. The living room and kitchen open on to a garden patio with a fountain. Accommodations include a double bed with private bath or a room with two twin beds and private bath. Limited French is spoken. The beaches are 20 minutes away, and many historic sites, museums, and excellent restaurants begin almost right out the door. Children over six are welcome. (Top 100.)

■ A "Kitchen House" in the historic district of Charleston, South Carolina. In Colonial days the kitchen was separated from the main house, primarily as a way of preventing the spread of fire. This restored kitchen now has two bedrooms, two baths, a living room and—true to its origin—a little eat-in kitchen stocked with wine, fresh fruits, milk, eggs, cereal, and coffee cake or croissants. The hosts enjoy talking about interior design and history.

■ 1837 home in Charleston Village, South Carolina. Built in 1837, this B&B overlooks Colonial Lake. This is a convenient location for visiting nearby historic churches, house museums, galleries, and good restaurants. Your hosts are a realtor and a preservation activist. They also like to talk about their hobby, gardening.

■ Williamsburg-style house built before 1715, Charleston, South Carolina. You can stay in the oldest frame house in Charleston. Once this was the oldest drugstore in the U.S., but now it has been restored to its original use as a private residence. The rooms have cypress floors, heavy beams, and antique furnishings. *Insider's Tip:* Ask for the room with a fireplace.

■ Greek Revival home in Charleston, South Carolina. This B&B was built in 1838. As you approach you can see its impressive façade with four columns and a large classic garden. The home is furnished with 18th-century American antiques. It's an easy stroll from here to the historic district. Interested in restoring your own home? Talk with your hosts. They are retired interior decorators who have brought many plantations and historic houses back to their original grandeur. Full breakfast served.

■ A 1770s house in Charleston, South Carolina. This home was originally built in an orange grove. You can still see its 18th-century moldings and paneling. The original kitchen building behind the house has now become the B&B self-contained unit. It has a sitting room, a built-in kitchen unit, and an upstairs bedroom and bath. The furnishings are southern antiques. For breakfast you can expect homemade coffee cakes and breads. The refrigerator is stocked with breakfast staples (eggs, milk, butter). Your host's hobbies include travel, cooking, interior design, and gardening.

B&B Inns

EVERGREEN INN
1103 S. MAIN ST., ANDERSON, SC 29621

Reservations Phone: 803/225-1109
Description: The inn located in Anderson's Historic District is one of the

oldest mansions. The accommodations consist of seven rooms, six baths, and eight fireplaces. The house is on the National Register.
Amenities: Continental breakfast with fresh fruit, yogurt, and cheeses.

Nearby Attractions: Jane Hartwell Park, Anderson Historic District
Rates: On request

OLD POINT INN
212 NEW ST., BEAUFORT, SC 29902

Reservations Phone: 803/524-3177
Description: This 1898 Victorian Inn in the "Beaufort Style," with double porches, front and side, is located in the historic district half a block from the Beaufort River.
Amenities: Breakfast includes juice, fruit, homemade muffins.

Nearby Attractions: Hunting Island State Park, Hilton Head Island
Special Services: Mints and flowers in the rooms, bicycles
Rates: On request

RHETT HOUSE INN
1009 CRAVEN ST., BEAUFORT, SC 29902

Reservations Phone: 803/524-9030
Description: Romantic historic home that pre-dates the Civil War (or War Between the States as they prefer to say here). It was built by a Southern aristocrat named Thomas Rhett. There are eight guestrooms, all with private bath, and three have fireplaces.
Amenities: Homemade breads for breakfast, with an array of preserves and fresh fruit and honey. Antique pool table.

Nearby Attractions: The Intercoastal Waterway and the waterfront of Historic Beaufort.
Rates: $80 to $120 single or double.
Author's Note: This inn has been favored by some high rollers. Barbra Streisand stayed here recently and wrote, "Loved Beaufort and the Rhett House Inn."

We have received an astounding number of forms from readers recommending this inn. At first we were puzzled by the sheer number of letters until one reader let the cat out of the bag. The Rhett House apparently gave out the forms to their guests. We are frankly flattered that the inn would try so hard to get into this book. But the important point is that so many of their guests were enthusiastic enough to write endorsements about this inn.

These comments from Iris Abrons of New York are fairly typical, "Having traveled all over the U.S. and Europe, my husband and I feel the Rhett House Inn exemplifies the best qualities an inn should have—beautiful furnishings, congenial hosts, excellent food, and a beautiful setting. We can't wait to go back!"

INDIGO INN
ONE MAIDEN LANE, CHARLESTON, SC 29401

Reservations Phone: Toll free 800/845-7639
Description: Located in historic downtown Charleston, the Indigo Inn has 18th-century decor, a courtyard, down pillows and comforters, one or two queen-size beds in each room, and facilities for the handicapped. Pets are allowed.
Amenities: "Hunt breakfast" (ham biscuits, homemade breads, fresh fruits, coffee, and juice), daily Charleston newspaper, private parking.

Nearby Attractions: Within walking distance of the open-air market, historic churches and mansions, and fine restaurant
Rates: $95 to $105 double in summer, $75 to $105 double in winter

THE JASMINE HOUSE
64 HASELL ST., CHARLESTON, SC 29401

Reservations Phone: Toll free 800/845-7639
Description: The inn has pre–Civil War Greek Revival architecture, 14-foot ceilings, fireplaces, and Oriental rugs. This antebellum home is right across from the Indigo Inn; you check in at the Indigo Inn front desk.
Amenities: "Hunt breakfast" (ham biscuits, homemade breads, fresh fruit, coffee, and juice), complimentary wine

Nearby Attractions: Within walking distance of open-air markets, historic churches, and fine restaurants
Special Services: Jacuzzi and daily periodicals
Rates: $105 to $150 double

THE JOHN LAWTON HOUSE
159 3RD ST. EAST, ESTILL, SC 29918

Reservations Phone: 803/625-3240 or 803/625-2586
Description: Built around the turn of the century from lumber and materials brought by mule and wagon from nearby Jericho Plantation, and extensively renovated in 1985, the inn is decorated with antiques, rich woods, Oriental rugs, and painted porcelains. Original family oil portraits are softly lit by crystal chandeliers. The draperies, wall coverings, and fabrics are period reproductions.
Amenities: Specialties include pear pie and homemade sausage and steamboat mustard. Breakfast is served on silver, crystal, and fine china

Nearby Attractions: Charleston, Columbia, Hilton Head Island, and the South Carolina coast all less than two hours away
Special Services: A small kitchen and private entrance are available to guests, and there's parking on the premises for cars and campers
Rates: $60 double

LIBERTY HALL INN
S.C. BUSINESS HWY. 28, PENDLETON, SC 29670

Reservations Phone: 803/646-7500
Description: The inn is a restored Piedmont farmhouse with private baths, air conditioning, and TVs in rooms furnished with period antiques.
Amenities: Continental breakfast plus other meals

Nearby Attractions: Woodburn Plantation, Clemson University, John Calhoun's home, lakes for boating and fishing, golf
Rates: $57 to $67 double
Innkeeper's Tip: "The 200-year-old town of Pendleton is the center of a three-county district which includes five large lakes, five state parks, a wild and scenic river, mountain trails, and a national forest. The entire town is on the National Register of Historic Places. A walking or driving tour highlights 36 historic homes and sites. Two restored plantation houses are open Sundays April to October. The first weekend in April brings azaleas, dogwoods, and Spring Jubilee —an award winning festival offering crafts, entertainment, and food. An antiques fair is held on the Village Green every fall."

CHAUGA RIVER HOUSE
COBB'S BRIDGE ROAD, WESTMINSTER, SC 29691

Reservations Phone: 803/647-9587
Description: Located directly on the rapids of the Chauga River in the center of the Sumter National Forest, the inn has five guestrooms decorated with French country antiques.
Amenities: Continental breakfast plus cereal and fruit

Nearby Attractions: Whitewater Falls, Clemson University
Special Services: Barbecue area, swimming, TV lounge, white-water rafting packages
Rates: $44 to $69 double

VIRGINIA

_____ B&B Reservation Services _____

PRINCELY BED & BREAKFAST LTD.
819 PRINCE ST., ALEXANDRIA, VA 22314

Offers B&B Homes In: Alexandria (Old Town)
Note: The service specializes in historic (1750–1870) homes
Reservations Phone: 703/683-2159
Phone Hours: 10am to 6pm Monday through Friday
Price Range of Homes: $70 to $85 double
Breakfast Included in Price: Continental (juice, fresh fruit, home-baked breads, coffee or tea)
Reservations Should Be Made: One week in advance (no last-minute reservations accepted)

Attractions Near the B&B Homes: Washington, DC; Mount Vernon

Best B&Bs
■ Home of Washington's brother. That's right, this imposing three-story town house was built in 1750 for George's brother, Lawrence. Located right in the heart of Old Town Alexandria, Virginia, it welcomes guests

with double parlors with fireplaces and antiques. A large bedroom has its own fireplace, a four-poster bed, and a private bath. Lawrence must have loved gardens; this home has them on three levels with a huge magnolia tree on one level and an abundance of flowering shrubs. Private offstreet parking is available. Shops, restaurants, and historic sites are within walking distance. (Top 100.)

BED & BREAKFAST OF TIDEWATER VIRGINIA
P.O. BOX 3343, NORFOLK, VA 23514

Offers B&B Homes In: Norfolk, Virginia Beach, Portsmouth, Chesapeake, the Eastern Shore and Northern Neck of Virginia
Reservations Phone: 804/627-1983 or 804/627-9409
Phone Hours: 8am to 8pm daily (answering service 24 hours a day)
Price Range of Homes: $30 to $60 single, $35 to $95 double
Breakfast Included in Price: Continental or full breakfast, which may include spoonbread, country sausage, Smithfield ham, and homemade muffins. Fresh fruit and regional seafood dishes may also be served when in season.
Brochure Available: Free
Reservations Should Be Made: At least two weeks in advance, but the earlier the better (last-minute reservations accepted if possible)

Attractions Near the B&B Homes: Norfolk Naval Station, Chrysler Museum, MacArthur Memorial, Waterside Marketplace, fishing and water sports, Virginia Beach oceanfront, Harbor tours
Major Schools, Universities Near the B&B Homes: Old Dominion, Eastern Virginia Medical School, Virginia Wesleyan

Best B&Bs

■ Victorian town house in the historic Ghent area of Norfolk, Virginia. Ghent is the trendy place in the city, filled with restaurants and unusual shops. "Everyone wants to stay in Ghent," says the reservation service. "And they love staying in this town house." Two guestrooms are available, and a full breakfast is served.

■ Shingle house in Virginia Beach, Virginia. Located just a block and a half from the ocean, this attractive B&B has the charm of "Old Virginia Beach." The entire upstairs (two double rooms, a single room, and bath) is available for guests.

■ Country house near Accomac, Virginia. This B&B is located on Virginia's Eastern Shore. The architecture is typical of this part of Virginia—big house, little house, colonnade, and kitchen. You're a short drive from Chincoteague, that beautiful wildlife preserve where you can view hundreds of birds from your car and meet wild ponies (now quite tame) on the trails.

BENSONHOUSE OF RICHMOND AND WILLIAMSBURG

2036 MONUMENT AVE., RICHMOND, VA 23220

Offers B&B Homes In: Richmond, Williamsburg, and Fredericksburg
Reservations Phone: 804/363-6900
Phone Hours: 10:30am to 5pm Monday through Friday (24-hour answering service)
Price Range of Homes: $52 to $105 single, $60 to $115 double, $105 suites
Breakfast Included in Price: Continental or full American, depending on individual home; many homes serve home-baked breads and muffins.
Brochure Available: $2 with a stamped, self-addressed no. 10 envelope
Reservations Should Be Made: Three or more weeks in advance (last-minute reservations accepted if accommodations available)

Attractions Near the B&B Homes: St. John's Church, Edgar Allan Poe Museum, Museum of the Confederacy, John Marshall House, State Archives, Virginia Historical Society, Science Museum of Virginia, Virginia Museum, and Virginia Theater for the Performing Arts; within a short drive of Colonial Williamsburg, Busch Gardens, Kings Dominion, and James River plantations
Major Schools, Universities Near the B&B Homes: U. of Richmond, Medical College of Virginia, Virginia Commonwealth U., Randolph Macon, Union Theological Seminary, St. Catherine's School, St. Christopher's School; in Williamsburg adjacent to the College of William and Mary

Best B&Bs

■ A 1908 house in Richmond, Virginia. Known as the "Summerhouse," this residence has been carefully restored. You'll enjoy the brightly colored walls, fireplaces, and detailed windows. *Insider's Tip:* Ask about the honeymoon or anniversary package. It includes breakfast in bed (on silver trays no less), wine or champagne, fruit and cheese, and enough fresh flowers to prove that romance can still be wonderful. **(Top 100.)**

- "Sheldon's Ordinary" home in Williamsburg, Virginia. This house is a copy of the 18th-century Sheldon's tavern in Litchfield, Connecticut. Yet it was built just a few years ago, in 1983. Many unusual decorative touches, such as hand-painted tiles from the Caribbean in the living room fireplace, and antique heart of pine wide-plank floors, and beautiful oak paneling from an old church in Indiana. This unique house is in a wooded area near William and Mary and one mile from the Colonial Williamsburg restored area. The house provides a full Continental breakfast which includes homemade ham, rolls, apple coffee cake, and fresh fruit.

- The Emmanuel Hutzler House in Richmond, Virginia. This is a huge home (over 8,000 square feet) designed in the Italian Renaissance style. Natural mahogany raised paneling gives a classic touch to the entry, living room, and staircase—complemented by leaded glass windows and coffered ceiling with dropped beams. The large living room has a marble fireplace flanked by bookcases, where guests can meet and relax. There is a choice of four guestrooms on the second floor, each with a private bath. *Insider's Tip:* Ask for the largest room with a marble fireplace, four-poster mahogany bed, and antique sofa and dresser. The adjoining private bath has a Jacuzzi, separate shower, and double sink.

THE TRAVEL TREE

P.O. BOX 838, WILLIAMSBURG, VA 23187

Offers B&B Homes In: Williamsburg
Reservations Phone: 804/253-1571
Phone Hours: 6 to 9pm Monday through Friday
Price Range of Homes: $50 to $90 single or double.
Breakfast Included in Price: Continental (juice, breads or pastries, coffee)
Brochure Available: Free
Reservations Should Be Made: Several weeks in advance

Attractions Near the B&B Homes: Colonial Williamsburg, Busch Gardens, Yorktown, Jamestown
Major Schools, Universities Near the B&B Homes: College of William and Mary

Best B&Bs

- New replica of an 18th-century home in Williamsburg, Virginia. You can walk to the historic district. This B&B is furnished with period pieces and each of the two double guestrooms has a private bath.

■ Large brick home in Williamsburg, Virginia. Sits on a beautifully landscaped property in a wooded residential area. The guestroom is large, with a private bath and private entrance. You can park off the street.

B&B Inns

THE BAILIWICK INN
4023 CHAIN BRIDGE RD., FAIRFAX, VA 22030

Reservations Phone: 703/691-2266
Description: Built in 1800, this historic landmark has been restored and refurbished with rooms patterned after Virginia's great mansions and furnished in antiques. Guests may choose rooms with fireplaces, Jacuzzi tubs, or the bridal suite.
Amenities: Full breakfast and afternoon tea are included. Laundry facilities are available. Guests may participate in parlor games or murder mystery weekends.

Nearby Attractions: Mount Vernon, Gunston Hall, George Mason University, and Civil War battlefields of Manassas and Bull Run.
Special Services: Shuttle bus to the Vienna Metrorail stop, which is 20 minutes from Washington, DC
Rates: $95 to $175 single or double
Innkeeper's Tip: "You can tour Mount Vernon during the day and continue your step back into history by staying in the George Washington bedroom at night."

CHESTER HOUSE
43 CHESTER ST., FRONT ROYAL, VA 22630

Reservations Phone: 800/621-0441
Description: This Georgian mansion with extensive formal gardens is located on two acres in Front Royal's historic district.
Amenities: Fresh-squeezed orange juice, fresh fruit, and home-baked pastries

Nearby Attractions: Skyline Caverns, Skyline Drive, Shenandoah River, golf, tennis, hiking, skiing, horseback riding, fine wineries

Special Services: antiques shop, badminton, complimentary beverages
Rates: $65 to $125 double
Innkeeper's Tip: "We have been described as an 'oasis' in the heart of town, and are within easy walking distance of antiques shops and historic attractions."

THE JOSHUA WILTON HOUSE INN AND RESTAURANT
HARRISONBURG, VA 22801

Reservations Phone: 703/434-4464
Description: 100-year-old Victorian home. The manager describes it as an "urban inn" located right in the center of Harrisonburg. Five guestrooms are furnished with antiques and reproductions.
Amenities: Complimentary beer, wine, or cocktails are served at check-in. The house specialty at breakfast is smoked salmon with poached eggs and herbed Hollandaise.

Nearby Attractions: Numerous antiques shops, the famous Skyline Drive, skiing, golf.
Rates: $85 to $100 single or double.

ABBIE HILL BED & BREAKFAST
P.O. BOX 4503 RICHMOND, VA 23220

Reservations Phone: 804/353-4656
Description: Early 1900s Federal town house located in the urban historic area (the "Fan District"). Rooms are furnished with period antiques.
Amenities: Many of the guestrooms have fireplaces. There are guest laundry facilities and a BYOB bar. Tea or sherry served on arrival.

Nearby Attractions: Virginia Museum of Fine Arts, Virginia State Capitol. Walk to good restaurants.
Special Services: Copy machine available (especially handy for business travelers)
Rates: $55 to $65 single, $65 to $95 double.

THE CEDARS
616 JAMESTOWN RD., WILLIAMSBURG, VA 23185

Reservations Phone: 804/229-3591

Description: This stately three-story brick Colonial home is within a ten-minute walk of the restored area. It has a lovely sitting room and porch, plus nine rooms and a cottage in the back which can be rented by a family.

Amenities: Blueberry muffins, juice, coffee and tea; afternoon tea

Nearby Attractions: Colonial Williamsburg, Busch Gardens, Yorktown, Jamestown, Colonial Parkway

Rates: $55 to $65 double

The Great Lakes Area

────────── **B&B Reservation Services** ──────────

BED & BREAKFAST/CHICAGO, INC.
P.O. BOX 14088, CHICAGO, IL 60614

Offers B&B Homes in: Chicago, North Shore suburbs
Reservations Phone: 312/951-0085.
Phone Hours: 9am to 5pm Monday through Friday
Price Range of Homes: $40 to $65 single, $50 to $75 double
Breakfast Included in Price: Continental
Brochure Available: Free
Reservations Should Be Made: Two weeks in advance (last-minute
   reservations accepted if possible)

Attractions Near the B&B Homes: Lake Michigan, McCormick Place,
   Glencoe Botanic Garden, Ravinia Festival, Old Town, Wrigley Field
Major Schools, Universities Near the B&B Homes: Northwestern,
   Loyola, U. of Chicago, U. of Illinois at Chicago, DePaul

Best B&Bs ────────────────────────────────────
■ Studio apartment in Chicago, Illinois. This is an unhosted B&B in a
prime high-rise building complex which has its own restaurants, dry
cleaners, and grocery store. The air-conditioned apartment has a double bed, sleeper sofa, TV, telephone, and a magnificent skyline view. A
self-serve Continental breakfast is provided. You can walk to business
appointments, excellent shopping, and the trendy art gallery district.
(Top 100.)

■ Apartment on the Magnificent Mile, Chicago, Illinois. This B&B is in
the heart of the city's premier shopping area, only a few steps from the
Water Tower Place. It's located in a luxury high-rise and is furnished
with antiques. The guestroom has a single bed, air conditioning, TV,
telephone, and private attached bath. Your host is a congenial semi-
retired businessperson who is active in community affairs.

■ Old Town in Chicago, Illinois. Ever think of living in a garage? You
may when you see the beautiful restoration job done by the current
owner on a 1920s chauffeur's garage. A catwalk on the second level
allows open space between the first and second floors. The home is

furnished with antiques and features skylights, recessed lighting, Oriental rugs, and TV. You have a choice of two air-conditioned guestrooms, one with twin beds and the other with a double bed. Weather permitting, a Continental breakfast is served in the garden. You are close to Lincoln Park and its famous zoo, the beach, and miles of lakefront.

■ A bargain on Chicago, Illinois's River North. This B&B in a two-bedroom, two-bath contemporary loft apartment has many attractive touches—fireplace, parquet floors, and antiques. The price for a single business traveler is very modest by Near North standards.

■ Victorian mansion just north of Old Town, close to Lincoln Park. Go ape at the famous nearby zoo. The home is a blend of old detail and contemporary amenities. The guestroom has a double bed with a private attached bath. A self-contained apartment is also available.

■ Self-contained one-bedroom garden apartment in a renovated frame building in Old Town. The hostess owns the reservation service, so this place must really be up to snuff. The host is a TV reporter for the Chicago ABC station.

B&B Inns

MISSISSIPPI MEMORIES BED & BREAKFAST
BOX 291, RIVERVIEW HEIGHTS, NAUVOO, IL 62354

Reservations Phone: 217/453-2771
Description: Large B&B home/inn on the banks of the Mississippi. Five antique-filled rooms. *Insider's Tip:* Ask for a room with a river view.
Amenities: Homemade cinnamon rolls, pancakes, individual fruit plates

Nearby Attractions: Only five minutes from the restored Mormon city of Nauvoo. Near antiques shops and malls.
Special Services: Thick terry-cloth robes for guests to use. Mints and fresh flowers in each room.
Rates: $40 single, $48 to $58 double
Innkeeper's Tip: "Try an outstanding dinner at Hotel Nauvoo (built about 1850). Attend a performance of the *City of Joseph,* an outdoor musical in August. Don't miss the Grape Festival every Labor Day."

MICHIGAN

―――――― **B&B Reservation Services** ――――――

BED & BREAKFAST IN MICHIGAN
701 E. LUDDING AVE. LUDDING, MI 49431

Offers B&B Homes In: All over the state of Michigan, including the Upper Peninsula
Reservations Phone: 616/843-1888
Phone Hours: 4pm to 6pm weekdays, or weekends
Price Range of Homes: $35 to $55 single, $40 to $80 double
Breakfast Included in Price: Some homes serve Continental, but many offer a full breakfast, featuring special dishes. There is also a "Howell Festival" celebrating the Howell melons and hand-blended coffee in one of the homes.
Brochure Available: Free if you send a stamped, self-addressed no. 10 envelope
Reservations Should Be Made: Two weeks in advance (last-minute reservations accepted if possible)

Attractions Near the B&B Homes: Henry Ford Museum, Greenfield Village, Fisher Theater, Cranbrook Art Museum, Sleeping Bear Dunes National Park, Marshall Homes Tour, Meadow Brook Hall, Michigan Space Center, ethnic festivals, Downtown Detroit, Grand Prix racing, convention center, Detroit Zoo, Irish Hills, resort areas
Major Schools, Universities Near the B&B Homes: U. of Michigan, Michigan State, Wayne State, Albion, Cranbrook schools, Oakland

Best B&Bs
■ Farmhouse on the National Historic Register near Troy, Michigan. This home is 145 years old, and filled with antiques. After breakfast you can enjoy the walking trail along Paint Creek. Or on cooler days you may want to watch all the varieties of birds that gather at the feeder right outside the living room picture window.

■ Estate home on the shore of a bay, Northport, Michigan. Every afternoon guests are served complimentary beverages in the Common Room with a bay window overlooking the water. You have a choice of four guestrooms. *Insider's Tip:* If you'd like some space, choose the suite with its own kitchen and private bath.

BED & BREAKFAST OF GRAND RAPIDS
455 COLLEGE AVE. SE, GRAND RAPIDS, MI 49503

Offers B&B Homes In: Heritage Hill Historic District in downtown
  Grand Rapids
Reservations Phone: 616/451-4849 or 616/459-7055
Phone Hours: 9am to 9pm daily
Price Range of Homes: $45 single, $55 double
Breakfast Included in Price: Deluxe Continental
Brochure Available: Free
Reservations Should Be Made: Two weeks in advance (last-minute
  reservations accepted if possible)

Attractions Near the B&B Homes: Gerald R. Ford Museum, Holland
  Tulip Festival, Lake Michigan, Heritage Hill District
Major Schools, Universities Near the B&B Homes: Grand Rapids
  Junior College, Davenport Business College, Grand Valley State,
  Kendall School of Design, Calvin College

Best B&Bs

■ Turn-of-the-century home in Grand Rapids, Michigan. Grand Rapids is
world famous as a furniture manufacturer. When you stay in this grand
house (known as the Barber House), you'll see much of his original
Mission-style furniture in the main living areas. The living room has a
copper-hooded fireplace and love seats. Every sleeping room is extra-
large. At night you can sink into one of those antique clawfoot bathtubs.

■ Victorian home in Grand Rapids, Michigan. This B&B is known as the
Heald Lear House, and it's big! The 17 rooms have many decorative
touches, such as a parquet floor in the foyer, leaded-glass windows,
and a gurgling fountain in the solarium. Guests are welcome to relax in
the living room or the library.

B&B Inns

THE KINGSLEY HOUSE
626 WEST MAIN ST., FENNVILLE, MI 49408

Reservations Phone: 616/561-6425
Description: Elaborate, ornate Victorian white-framed and red-roofed
  house was designed by a New York architect in 1886. The home was

originally built for Harvey Kingsley, who brought apple trees to the shores of Lake Michigan a century ago. Each of the guestrooms has been named after a variety of apples, for example, the McIntosh Room with country flowers, and a country painting on an easel.

Amenities: Full family-style breakfast served, including country ham, eggs, homemade breads and muffins.

Nearby Attractions: Hunting, fishing, skiing, Windmill Island, a Dutch village.
Rates: $55 to $65 single, $65 to $75 double.

WICKWOOD INN
510 BUTLER ST., SAUGATUCK, MI 49453

Reservations Phone: 616/857-1097
Description: An English country manor with several common rooms with Laura Ashley papers and fabrics and antiques, the inn has 11 air-conditioned rooms with private bath.
Amenities: Homemade coffee cake, fruit in season, coffee. Brunch is served on Sunday, and hot and cold hors d'oeuvres are served each night in the library bar.

Nearby Attractions: Cross-country ski area with 200 miles of mapped trails, charter fishing boats, two blocks from quaint Victorian village
Special Services: "Our London taxi is at our door to drive guests to dinner or town." Crabtree & Evelyn soaps and shampoo are in each bath.
Rates: $90 to $127 double, May 1 to December 31; $70 to $100 January 1 to April 30

CLIFFORD LAKE HOTEL
561 CLIFFORD LAKE DR., STANTON, MI 48888

Reservations Phone: 517/831-5151
Description: A Michigan historic site overlooking Clifford Lake, the inn contains rooms in the hotel and cottages with two, three, and four bedrooms. The rooms are furnished with antiques, and have corner sinks and country furniture.
Amenities: Continental breakfast; complete food and beverage service

Nearby Attractions: Crystal Speedway, Morelands Moto-Cross, swimming, paddleboats, snowmobiles, fishing-boat rentals

Rates: $55 single, $65 double, in summer; $45 single, $55 double, in fall and winter

---

CHICAGO PIKE INN
215 E. CHICAGO ST., COLDWATER, MI 49036

Reservations Phone: 517/279-8744
Description: This large turn-of-the-century colonial mansion has been restored and furnished in period antiques. The six guestrooms have private baths and queen-size beds.
Amenities: Full country breakfast

Nearby Attractions: Shipshewana, Amish country, antiques capital of Michigan, Battle Creek International Balloon Championship, 150 lakes, parks, Tibbits Professional Summer Theatre.
Special Services: Library, games, puzzles, seasonal refreshments
Rates: $75 to $130 single or double
Innkeeper's Tip: "Every season has its charm here. In spring and summer, guests enjoy our large wrap-around porch with comfortable rocking chairs and the gazebo for breakfast and in the fall and winter, our fireplaces are a cozy gathering place."

OHIO

B&B Reservation Services

COLUMBUS BED & BREAKFAST
769 S. 3RD ST., COLUMBUS, OH 43206

Offers B&B Homes In: Columbus, Ohio, area
Reservations Phone: 614/443-3680 or 614/444-8888
Phone Hours: 8am to 11pm daily (closed in January)
Price Range of Homes: $45 single, $55 double
Breakfast Included in Price: Continental (juice, roll or toast, coffee)
Brochure Available: Free

Reservations Should Be Made: Two weeks in advance (last-minute reservations accepted if possible)

Attractions Near the B&B Homes: German Village, restored residential area listed in the National Register
Major Schools, Universities Near the B&B Homes: Ohio State, Franklin, Denison, Otterbein, Kenyon, Capital

BUCKEYE BED & BREAKFAST
P.O. BOX 130, POWELL, OH 43065

Offers B&B Homes In: Akron, Athens, Belmont, Canton, Bethel, New Richmond, Tipp City, West Milton, Vandalia, Troy, Piqua, Poland, DeGraft, Peninsula, Port Clinton, Johnstown, Columbus, Cincinnati, Delaware, Cambridge, Spring Valley, Dublin, Muirfield, Westerville, Worthington, Marietta, Dayton, Logan, North Olmstead, and Seville, all in Ohio
Reservations Phone: 614/548-4555
Phone Hours: 24 hours daily
Price Range of Homes: $22 to $35 single, $30 to $65 double
Breakfast Included in Price: Some homes serve Continental; others, full American. Many hosts who are gardeners and "nutrition-oriented" serve organically grown specialties.
Brochure Available: Free
Reservations Should Be Made: 10 days in advance (last-minute reservations accepted if possible)

Attractions Near the B&B Homes: Kings Island, Cincinnati Opera/ Zoo, Ohio Historical Center, Muirfield Golf Course, Mound Builders' Sites, Little Brown Jug Harness Classic, Vandalia Trap Shoot, Marietta River Festival
Major Schools, Universities Near the B&B Homes: Ohio State, Ohio U., Ohio Wesleyan, Otterbien, Capital, Kenyon, Muckingum, Marietta, Wilmington, Wright State, U. of Cincinnati, Wittenberg, Concordia College, Antioch, U. of Dayton, Columbus Tech, Ohio Dominican

Best B&Bs _____

■ Manor house in Delaware, Ohio. Located just north of Columbus is a lovely old home known as Delaware Manor. Built in 1906, it offers a parlor crammed with books and games. Or you can play games outdoors under the maple trees. Mallets are available for croquet on the lawn. Breakfast is really special, with home-baked breads and muffins, Ohio honey, and maple syrup (with Ohio apple cider in season). *Insider's Tip:* Want to watch a great movie? *Out of Africa, The Wizard of Oz,* and *The Sound of Music,* among other classics, are available for guest showings on the VCR. **(Top 100.)**

■ Rural home in Spring Valley, Ohio. The hosts of this B&B have traveled in Germany, France, and India—and the decorations reflect their purchases along the way. It's located between Dayton and Cincinnati in the rolling countryside of the Miami Valley. Many crafts shops, antiques stores, and fine restaurants are nearby. *Insider's Tip:* Visit neighboring Waynesville; your hosts call it an "antique browser's paradise."

■ Something special near Cincinnati: Amos Shinkle Townhouse in Covington, Kentucky. You may have never heard of Mr. Shinkle but he headed the company that constructed the famous Roebling Suspension Bridge between Ohio and Kentucky. In 1850 he built a more modest structure, a town house near the river his new bridge spanned. Enter Bernie Moorman years later, who has completely restored this home into a handsomely decorated B&B. Mr. Moorman had been the mayor of Covington. Now most mornings you will find Bernie in the kitchen preparing eggs, pancakes, pastries, and fresh fruit. You can stay in one of three guestrooms in the main house, which has awesome chandeliers, oak floors, and a grand entrance hall. The carriage house right behind the main house is a restored stable right out of the 1800s. Children can stay in the horse stalls redesigned as sleeping accommodations. You're close to Cincinnati and many of the attractions of Kentucky. For reservations or more information, write: Amos Shinkle Townhouse, 215 Garrard St., Covington, KY 41011. Or call 606/431-2118.

WISCONSIN

—————— B&B Reservation Services ——————

BED & BREAKFAST GUEST HOMES
698 COUNTY U, ALGOMA, WI 54201

Offers B&B Homes In: Wisconsin, particularly Door County
Reservations Phone: 414/743-9742

Phone Hours: 7am to 9pm daily

Price Range of Homes: $45 to $60 single, $49 to $80 double

Breakfast Included in Price: "Practically all hosts serve a generous full breakfast."

Brochure Available: Free if you send a stamped, self-addressed no. 10 envelope

Reservations Should Be Made: Preferably one or more weeks in advance (last-minute reservations filled if possible)

Attractions Near the B&B Homes: State parks, fishing, villages, cherry orchards, farms, urban and rural settings

Best B&Bs

■ Large, newer home overlooking the water, close to all of the attractions of Door County, Wisconsin, located between Sturgeon Bay and Egg Harbor. The host, Mrs. Martens, describes her home as "modest, but we do our best to make our guests happy." That includes asking them what they would really enjoy for breakfast while they're on vacation. Then Mrs. Martens brings out many foods from Door County, including a wonderful plum and cherry jam, maple syrup, and a special baked egg dish that includes bread, ham, and cheese. Two rooms are available with queen-size beds. The hosts are a retired IBM engineer and a former nurse. Both very friendly people. *Insider's Tip:* This is great biking country because the roads are relatively flat. **(Top 100.)**

■ "Guest's Delight" Colonial home in Maplewood, Wisconsin, is located right next to the Annaphee State Trail, just south of Sturgeon Bay in Door County.

■ Country home in Jackson Port, Wisconsin, in Door County. This is a rural retreat in some 31 acres of woods just two miles from Whitefish Dunes State Park. In winter you can snowmobile over nearby trails which are also ideal for hiking in warmer weather.

■ Stone farmhouse in Mequon, Wisconsin. Only 20 miles north of Milwaukee and centuries away in flavor. Each of the three guestrooms is decorated in early American antiques and reproduction furniture.

■ Brick farmhouse in Manitowoc, Wisconsin. Great area for an outdoors vacation—fishing, skiing, horseback riding. You have a choice of four guestrooms. Your host is certainly an interesting person. He builds sailboats and once studied to be a concert pianist.

■ New home in Lake Delton, Wisconsin. This place was built especially as a B&B, and is close to all the water activities of Wisconsin Dells.

Each of the four guestrooms has a private bath. It is furnished not only with antiques but with an unusual collection of old gas station memorabilia.

WISCONSIN SOUTHERN LAKES BED & BREAKFAST RESERVATION SERVICE
P.O. BOX 322, FONTANA-ON-GENEVA LAKE, WI 53125

Offers B&B Homes In: Southeastern Wisconsin, primarily Walworth County
Reservations Phone: 414/275-2266
Phone Hours: 3 to 10pm daily
Price Range of Homes: $30 to $50 single, $40 to $60 double
Breakfast Included in Price: Full country-style breakfast of beverage, juice, fresh fruit, specialty, and meat. The specialty might be pineapple crêpes with sherry cream, creamed mushrooms on toast, buttermilk pancakes, or French toast; most hosts offer afternoon refreshments
Brochure Available: Free with stamped, self-addressed envelope
Reservations Should Be Made: Two to three weeks in advance; last-minute reservations accepted if guaranteed with a credit card

Attractions Near the B&B Homes: Cruises, Yerkes Observatory, Outdoor Ethnic Museum, Clown Hall of Fame, Electric Railroad Museum, Southern Kettle Morraine State Forest
Major Schools, Universities Near the B&B Homes: Northwestern Military & Naval Academy in Fontana, Wisconsin School for the Deaf, George Williams College, U. of Wisconsin at Whitewater

Best B&Bs
■ Emerald View House in the hills above Geneva Lake, Wisconsin. The home overlooks soft rolling hills and a golf course. The family suite is particularly spacious with a bedroom decorated with a country geese motif and a private bath. "Emerald Cream coffee is served at breakfast, along with fruit juice, seasonal fresh fruits, and specialties such as blueberry buttermilk pancakes with bacon, and ham and cheese blended into great scrambled eggs, and French toast with Canadian bacon."
Insider's Tip: Be sure to see the rose garden. It recently won top honors from the local garden club.

■ Small country home in Fontana, Wisconsin. This home is surrounded by gardens and sits right on a golf course. The hosts have visited many B&Bs in Europe, and guests benefit from their experience. Breakfast is definitely a gourmet affair. *Insider's Tip:* This is the B&B that serves pineapple crêpes—as described above.

B&B Inns

LOUE HOUSE
1111 S. MAIN ST., ALMA, WI 54610

Reservations Phone: 608/685-4923

Description: This Italianate house was designed by Charles Maybury in 1853 and is on the National Register of Historic Places. There are sinks in most rooms, and baths down the hall.

Amenities: Continental breakfast: "Help yourself—toast your own muffin."

Nearby Attractions: Beautiful swamp, canoeing, excellent fishing, tennis, and golf

Special Services: Fish-cleaning facilities, gas grill, and picnic table

Rates: $16 single, $30 double

Innkeeper's Tip: "We now have a coffee bar in the lobby where all guests can meet and get acquainted. Alma is located in some of the most scenic areas along the Mississippi River. A walking trail leads to a good scenic view."

The Northwest & Great Plains

IDAHO

B&B Inns

INDIAN CREEK GUEST RANCH
HC. 64 (P.O. BOX 105), NORTH FORK, ID 83466

Reservations Phone: 208/394-2126
Description: The rustic main lodge with three cabins is hidden in a mountain valley. A fishing stream runs through the front yard.
Amenities: Juice, eggs, hotcakes, sausage, hashbrowns, coffee or tea

Nearby Attractions: Ride on horseback to the old ghost town of Ulysses, the scenic Salmon River
Special Services: Pickups from the airport or from Salmon
Rates: $35 single, $70 double
Innkeeper's Tip: "Our ranch borders the Frank Church Wilderness area," says Jack Briggs. "There are many scenic drives to enjoy in this area. Float trips on the Salmon River can be arranged. We're located very close to the spot where Captain William Clark of the Lewis & Clark expedition was forced to turn back and try another route,"

SAWTOOTH HOTEL
P.O. BOX 52, STANLEY, ID 83278

Reservations Phone: 208/774-9947
Description: Each room is decorated with a lodgepole double bed and old-fashioned furnishings.
Amenities: Breakfast highlights include sourdough pancakes, cinnamon rolls, and country sausage.

Nearby Attractions: Sawtooth Recreation Area, Salmon River, Sawtooth National Fish Hatchery, rafting, field trips, horseback riding
Special Services: Will serve predawn breakfast and pack a lunch for day-trippers.
Rates: $20 to $25 single, $25 to $40 double

IOWA

———————— B&B Reservation Services ————————

BED & BREAKFAST IN IOWA LTD.
P.O. BOX 430, PRESTON, IA 52069

Offers B&B Homes In: Iowa
Reservations Phone: 319/689-4222
Phone Hours: Anytime in person or via an answering machine
Price Range of Homes: $30 to $50 single, $45 to $75 double
Breakfast Included in Price: Full, with Iowa breakfast specialties, or Continental
Brochure Available: Send $1 for a directory of homes
Reservations Should Be Made: Two weeks in advance; short notice also accepted by most homes when space is available

Attractions Near the B&B Homes: Iowa Great Lakes, historic homes, Iowa farms
Major Schools, Universities Near the B&B Homes: Drake, U. of Northern Iowa, Iowa State, U. of Iowa, Grand View

Best B&Bs —————————————————————————————

■ B&B in Amish community of Oelwein, Iowa. The reservation service says, "People coming to Iowa expect to be corn fed, and that's certainly what they are in this home. The host is a former baker, and she loves to cook." The home is a restored red brick Victorian built at the turn of the century. Two rooms are available to guests. The rates are a real bargain for a room and that "corn-fed" breakfast. **(Top 100.)**

■ Stagecoach inn B&B in Burlington, Iowa. Yes, the original building was once a stopping place for bounce-weary east—west travelers coming by stagecoach. Now the building has been completely restored and you have a choice of four guestrooms. Burlington is an interesting little town that boasts of the world's most crooked street.

■ Working farm in Ogden, Iowa. Here's your chance to introduce your children to farmlife. You may want to visit Boone, about 20 miles away, birthplace of Mamie Eisenhower.

B&B Inns

THE REDSTONE INN
504 BLUFF, DUBUQUE, IA 52001

Reservations Phone: 319/582-1894
Description: This restored Victorian mansion is in the heart of the city and has undergone extensive renovations in the last few years. It is furnished in antiques, and has a plaster crown molding with gold-leaf cherubs in the parlor. The four double suites have whirlpool baths.
Amenities: Continental breakfast; with suites only, full valet and room service

Nearby Attractions: River rides, Woodward Riverboat Museum, the Fenelon Rivers Hall of Fame, arboretum, cross-country and downhill skiing
Special Services: Turn-down service and morning coffee
Rates: $65 to $165, double occupancy

STOUT HOUSE
1105 LOCUST, DUBUQUE, IA 52001

Reservations Phone: 319/582-1894
Description: Purchased in 1985 from the archdiocese of Dubuque, the house was built in the Richardsonian Romanesque style by lumber baron F.D. Stout. It is a massive red sandstone home with a hexagonal tower and stone archways, now an elegant accommodation for guests.
Amenities: Continental breakfast

Nearby Attractions: Dubuque Greyhound Park, Fenelon Rivers Hall of Fame, Fenelon Place Elevator, skiing
Special Services: Complimentary beverages
Rates: $65 to $80 double
Innkeeper's Tip: "The movie, *Field of Dreams,* was filmed in nearby Dyersville. Take a ride on the Fenelon Place Elevator, shortest, steepest cable car in the country."

MINNESOTA

―――――――― B&B Reservation Services ――――――――

MINNESOTA OFFICE OF TOURISM
375 JACKSON STREET, ST. PAUL, MN 55101

Information Phone: 800/657-3700. In the twin cities of Minneapolis and St. Paul, call 296-5029.

Special Note: Even though B&B's are flourishing in Minnesota, reservation services don't seem to last long in the state according to the Minnesota Office of Tourism. This state tourism office is not a reservation service as such but it does function as a clearinghouse of information about available B&B's. Call or write them for the free booklet "Explore Minnesota—Bed and Breakfast and Historic Inns." You then make your own reservations directly with the individual B&B owners.

Best B&B's ――――――――――――――――――――――――
- (Author's selection based on information provided by the Minnesota Office of Tourism)

――――――――――――――― B&B Inns ―――――――――――――――

GUNFLINT LODGE
GT100, GRAND MARAIS, MN 55604

Reservations Phone: Toll free 800/328-3325; 800/328-3362 in Minnesota

Description: This rustic lodge and cottages are set in Minnesota's North Woods on a glacial lake surrounded by towering bluffs. Chalets available with fireplace and whirlpool tub.

Amenities: Full breakfast

Nearby Attractions: Gunflint Trail, Boundary Waters Canoe Wilderness Area
Rates: $69 to $159 double

MONTANA

────────── B&B Reservation Services ──────────

BED & BREAKFAST WESTERN ADVENTURE
P.O. BOX 20972, BILLINGS, MT 59104

Offers B&B Homes In: Montana and Wyoming
Reservations Phone: 406/259-7993
Phone Hours: Weekdays from noon to 5pm in winter, 9am to 5pm in summer; answering machine always on
Price Range of Homes: $35 to $115, single and double
Breakfast Included in Price: "Full breakfast in 90% of the homes"; Continental plus in others
Brochure Available: Free; directory available for $5
Reservations Should Be Made: Three weeks in advance

Attractions Near the B&B Homes: Most are located in the Rocky Mountain Range near Yellowstone and Glacier National parks. Many are on the blue-ribbon trout streams and rivers for which the two states are famous. They are also located on ranches and in historic districts.
Major Schools, Universities Near the B&B Homes: U. of Montana, Montana State U., Carroll College, Rocky Mountain College, Eastern Montana College

Best B&Bs ─────────────────────────────

■ An 1875 Victorian home in Helena, Montana. This B&B is known as Sanders. It offers seven spacious guestrooms that have been restored to reflect turn-of-the-century living in the state's capital. All have private baths and are furnished with canopied beds, tiger oak armoires, clawfoot tubs, and many other of the original furnishings. This home is located within three blocks of the original Governor's Mansion, St. Helena's Cathedral, and the historic Last Chance Gulch. Says Paula Diegert, head of the reservation service, "Whenever I travel to Helena,

I enjoy the company of these gracious and interesting hosts while entering a part of Montana's elegant history. It's an honor to recommend them as an exceptional bed-and-breakfast." **(Top 100.)**

■ A colonial home in Missoula, Montana, surrounded by 25 acres of woods and meadows. It provides a relaxing country atmosphere while being only a few minutes from Missoula, one of Montana's major cities, and home of the University of Montana. Three bedrooms, furnished with period pieces from all over the world, share a large bath. The Clark Fork River and rafting are available within two blocks. It is also 20 minutes from two ski areas. There is a library/lounge with fireplace and television for guests. The University of Montana and a variety of events are just ten minutes from this home. A full breakfast, with home-baked breads and jams, is served in the formal dining room or on the deck. Tea and coffee are available to guests at any time. The hosts enjoy hiking, skiing, rafting, and attending the concerts, plays, and athletic events at the University of Montana. They are excellent resources for the many attractions in the area. Children over 16 are welcome, but no smoking or pets please.

■ 1903 Queen Anne Victorian home in the middle of the quaint mining town of Red Lodge, Montana. The living room is appointed with bright flowered pillows, polished carved woodwork, overstuffed sofas, and interesting pictures depicting life at the turn of the century. Guests look out from a multitude of leaded glass window panes to mountain vistas. There are five bedrooms; the three on the second floor have private baths, and two rooms on the third floor share a shower bath. All bedrooms have flowered comforters, lace pillows, comfortable chairs, and an array of antiques. Guests are one block from the antiques shops, museums, and little restaurants of Red Lodge. Relax with afternoon lemonade or hot cider. Fish in famous Rock Creek just behind the inn or ski at Red Lodge Mountain. Both Alpine and Nordic skiing are superior in Red Lodge and ski storage is available. The highway leads to the scenic Beartooth Pass and the northeast entrance of Yellowstone Park, just 60 miles away. A Continental breakfast is served with home-baked pastries and breads, an accompaniment to fresh fruits, cheeses, and homemade jams. Fresh brewed coffee and tea are available any time. The host is a native of the Red Lodge area who loves meeting new people, gardening, and baking her prized Finnish recipes. Children over 10 are welcome, but no pets please. Smoking is allowed on the deck.

■ B&B lodge in Whitefish, Montana, constructed of locally harvested larch logs and located on 48 wooded acres adjoining a 27-hole golf course and winter Nordic ski trails. This B&B has a good view of Flathead Valley, the snow-capped peaks of Glacier National Park, and Big Mountain ski area. The eclectic interior is furnished with Native American and European antiques. There are two guest suites, each with private baths and direct access to the outdoor gazebo covered Jacuzzi located on the redwood deck. A large third suite is available for children. This home is located in the northwest town of Whitefish about 2 miles off U.S. 93 North. There are afternoon refreshments, outdoor Jacuzzi tub, indoor sauna, and TV and telephones in suites. Horse boarding is available. It is within 20 minutes of skiing, fishing, and golfing. A full gourmet breakfast is served in the formal dining room on fine china. Smoking is allowed on the outdoor deck and children are welcome.

■ B&B in West Yellowstone, Montana, tucked into national forest land. Deer and moose are often at the salt lick in the backyard at dusk. Birds, chipmunks, and squirrels are always skittering at the edge of ponds and feeders hanging from the numerous trees. Tie your own flies and view video tapes about fly-fishing in the area. Just 15 miles away is the famed Big Spring, the origin of the Henrys Fork Snake River trout spawning refuge. Drift boating on the Madison and Gallatin rivers and Hebgen Lake are all within 20 miles. There are three bedrooms, one on the first floor with private shower; two on the second floor share a full bath. West Yellowstone is located at the west entrance to Yellowstone National Park on U.S. 20 and within 30 minutes or less of the blue ribbon trout streams and lakes. The house is 10 miles from the entrance to the park. A hot tub is available. Fly-tying facilities and instructions are available. Fishing guide service with a licensed guide can be arranged. Craft gifts are available for purchase. All guests receive a memento from the hosts. A Continental-plus breakfast is served with home-baked breads, fresh fruit, and plenty of coffee. The host is an accomplished carpenter, fly-tyer expert, tole and decorative painter, antique collector, and wood refinisher. The other host is a self-employed gregarious fly fisherman. Both enjoy all kinds of outdoor activities. Smoking and pets are not allowed.

■ Home in Whitefish, Montana, circa 1920, offers comfortable sur-roundings amidst authenic period furnishings. The inviting living room offers guests a place to read, converse, and relax in front of a crackling fire. The inn is located in the center of Whitefish, tucked at the base of the Big Mountain Ski Resort in Flathead Valley and offers unlimited opportunities for recreation, relaxation, and hospitality Mon-tana style. Five bedrooms, each with private bath, are individually decorated with specially chosen linens, wallpapers, and distinctive an-tique furniture. Whitefish is located on U.S. 93 in northwest Montana less than 30 miles from Glacier National Park's west entrance, near beautiful Whitefish Lake. It is less than one hour from Flathead Lake. World class Nordic (cross-country) skiing is within one mile. Walk one block to downtown, famous for the Christmas Stroll the first weekend of December. Within walking distance from Amtrak. Full gourmet break-fasts are prepared each morning and served in the sunny dining room.

Guests are invited to linger over coffee with the hosts, who are an excellent resource for all activities in the area. Your host, Mike from the New England seacoast, owns a cross-country ski shop and is an expert skier, hiker, cyclist, and canoer. He is a collector of artwork and antiques and is interested in historic preservation through the Glacier Natural History Association. Rhonda is a partner in the ski shop, an avid skier, and involved in the Junior Ski Program. She is contributing editor to the *Whitefish Magazine*. Terri has a part-time catering business, is interested in the theatre, and is a gourmet chef. No smoking allowed in bedrooms or dining room. Weekly rates are available.

B&B Inns

IZAAK WALTON INN
P.O. BOX 653, ESSEX, MT 59916

Reservations Phone: 406/888-5700
Description: Built in 1939 by the Great Northern Railway, the inn is now listed on the National Register of Historic Places. The inn's walls are lined with railroad pictures and memorabilia, and some rooms have private bath

Nearby Attractions: Cross-country skiing, fishing, annual eagle migration, railfanning, Glacier National Park with the Bob Marshall and Great Bear Wilderness
Special Services: Sauna, laundry facilities
Rates: $55 to $74 single, $60 to $79 double (cabooses $350-3 nights, $600-7 nights).

WILLOWS INN
224 SOUTH PLATTE, RED LODGE, MT 59068

Reservations Phone: 406/446-3913
Description: This 1903 Queen Anne Victorian has five guestrooms and a two-bedroom family cottage that features Shaker country decor. Each room has a view of the surrounding Big Sky Country.
Amenities: Continental breakfast served around an authentic woodburning stove. Complimentary wine for honeymoons and anniversaries.

Nearby Attractions: Wildflower hikes, skiing, horseback riding, fishing, golf, whitewater rafting, scenic Beartooth Highway and Rock Creek, and Yellowstone Park.

Special Services: Guest refrigerator, turn-down service, afternoon refreshments.

Rates: $45 to $60 single or double

NORTH DAKOTA

B&B Reservation Services

OH WEST B&B
P.O. BOX 211, REGENT, ND 58650

Offers B&B Homes In: North Dakota
Reservations Phone: No phone listed
Price Range of Homes: $20 to $45 single, $25 to $50 double
Breakfast Included in Price: Full American breakfast, with specialties including Swedish and Ukrainian breads, and home-processed maple syrup
Brochure Available: Send a stamped, self-addressed envelope for a directory
Reservations Should Be Made: Two weeks in advance

Attractions Near the B&B Homes: State and national parks, Badlands, state capitol
Major Schools, Universities Near the B&B Homes: Minot State College, U. of North Dakota

Best B&Bs

■ **Volden Farm.** A 1926 farmhouse in rural Laverne, North Dakota, with a modern 1978 addition in the heart of fishing, hunting, and canoeing land. The host has filled this home with antiques and collectibles gathered during 27 years in the air force. The farm is located a mile from the Sheyenne River. You can have real privacy in two guestrooms. Scandinavian breakfast is served. Children are always welcome. **(Top 100.)**

■ Prairie view log home in New Salem, North Dakota. Finnish craftspeople hoisted these logs into place in 1980. The home has a front and back porch and something pretty unusual—a petrified wood fireplace. *Insider's Tip:* Don't miss nearby Fort Lincoln on the Lewis and Clark trail. This historic site also includes General Custer's newly restored home.

■ Great retreat for sports buffs in rural Regent, North Dakota. In summer months this B&B offers a heated swimming pool, volleyball and croquet. You can climb a nearby butte for a panoramic view. *Insider's Tip:* Ask the host about fishing. He can set up a special trip for you.

■ Swing your partner to this Lidgerwood, North Dakota, B&B. The host loves to square dance and can direct you to some local doings. You will be only a short distance from the Tewaukon National Wildlife Refuge and the Sisseton Yellowstone state parks. Children are welcome and you can even bring your pets.

OREGON

—————— B&B Reservation Services ——————

GALLUCCI HOSTS HOSTEL, BED & BREAKFAST
P.O. BOX 1303, LAKE OSWEGO, OR 97035

Offers B&B Homes In: Oregon
Reservations Phone: 503/636-6933
Phone Hours: 10am to 6pm daily
Price Range of Homes: $12 to $35 single, $15 to $50 double
Breakfast Included in Price: Continental (juice, roll or toast, coffee)
Brochure Available: For a $1 fee, plus a stamped, self-addressed no. 10 envelope
Reservations Should Be Made: Three days in advance (last-minute reservations accepted if possible)

Attractions Near the B&B Homes: Mount St. Helens, Fort Vancouver, state parks, zoos, historic homes

B&B Inns

THE AUBURN STREET COTTAGE
549 AUBURN ST., ASHLAND, OR 97520

Reservations Phone: 503/482-3004
Description: The inn is newly built in 1900s style, with separate
    cottages in a quiet garden setting. Each cottage contains a kitchen-
    ette (with microwave oven), skylights, and large windows, and sleeps
    four.

Nearby Attractions: Shakespeare Festival Theater, Britt Garden Music
    Festival, mountain lakes, many rafting rivers, Crater Lake Park,
    Oregon Caves
Rates: $76 double in summer, $66 double in winter

FOX HOUSE INN
269 B ST., ASHLAND, OR 97520

Reservations Phone: 503/488-1055
Description: This is a historic, award-winning Victorian home, furnished
    with antiques, velvet draperies, and stained glass. Guests enjoy
    canopied beds, private baths, and phones.
Amenities: Gourmet breakfast, afternoon refreshments.

Nearby Attractions: Oregon Shakespeare Theatre; festivals; Emigrant
    Lake; Crater Lake with skiing, rafting, fishing, hiking, and white-
    water activities
Special Services: Turn down service, TVs, stereos
Rates: $85 to $125 double
Innkeeper's Tip: "Guests can enjoy the Winter Wine and Food and
    Arts Festival in early February and a Garden Festival in the Spring."

OREGON CAVES CHATEAU
20,000 CAVES HWY., CAVE JUNCTION, OR 97523

Reservations Phone: 503/592-3400
Description: This six-story structure (no elevator) was built in 1934 in
    rustic style. The rooms are comfortable, and the lobby is framed with
    fir timber, with two large marble fireplaces. There's also a camp-
    ground.

Nearby Attractions: Redwood National Park, Crater Lake National
  Park, Illinois and Rogue rivers
Special Services: Cave tours, hiking trails
Rates: $53 to $56 double

PARADISE RANCH INN
7000 MONUMENT DR., GRANTS PASS, OR 97526

Reservations Phone: 503/479-4333
Description: Set in the Rogue River Valley, the inn has comfortably
  furnished rooms and an indoor recreation center.

Nearby Attractions: Crater Lake, Oregon Caves, Ashland Shakespeare
  Theater, Peter Britt Music Festival, salmon and steelhead fishing,
  rafting on the Rogue River
Special Services: Heated pool and spa, lighted tennis courts, triangu-
  lar golf, hot tub, recreational facility, mountain bikes, jogging trails,
  fishing
Rates: $73 to $125 single, $83 to $125 double, in summer; $53 to
  $80 single, $58 to $80 double, in winter
Innkeeper's Tip: "Why not try a country picnic on an island." Just ask.

THE BIRCH LEAF LODGE
RTE. 1, BOX 91, HALFWAY, OR 97834

Reservations Phone: 503/742-2990 or 503/223-4685
Description: A lodge located on a 42-acre farm surrounded by national forest, the Eagle Cap Wilderness and Hells Canyon National
  Recreation Area. There is a choice of five guestrooms, each with a
  library and wide views of the surrounding valley, and the home has a
  two-story wrap-around deck.
Amenities: Full breakfast includes farm eggs and fresh seasonal fruit
  from the orchard, with homemade breads.

Nearby Attractions: Trout stream, hiking and skiing trails, excellent
  birding
Rates: $45 single, $60 double

WASHINGTON

──────── B&B Reservation Services ────────

TRAVELLER'S BED & BREAKFAST
P.O. BOX 492, MERCER ISLAND, WA 98040

Offers B&B Homes In: Washington State, northern Oregon, and Vancouver and Victoria, British Columbia
Reservations Phone: 206/232-2345
Phone Hours: 8:30am to 4:30pm Monday through Friday
Price Range of Homes: From $35 single, $45 to $145 double
Breakfast Included in Price: Varies; some may include regional and gourmet specialties
Brochure Available: Free; $6 for a descriptive directory with maps and photos
Reservations Should Be Made: As early as possible (last-minute reservations dealt with on an availability-only basis)

Attractions Near the B&B Homes: Mount Rainier National Park, Olympic National Park (includes Rain Forest), Mount St. Helens tours, San Juan Island, Snoqualmie Falls, North Cascades loop, Columbia River Gorge, Grand Coulee Dam, Lake Chelan, 1986 Expo site, Grouse Mountain, Provincial Museum, and Butchart Gardens in Victoria
Major Schools, Universities Near the B&B Homes: U. of Washington, Seattle College, Seattle Pacific College, U. of British Columbia

Best B&Bs ────────────────────────────

■ Yes, Clark Gable stayed here. And so did many other 1930s and 1940s movie stars—at this waterfront mansion on the Hood Canal, Washington. This great house was built in the 1930s, with each of the guestrooms angled so that each had a view of the canal and the Olympic Mountains. Located an hour's ferry ride from downtown Seattle, all rooms have king-size beds and private bathrooms. A full breakfast is served in the dining room, also with its own view. Guests can use the library and the lounge. This is a great place for an anniversary or a honeymoon. (Top 100.)

■ 1910 home in Kirkland, Washington. The building has been converted to a B&B inn with eight rooms reserved for guests. All rooms have queen-size beds and private bathrooms. The rooms are furnished with antiques, selected and imported from Europe by the host.

■ English Tudor home in Port Angeles, Washington. This home is furnished throughout with English antiques. Port Angeles is convenient to the ferry to Victoria, British Columbia, and for exploring the northern part of the Washington coast.

■ Victorian farmhouse on Orcas Island, Washington. This beautiful part of the San Juan Islands sports a lovely old B&B with seven rooms. You'll find 19th century touches such as claw-foot tubs and pedestal sinks, and down comforters.

■ Tudor mansion in West Seattle, Washington. This home was designed by an architect in 1907, especially for its historical site. The B&B has now been carefully restored. *Insider's Tip:* Ask for the room with the fireplace and deck.

■ An 1890 Victorian home in Seattle, Washington. This is a true Victorian: stained-glass windows, original woodwork, fine refinished furniture. One writer/guest published this account in a national magazine: "The skylight view from the shower will make your spirits soar."

PACIFIC BED & BREAKFAST
701 N.W. 60TH ST., SEATTLE, WA 98107

Offers B&B Homes In: Greater Metropolitan Seattle area and throughout the state of Washington, including Mount Rainier and the San Juan Islands; also British Columbia, Canada
Reservations Phone: 206/784-0539
Phone Hours: 9am to 5pm Monday through Friday
Price Range of Homes: $35 to $60 single, $40 to $145 double
Breakfast Included in Price: "Gourmet" Continental or full American (homemade breads, muffins, and croissants a specialty)
Brochure Available: Free if you send a stamped, self-addressed no. 10 envelope (or $5 for the listing directory)
Reservations Should Be Made: Three weeks in advance (last-minute reservations accepted if possible)

Attractions Near the B&B Homes: City and national parks, museums, theaters, opera house, ferry rides
Major Schools, Universities Near the B&B Homes: U. of Washington and more than eight other universities and colleges (inquire about a specific school when you call for reservations)

Best B&Bs

■ A 1928 brick Colonial home high in the hills above Seattle, Washington. The view is splendid, with much of Seattle stretching out before you as you stay in the home surrounded by formal English gardens. Antiques from all over Europe fill this home. You can stay in any of three bedrooms, all with double beds. You might prefer the room with a private deck (with immediate access day and night to that great view). You can walk to two bus lines or even to the Seattle Center. During the week the host provides help-yourself breakfast fixings; on weekends, a home-cooked breakfast is served in the formal dining room. One recent guest wrote to the reservation service organization, "We are indebted to you for this guesthome. The location was perfect, the view terrific, the home and gardens lovely and the host is both a fine cook and a warm and gracious host." What more can you ask for? (Top 100.)

■ B&B on Queen Anne Hill in Seattle, Washington. You are right on top of downtown Seattle when you stay in this contemporary home. You will stay in a private suite. Step outside on the deck for a view of Puget Sound and the Olympic Mountains. Make yourself right at home. You will have a European-style kitchen with some staple foods. A private entrance, TV, and phone complete the amenities. Good quarters particularly for a business traveler.

■ An 1890 Victorian home with stained-glass windows and fine period furniture in Seattle, Washington. There are many nice touches here— including lace bedspreads, a skylight view from the shower, and "legendary" breakfasts with some of the host's recipes featured in national magazines.

■ The Mansion guesthome in Seattle, Washington, on Capitol Hill. You will stay on a street known as "Millionaire's Row" and you will feel like one in this huge (14,000 square feet) home with a ballroom, a billiard room, and an oak-paneled entry hall. The second-floor guestrooms have antiques and original tile baths with pedestal sinks and showers. Feeling musical? You can do what musical millionaires once did—play one of the five available grand pianos. Afterward take a stroll in the gardens.

■ Dutch Colonial home in Seattle, Washington. Built in 1914, this home offers everything from French door elegance to oversized showers and a private deck overlooking Lake Washington and the Cascade Mountains. It is only two miles to downtown.

■ A recently renovated house near downtown Seattle, Washington, and the University of Washington. You can check into a private suite upstairs with a living room and a view of the city skyline. You can use the TV and VCR or spread your business work on the desk. A second large room features a kitchenette with microwave oven, refrigerator (where you will find the breakfast fixings), and a comfortable sitting area with a private phone and a queen-size bed under a skylight.

B&B Inns

THE COUNTRY KEEPER BED AND BREAKFAST INN
61 MAIN ST., CATHLAMET, WA 98612

Reservations Phone: 206/795-3030
Description: This historic 1907 home is located on a hill overlooking the Columbia River and Puget Island. It has extensive ornate woodwork and polished inlaid floors and is furnished with original furniture.
Amenities: The candlelight breakfast includes Australian specialties.

Nearby Attractions: National whitetail deer game refuge, salmon and sturgeon fishing, tennis, pool, museums, Mt. St. Helens Volcano Visitor Center.
Special Services: Library of local history and art books, bikes, river tours.
Rates: $45 to $65 double
Innkeeper's Tip: "Cathlamet is an 1846 fishing village. You can take the last ferry on the Columbia to Puget Island for a picnic on the beach, stop for refreshments at the Rat-Tap, a 100 year old tavern on the waterfront, and then visit the marina and see the old fishing boats. Your visit should include a shopping excursion to Mylett's Store for quality clothing and free advice on any subject."

THE INN AT PENN COVE
702 NORTH MAIN, COUPEVILLE, WA 98239

Reservations Phone: 206/678-8000
Description: Two historic 1880s houses have been restored and furnished with period antiques. Baths have been renovated with spa tubs. Beds are fitted with down comforters and pillows. Most rooms have a view of Puget Sound and snow covered Mt. Baker.
Amenities: Gourmet breakfast

Nearby Attractions: 54 registered historic landmarks, sailing, boating, fishing, biking, hiking, bird-watching, arts & crafts festivals.
Rates: $75 to $125 double

HAUS ROHRBACH PENSION
12882 RANGER RD., LEAVENWORTH, WA 98826

Reservations Phone: 509/548-7024
Description: In the foothills of the Washington Cascades, the inn has ten comfortable rooms (six with private bath) and a separate chalet with kitchen and accommodations for six.
Amenities: In fine weather, breakfast and desserts are served on the deck.

Nearby Attractions: The Bavarian village of Leavenworth, skiing, tobogganing, sleigh rides
Special Services: Heated pool, hot tub
Rates: $50 to $70 single, $60 to $80 double; $98 for the chalet (no breakfast)

PALACE HOTEL
1004 WATER ST., PORT TOWNSEND, WA 98368

Reservations Phone: 206/385-0773 or toll free 800/962-0741 in Washington
Description: In this three-story restored Victorian building overlooking the harbor in historic downtown Port Townsend are 15 units, 12 with private bath, several with kitchens. Children are welcome. The hotel is listed on the National Historic Register.
Amenities: Continental breakfast

Nearby Attractions: Fort Worden State Park, biking, fishing, beachcombing, boating
Special Services: Coffee and tea in each room
Rates: $40 to $79 double in spring and summer, $36 to $72 double in fall and winter

STARRETT HOUSE INN

744 CLAY, PORT TOWNSEND, WA 98368

Reservations Phone: 206/385-3205

Description: This 1889 Victorian mansion has frescoed ceilings and a free-hung three-tiered spiral staircase, which leads to an unusual eight-sided dome. A dozen rooms with elaborate carved mouldings are furnished with period antiques. Each room features a view of the Olympic Mountains or Puget Sound.

Amenities: Gourmet breakfast.

Nearby Attractions: Fort Worden State Park, Olympic National Park's Hurricane Ridge and Rain Forest, historic tours, festivals, concerts

Rates: $70 to $125 double

Innkeeper's Tip: The inn is located in a national historic district with an 1800s Victorian shopping district.

The Southeastern States

ALABAMA

B&B Reservation Services

BED & BREAKFAST MONTGOMERY
P.O. BOX 886, MILLBROOK, AL 36054

Offers B&B Homes In: Montgomery
Reservations Phone: 205/285-5421
Phone Hours: 7am to 9pm daily
Price Range of Homes: $32 to $65 single, $40 to $75 double
Breakfast Included in Price: Continental (juice, roll or toast, coffee); hosts serve full breakfasts if guests desire, and at least two will serve dinner (for a fee) if requested
Brochure Available: Free
Reservations Should Be Made: One to two weeks in advance (last-minute reservations accepted if possible)

Attractions Near the B&B Homes: Montgomery, the capital and a pre—Civil War city on the Alabama River; many beautiful antebellum homes in nearby Lowndesboro; home of nationally famous Alabama Shakespeare Theater, first White House of the Confederacy
Major Schools, Universities Near the B&B Homes: Auburn, U. of Montgomery, Huntingdon College, Alabama State, Faulkner U.

Best B&Bs

■ "Red Bluff Cottage" in Montgomery, Alabama. This is a newly built home in one of the city's oldest historical districts, conveniently located to I-65, I-85, and downtown. Choice of four guestrooms with private baths. *Insider's Tip:* You can get a great view of the Alabama River from the deep upstairs porch. (Top 100).

■ Restored farmhouse near Montgomery, Alabama. The specialty of the house is a great breakfast. After breakfast you can take a walk by the red barn and take some pictures of the pastoral scenes. Don't miss a shot of that antebellum church nearby!

■ A country contemporary near Montgomery, Alabama. Located on 60 acres, East Fork Farm offers four guestrooms and private entrances opening to a covered pool and terrace.

—————————— **B&B Inns** ——————————

THE MENTONE INN
P.O. BOX 284, MENTONE, AL 35984

Reservations Phone: 205/634-4836 (Closed during the winter)
Description: This rustic inn on top of Lookout Mountain offers 12
   guestrooms. Rooms are furnished simply but comfortably. One of the
   popular activities is watching the sunset from the big front porch
   (there's a beautiful view of the valleys).
Amenities: Full breakfasts are served. The fare is varied and can
   include eggs, country ham, waffles (if there aren't too many guests),
   pancakes, and French toast.

Nearby Attractions: An old log church, St. Joseph's on the Mountain,
   DeSoto State Park and Falls, many antiques shops
Rates: On request

FLORIDA

—————— **B&B Reservation Services** ——————

BED & BREAKFAST OF THE FLORIDA KEYS, INC.
5 MAN-O-WAR DR., MARATHON, FL 33050

Offers B&B Homes In: The Florida Keys and along the east coast of
   Florida
Reservations Phone: 305/743-4118
Phone Hours: 8am to 5pm Monday through Friday, on Saturday and
   Sunday to noon
Price Range of Homes: $40 to $50 single, $45 to $110 double
Breakfast Included in Price: Continental (juice, roll or toast, coffee)
   or full American; banana bread is one of the specials served
Brochure Available: Free
Reservations Should Be Made: Two weeks in advance (last-minute
   reservations accepted if possible)

Attractions Near the B&B Homes: John Pennekamp State Park, Bahia
   Honda State Park, Theater of the Sea, Seven Mile Bridge

Major Schools, Universities Near the B&B Homes: Florida Atlantic U.

Best B&Bs

▪ Contemporary home in Jupiter, Florida. "One of the best homes in town," says the reservation service. It is located only a block from the ocean and two blocks from the Burt Reynolds Theater, and 20 miles from Florida's most prestigious (and pricey) shopping streets: Worth Avenue in Palm Beach. The host, born in Scotland, serves a Continental breakfast. The B&B guestroom has a private entrance, and you are welcome to use the pool. Golf and tennis are nearby. **(Top 100.)**

▪ A B&B in the Florida Keys right on the ocean with a private bath, color TV, air conditioning, and Bahama fans.

▪ An oceanview home in the Florida Keys with a king-size bed in the guestroom, which has a private bath.

▪ A contemporary home in the Florida Keys on a canal with an ocean view. Breakfast is served on the deck overlooking the ocean (weather permitting).

BED & BREAKFAST CO. TROPICAL FLORIDA

P.O. BOX 262, SOUTH MIAMI, FL 33243

Offers B&B Homes In: Florida (also the Caribbean and London)
Reservations Phone: 305/661-3270
Phone Hours: 9am to 5pm Monday through Friday, plus an answering machine to 10pm and on weekends
Price Range of Homes: $30 to $90; some guesthouses higher
Breakfast Included in Price: Continental to full American
Brochure Available: Free with stamped, self-addressed envelope
Reservations Should Be Made: Two weeks in advance (last-minute reservations accommodated when possible)

Attractions Near the B&B Homes: State parks of Florida, Everglades National Park, John Pennekamp Coral Reef State Park, Cape Canaveral, St. Augustine historic area, Orlando, state forests, Florida Keys, Sanibel/Captiva islands
Major Schools, Universities Near the B&B Homes: U. of Miami, Florida State U., U. of Southern Florida, Nova U.

Best B&Bs

■ Ultra luxury "cottage" in Miami, Florida, within walking distance of Coconut Grove village. The hosts reside in the main house on the property. The grounds are landscaped with specimen tropical plantings, splashy colored bromeliads, and ferns, around a natural pool with a fountain. Oriental styling is subtly reflected in the gardens, with art metalwork of Garland Falkner prominently featured. The cottage is equipped with a complete kitchen including microwave, dishwasher, and compactor. There is also cable TV with special programming, VCR, double bed, and sofa in the living room, which could be used for an additional guest. (Top 100.)

■ Large contemporary ranch home in Ormond Beach, Florida. Go for a dip in the pool, just a few steps from your bedroom. The home is a ten-minute drive to the world famous Daytona Beach and the fishing dock, the Daytona 500 track, jaialai, and only one hour to the Disney-Orlando attractions. Bikes are available for local browsing. A microwave, HBO, and small refrigerator are included in the bedroom with queen-size bed and private bath. Second bedroom available with shared bath.

■ Colonial mansion in the village of Tavarres, Florida, known as an antique shopper's paradise just 45 minutes west of Orlando. The leaded-glass windows, hand-carved newel posts, winding staircase, carved mouldings, and inlaid mahogany floors are reminiscent of a grand Southern era. There are huge bedrooms upstairs, a sun room that can also be used for extra guests, and beautiful antique furnishings. A pool is located between the house and the lake.

■ B&B in Ft. Myers, Florida, just a short distance from the causeway to Sanibel/Captiva, the world famous shelling beach and resort community. The sliding glass doors of the large guestroom overlook a small lake. A smaller guestroom shares a bath with the host, a native of Iceland. The location is also convenient to Ft. Myers Beach, Cape Coral, and Bonita Springs.

■ One-bedroom apartment on Ramrod Key in the Gulf of Mexico. This two-story building has a living/dining room, kitchen, and bath downstairs, and a bedroom upstairs with two single beds. The sofa in the living room could sleep a child or small adult. Swim, fish, snorkel. Only a five-minute drive to Loo Key, the best diving in the Keys. The host's Victorian home is on three lots, with a large pool and hot tub for guests' use. The host offers discount rates to take guests out fishing or to the reefs for diving. The property adjoins the Key Deer Refuge and is abundant with wildlife and birds.

■ Mansion on a residential island in Biscayne Bay, Florida. From this home you're within a five-minute drive of Atlantic Ocean beaches and some excellent restaurants and shops. The home is decorated with mementos of the host family's world travels. The family is originally from Denmark. They are very interested in the arts and enjoy talking about plays, music, and ballet. When you break bread with this host, she may also talk about another family passion, sailing.

OPEN HOUSE BED & BREAKFAST REGISTRY
P.O. BOX 3025, PALM BEACH, FL 33480

Offers B&B Homes In: Palm Beach County
Reservations Phone: 407/842-5190
Phone Hours: Evenings and weekends
Price Range of Homes: $45 to $85, single and double
Breakfast Included in Price: Continental to full American
Brochure Available: Free
Reservations Should Be Made: As soon as possible

Attractions Near the B&B Homes: Lion Country Safari, Palm Beach Polo and Country Club, Worth Avenue in Palm Beach (renowned shopper's paradise)
Major Schools, Universities Near the B&B Homes: Florida Atlantic U., Palm Beach Jr. College

Best B&Bs

■ Contemporary ocean villa in Jupiter, Florida. If you love water, you're right between two comfortable choices—a dip in the ocean or in a private heated swimming pool. This B&B offers just one guestroom but it has its own walled garden. Breakfast is served poolside. Bring your racquet and clubs; tennis is available on the premises and golf nearby.

■ Early century restored home in West Palm Beach, Florida. Located in the old Northwood historic district, this B&B offers twin accommodations with private baths and swimming pool. You're only ten minutes from the beach.

■ Lakeside home in Lake Worth, Florida, on 2½ acres. You can fish in the lake and swim in a private pool.

■ Canalside home in Boca Raton, Florida, one mile from the beach. Boats glide right by on this navigable canal. Your bedroom opens on to a screened patio and pool. You can walk to some of the fine restaurants and shopping of Boca Raton.

■ B&B in Lantana, Florida, west of I-95, right across from a pretty lagoon. Only 10 minutes from the Lantana Municipal Beach. There are a screened patio and pool.

B&B SUNCOAST ACCOMMODATIONS
8690 GULF BLVD., BEACH ISLAND, FL 33706

Offers B&B Homes In: Florida, specializing in the Gulf Coast (Pinellas County)
Reservations Phone: 813/360-1753
Phone Hours: 9am to 10pm daily
Price Range of Homes: $30 to $50 single, $45 to $90 double
Breakfast Included in Price: Continental (juice, roll or toast, fruit, coffee); "But a few hosts are gourmet cooks and enjoy whipping up a full, delicious breakfast"; many breakfasts are "Help yourself."
Brochure Available: Free for Florida ($3 for listings throughout the U.S. and foreign countries); send a stamped, self-addressed envelope
Reservations Should Be Made: Two weeks to one month in advance (last-minute reservations accepted in the St. Petersburg area)

Attractions Near the B&B Homes: Walt Disney World, Sea World, Sunken Gardens, Dali Museum
Major Schools, Universities Near the B&B Homes: St. Petersburg Jr. College, Eckard College, U. of Florida, Tampa College, Stetson Law School, Bay Pines VA Hospital

Best B&Bs
■ Waterfront B&B near Tampa, Florida. The room has an outside entrance, queen-size bed, private shower/bath, phone, TV, refrigerator, microwave, a dock, and heated 'spa'. Walk to Gulf of Mexico beach. The host provides fishing poles, beach towels, chairs, mats, laundry privileges, and kitchen. The rate includes Continental breakfast, or 'help yourselves,' or full breakfast. The hosts are nonsmokers, there are no pets in residence, moderate drinking allowed, and smoking is permitted on the patio. This home is 40 minutes west of the Tampa airport. **(Top 100.)**

■ B&B in ocean-front home in northeast Florida. VCR available and you can also listen to old-time radio tapes. The apartment is stocked with food for a do-it-yourself breakfast.

■ Cottage on the bay in Tampa, Florida, with a self-contained kitchen. The house is stocked with breakfast items and is only minutes to downtown Tampa, and 40 minutes to the Gulf beaches.

■ Restored two-story home in Cortez, Florida, minutes to Bradenton Beach along the historical walk to Fisherman's Bay. The home has a queen-size room, featherbeds, and private bath. There is a lovely patio with pool. A bargain.

■ Lovely room in restored older home in Havana, Florida, 12 miles north of Tallahassee. The village is full of antiques shops. Another bargain.

B&B Inns

THE PINK CAMELIA INN & GALLERY
145 AVENUE E, APALACHICOLA, FL 32320

Reservations Phone: 904/653-2107
Description: This B&B inn is located in a restored, turn-of-the-century home. It offers four guestrooms with private baths. All rooms are furnished with antiques and artwork (both hosts are professional artists).
Amenities: Full three-course gourmet breakfast served on china and crystal. Complimentary dessert in the evening, served with wine.

Nearby Attractions: Four blocks from Apalachicola Bay.
Special Services: Bicycles provided
Rates: $60 to $70 single, $65 to $75 double

HARRINGTON HOUSE BED & BREAKFAST
5626 GULF DR., HOLMES BEACH, FL 34217

Reservations Phone: 813/778-5444
Description: Old style Florida home right on the beach. Choice of seven attractive guestrooms with private bath. Living room has an 18-foot-high ceiling and a working fireplace.

Nearby Attractions: Ringling Mansion and Museum, Selby Gardens, Bishops Planetarium
Special Services: Hosts provide restaurant menus and maps for the local area

Rates: $79 to $95 double May through November, $95 to $115 double December through April
Insider's Tip: Request one of the rooms that has a gulf view.

CABBAGE KEY, INC.
P.O. BOX 200, PINELAND, FL 33945

Reservations Phone: 813/283-2278
Description: On a unique hideaway island, the main house was constructed in 1930 by novelist Mary Roberts Rinehart. There are rooms with private baths, a suite for four, and three cottages.

Nearby Attractions: Intracoastal Waterway, the islands of Sanibel and Captiva, Fort Myers, fishing, sailing, water sports
Rates: $65 to $145 double

SEMINOLE COUNTRY INN
15885 WARFIELD BLVD. (P.O. BOX 625), INDIANTOWN, FL 33456

Reservations Phone: 407/597-3777
Description: The historic inn was built by the uncle of the Duchess of Windsor, and the lobby has an open fireplace, twin white staircases, pecky cypress ceilings, and brass chandeliers molded with the crest of royalty.

Nearby Attractions: Indiantown with its $1-million marina; the largest citrus grove in Florida, four miles away; Lake Okeechobee, less than ten miles from the inn
Special Services: Grass airfield, tennis courts, racquetball courts, 18-hole golf course, swimming pool, restaurant
Rates: $45 single, $50 to $65 double

GEORGIA

_____ B&B Reservation Services _____

ATLANTA HOSPITALITY—A B&B RESERVATION SERVICE
2472 LAUDERDALE DR. NE, ATLANTA, GA 30345

Offers B&B Homes In: Atlanta (Georgia), Massachusetts, Barbados (West Indies)
Reservations Phone: 404/493-1930
Phone Hours: 9am to 10pm daily
Price Range of Homes: $20 to $30 single, $35 to $55 double
Breakfast Included in Price: Mostly Continental, but may include grits and country ham, pecan rolls, red-eye gravy
Brochure Available: Free
Reservations Should Be Made: Two weeks in advance (last-minute reservations accepted if possible)

Attractions Near the B&B Homes: Martin Luther King Memorial Site, High Museum, Stone Mountain Park, largest shopping mall in the Southeast
Major Schools, Universities Near the B&B Homes: Emory, Atlanta U., Mercer

Best B&Bs

■ Home in northeast Atlanta, Georgia. This B&B is about 35 minutes by car from downtown Atlanta. You reach the house via a long winding driveway flanked by beautiful landscaping. A collie may greet you on arrival. The guestroom has a private bath and a private entrance. **(Top 100.)**

■ Home near downtown Atlanta, Georgia. Each guestroom has a private bath. You'll like talking with your host, a charming woman who is a professor of sociology at a local college and has traveled extensively.

BED & BREAKFAST ATLANTA
1801 PIEDMONT AVE. NE, ATLANTA, GA 30324

Offers B&B Homes In: Metropolitan Atlanta, Stone Mountain, Marietta, Decatur, Roswell, McDonough, Norcross, Smyrna, and other areas of Metro Atlanta
Reservations Phone: 404/875-0525
Phone Hours: 9am to noon and 2 to 5pm Monday through Friday
Price Range of Homes: $32 to $80 double; $48 to $100 double for guesthouses, suites, condominiums, and B&B inns; monthly rates starting at $750
Breakfast Included in Price: Continental or full American; southern breakfasts sometimes served at the discretion of the individual hosts
Brochure Available: Free if you send a stamped, self-addressed no. 10 envelope
Reservations Should Be Made: Two weeks or more in advance (last-minute reservations accepted on a space-available basis)

Attractions Near the B&B Homes: Underground Atlanta, Stone Mountain, Cyclorama, Civil War monuments, World Congress Center, the High Museum of Art, Six Flags, Atlanta Historical Society
Major Schools, Universities Near the B&B Homes: Emory, Georgia Institute of Technology, Atlanta U., Oglethorpe, Georgia State, Agnes Scott

Best B&Bs

■ 1920s Tudor home in Atlanta, Georgia, off Peachtree Road. Surrounded by towering trees and beautifully kept grounds, the home and area invite enjoyment of Atlanta's beauty. Downtown is about five miles away; Midtown about two miles. Three bedrooms are offered, each with full private bath, cable TV with VCR, and a closet containing a small refrigerator and microwave. The Brass King Room (king-size bed) view is of the rear of the home and its well-tended garden and a small putting green; the Queen Poster Room (queen-size bed) looks out on the sloping front yard and one of the city's loveliest streets. Julie's Suite features a charming bedroom with double bed and lovely sitting room (another TV and VCR) across the hall. Additional amenities are an exercise room with both steam and sauna; and an in-house office with access to Fax, computer, and copier. Furnishings throughout the home reflect the discriminating taste of its hosts, a dentist and a realtor. Interesting and beautiful art, antiques, and porcelains abound. Continental-plus breakfast is served in a formal dining room; residence pets are two dogs and three cats who spend part of their time indoors. **(Top 100.)**

■ B&B housed in a 1930s bungalow in one of Atlanta, Georgia's most desirable intown neighborhoods. Public transportation is excellent—Morningside is a favored area for walking and jogging with its lovely older homes, parks, restaurants, and shops nearby. A well-tended patio garden provides entry to the interesting eclectic, art-filled interior. The guestroom affords comfort and privacy with a queen-size poster bed, adjoining full bath, and view of the rear garden. The native Atlanta host is a talented and successful artist (painter and papermaker). "A resident dog and cat join the host in non-smoking preference."

■ Springvale B&B is a small Victorian home in Atlanta, Georgia's first planned community, Inman Park. The neighborhood was developed in the 1880s, making it one of the nation's first "garden suburbs." Designed and built by longtime residents of this historic neighborhood, Springvale is a combination of old and new. This B&B offers three beautiful guestrooms, each with private bath. The Walnut Room derives its name from the antique furniture used—double bed with carved headboard, dresser, loveseat, and chair. A full bath adjoins this room. Sandy's Room offers guests antique twin beds, dresser, telephone, and cable TV. Both rooms are located on the second floor. The Oak Room, located on the third floor offers optimum privacy—with the name derived from the use of oak furniture. There is a double bed, built-in desk, dresser, rocking chair, telephone, and cable/remote control TV. This room has its own heating-cooling controls. Spacious bath, shower only, adjoins this room. Hosts are retired educators who enjoy travel, gardening, and interaction with B&B guests.

■ Guest cottage north of downtown Atlanta, Georgia, between Peachtree and Piedmont roads. Early 1900s neighborhood is on the Historic Register. This is a highly desirable and interesting intown neighborhood, with special appeal for the walking and jogging set. Some nearby points of interest are the Woodruff Arts Center, High Museum, botanical gardens, Colony Square, Piedmont Park, and many appealing restaurants and shops. Public transit is excellent, with access to downtown meetings only minutes by car as well. A bright, cheery, spacious unit has been lovingly redone by expert B&B hosts. A bedroom alcove has double bed and desk. The living/dining space offers a couch (double sleep-sofa) and chair, and a breakfast table and chairs overlooking a private outdoor area. Newly done full bath is another plus as is the galley kitchen (microwave, toaster oven, sink, small refrigerator, etc.). Cable TV and phone are available. Ample provisions are furnished for self-catered breakfast. There are no pets; smoking is allowed. Host couple resides in Dutch colonial home in "front yard" of this private unit. They are active retirees.

■ Air-conditioned traditional two-story house with swimming pool is located on 12 beautifully wooded acres in northeast Atlanta, Georgia. Two guestrooms, each with double bed, share one bath. One room is done in yellow, with handmade quilts and an antique doll collection. The other provides a view of the pool, woods, and flowers. A Continental plus breakfast is served in the charming down-stairs dining room. One of your hosts, a retired engineer, builds beauti-ful reproduction furniture; an impressive silver chest in the front entry is evidence of his skill. The other host's skills include a specialty in baking.

■ Northwest Atlanta, Georgia, home a few feet from the banks of the Chattahoochee River. Good location for antiquing, shopping, sightsee-ing, or reaching downtown meetings by car. Two spacious bedrooms, each with twin poster beds and traditional decor, share one full bath. Sliding glass doors open from each room onto a large screened porch with pool and river vista. The hosts designed and built this home when their now-grown family was young. Continental-plus breakfasts are served.

R.S.V.P. GEORGIA & SAVANNAH BED & BREAKFAST RESERVATION SERVICE
417 E. CHARLTON ST., SAVANNAH, GA 31401

Offers B&B Homes In: Throughout Georgia, South Carolina, and northern Florida
Reservations Phone: 912/232-7787 or toll free 800/729-7787
Phone Hours: 9:30am to 5:30pm weekdays; answering service week-ends
Price Range of Homes: $50 to $175 per room
Breakfast Included in Price: Provided in many different ways: sit-down, tray service in room, guests self-serve in their own kitchens
Brochure Available: Free
Reservations Should Be Made: As far in advance as possible. Mini-mum one-night's deposit required with all reservations. Personal checks and traveler's checks preferred; some credit cards accepted.

Attractions Near the B&B Homes: National historic districts and monuments, Atlantic Ocean and coastline, barrier islands along the Intra-Coastal Waterway, north Georgia mountains and state parks

Best B&Bs

- Brick town house in Savannah, Georgia. Built in 1854, this elegant home has antique furnishings. Did you ever hear harp music at breakfast? You may well at this B&B. The host is a famous concert harpist, and she enjoys playing for guests.

- Town house in the Central Savannah Historic District. You can have a complete suite of rooms in this 1872 home. A family could occupy two bedrooms, a living room with working fireplace, and a full country kitchen. Breakfast is in the refrigerator and you fix your own. If the house looks familiar, you may have seen it featured in various national magazines.

- Early 1800s stagecoach stop, now a colorful B&B in the foothills of north Georgia. The home is filled with antiques and several excellent antiques stores are nearby for shopping. You can ride horseback on the mountain trails, and fish in the streams.

QUAIL COUNTRY BED & BREAKFAST, LTD.
1104 OLD MONTICELLO RD., THOMASVILLE, GA 31792

Offers B&B Homes In: Thomasville, Georgia (city and country)
Reservations Phone: 912/226-7218 or 912/226-6882
Phone Hours: 8am to 10pm daily
Price Range of Homes: $30 to $40 single, $40 to $50 double
Breakfast Included in Price: Continental (juice, roll or toast, coffee)
Brochure Available: Free if you send a stamped, self-addressed no.
  10 envelope
Reservations Should Be Made: One week in advance (last-minute reservations accepted if possible)

Best B&Bs

- Beautiful Victorian mansion in Thomasville, Georgia. If you have seen *Gone with the Wind* recently, this place may well remind you of the famous Tara in the movie. The house has white columns, too. The host is a retired school teacher and you can expect to find some homemade grits (her specialty) on your breakfast plate. The guestroom has a separate entrance. (Top 100.)

- Neoclassical home in Thomasville, Georgia. Located in pecan groves, this house has large columns on three sides. Each bedroom has its own bath and fireplace. The floors throughout are heart of pine and the rooms are furnished with antiques.

■ Williamsburg-style guesthouse in Thomasville, Georgia. Take a trip back to the 18th century as you walk through this B&B's garden and dependencies (early buildings constructed to provide services to the main house). Guests are welcome to use the swimming pool.

B&B Inns

THE PITTMAN HOUSE
105 HOME ST., COMMERCE, GA 30529

Reservations Phone: 404/355-3823 (A Reader Recommendation) "I do not see how it can be improved upon," says Mary Hall of Decatur, GA.

NOTE TO READERS: When you find a really spectacular B&B, share the information with other readers in the next edition of this book. Use the forms at the back of this book.

THE FORSYTH PARK INN
102 WEST HALL ST., SAVANNAH, GA 31401

Reservations Phone: 912/233-6800

Description: Queen Anne Victorian mansion with ten guest groups, including a cottage in a landscaped, walled courtyard. This home was built in 1893 with 16-foot ceilings, carved doors, and an impressive staircase.

Amenities: Complimentary wine, port, and sherry are served in the formal parlor during the evening social hour.

Nearby Attractions: 18 miles from Savannah Beach on the Atlantic Ocean. Several historic forts in the area. The Inn is located in the largest historic district in the country and overlooks 23 acres of a beautifully landscaped park.

Rates: $60 to $85 single, $85 to $145 double

Innkeeper's Tip: "Savannah Riverfront has many fine casual seafood restaurants, pubs, and shops. There are riverboat cruises and numerous street festivals."

SUSINA PLANTATION INN
RTE. 3 (BOX 1010), THOMASVILLE, GA 31792

Reservations Phone: 912/377-9644
Description: This antebellum mansion built in the Greek Revival style
was the plantation house for a cotton farmer who employed 100
slaves. This gracious inn still has 115 acres of lawns and woodlands
as an attractive setting. There are eight bedroom suites for guests.
Amenities: Full breakfast and dinner with wine included

Nearby Attractions: Pebble Hill Historic Plantation House, annual arts
and crafts fair, Rose Test Gardens
Special Services: Swimming pool, tennis court, stocked fish pond,
jogging trails, conference rooms, screened veranda
Rates: $100 single, $150 double. Includes five-course dinner with wine
and breakfast.

KENTUCKY

B&B Reservation Services

OHIO VALLEY BED & BREAKFAST
6876 TAYLOR MILL RD., INDEPENDENCE, KY 41051

Offers B&B Homes In: Southern Ohio, southeastern Indiana, and
northern Kentucky
Reservations Phone: 606/356-7865
Phone Hours: 9am to 6pm Monday through Friday; answering machine
at other times
Price Range of Homes: $30 to $60 single, $35 to $98 double
Breakfast Included in Price: Continental (juice, roll or toast, coffee),
full American (juice, eggs, bacon, toast, coffee), and homemade
breads, biscuits, yogurt
Brochure Available: Free if you send a stamped, self-addressed envelope
Reservations Should Be Made: Two weeks in advance (last-minute
reservations accepted if possible)

Attractions Near the B&B Homes: Major-league sports, zoo, Kings Island Park, College Football Hall of Fame, symphony, opera, ballet, repertory theater, state parks, recreational lakes

Major Schools, Universities Near the B&B Homes: U. of Cincinnati, Northern Kentucky, Xavier, Mount St. Joseph, Thomas More

Best B&Bs

■ Mt. Auburn, Ohio, town house with great views of downtown Cincinnati. You stay high on a hill in a country setting; yet you are only a short walk or taxi ride to the center of downtown. The guestrooms and baths have been restored in this historic home furnished with Victorian antiques. Within a mile of the University of Cincinnati. If you don't have a car, the host can arrange for airport pickup. (Top 100.)

■ Sprawling California-style home in Cincinnati, Ohio. The available B&B suite features a queen-size bed, TV, radio, telephone, private bath, and patio. A bargain rate of $45.

■ The Claire House, a 100-year-old brick row house in Covington, Kentucky. Two suites are available. Country kitchen, antique bath, fireplace, and original art on the walls. Close to downtown Cincinnati and the Mainstrasse German Village. Your host is a teacher and writer. Your hostess a teacher of ballroom dancing.

■ An 1880s home in Bellevue, Kentucky. Located in the historical Taylor Daughter's District, this home is listed with the National Trust for Historic Preservation. It is appointed throughout with fine Victorian antiques.

■ Restored farmhouse in New Richmond, Ohio. Natural surroundings: pond, wildlife, sheep. Private suite available. It includes a private bath and sitting room with TV and a fireplace. Breakfast is big—seven courses—and served on the outside patio or in the cozy kitchen. The host will make reservations for nearby restaurants and attractions.

BLUEGRASS BED & BREAKFAST
RTE. 1, BOX 263, VERSAILLES, KY 40383

Offers B&B Homes In: Central Kentucky (Lexington)
Reservations Phone: 606/873-3208
Phone Hours: 8am to 8pm daily
Price Range of Homes: $45 to $100 double
Breakfast Included in Price: Full American (juice, eggs, bacon, toast, coffee)

Brochure Available: Free
Reservations Should Be Made: Two weeks in advance (last-minute reservations discouraged)

Attractions Near the B&B Homes: Kentucky Horse Park, Mary Todd Lincoln House, Mammoth Cave, Lake Cumberland, Henry Clay's home, Shakertown
Major Schools, Universities Near the B&B Homes: U. of Kentucky, Transylvania U.

Best B&Bs

■ Scottwood—a 1795 Federal house in Midway, Kentucky—eight miles from Lexington. In the early seafaring days of the New Country, Blue Canton china was often used as ship's ballast. Today each piece has become a prized collector's item. But you will be served breakfast on Blue Canton in this B&B. The owners, as you might suspect, are antique buffs. Their love of antiques is evident throughout this house in hand-some New England and early Kentucky furniture. The home offers a choice of three guest bedrooms in the main house and a separate cottage with a sleeping loft right next door. The reservation service reports they picked this as their "best" because of the decor of the home and because "the hosts are so nice to be with. They have a gift for making people feel welcome." **(Top 100.)**

■ Welcome Hall—a 1792 home in central Kentucky. Want a taste of farm life? This stone house presides over a handsome country estate devoted now to raising blooded horses and general farming. One room is available with twin beds and private bath. A historic, restored two-room slave cabin is also available with a four-poster bed.

■ 18-acre minifarm in Kenton County, Kentucky. Want to fish and swim in a lake, or walk through an animal reserve? This is a good country retreat for just such activities. Yet you are only 20 minutes from downtown Cincinnati. Your host enjoys talking about theater, travel, and boating. Great bargain!

■ Springdale—a beautiful country home above a stone springhouse in central Kentucky. This house was actually started almost 200 years ago and has been expanded into an airy brick home shaded by tall old trees. One bedroom is available with double bed and private bath, with an additional bedroom for family or friends. Crib available.

■ An 1829 home (Peacham) near Lexington, Kentucky. Count 'em, nine fireplaces in this charming old home. The brick that built this B&B was fired right on the farm. The private first-floor suite includes a living room, bedroom, and private bath. The second-floor room has twin beds and a private bath.

■ Artist's studio near Lexington, Kentucky. Polly Place has been described as a "dream studio—beautiful, comfortable, yet with touches of whimsy." The first level is one great room oriented around a huge fireplace. Above are open balconied bedrooms and bath with Jacuzzi. The studio itself was built on a shaded knoll on a 200-acre farm. Four people can sleep here comfortably, "six in a pinch." The whole place can be taken over by couples traveling together or a family.

B&B INNS

JAILER'S INN

111 W. STEPHEN FOSTER AVE., BARDSTOWN, KY 40004

Reservations Phone: 503/348-5551

Description: This two-story limestone building was once the Nelson County jail, constructed in 1819. In recent years it has been converted into a one-of-a-kind B&B. The new owners have completely renovated the jailer's residence, decorating it with antiques and oriental rugs. Another bedroom was once the women's cell. Now it offers much more luxurious accommodations with a private bath and three bunk beds.

Amenities: Continental breakfast included (presumably not bread and water)

Nearby Attractions: My Old Kentucky Home State Park (a house in this area inspired Stephen Foster to write his famous song), Lincoln Homestead Park, Old Bardstown Village and Civil War Museum.

Rates: $50 to $65 single or double.

MISSISSIPPI

———————— B&B Reservation Services ————————

LINCOLN LTD. BED & BREAKFAST; MISSISSIPPI RESERVATION SERVICE

P.O. BOX 3479, MERIDIAN, MS 39303

Offers B&B Homes In: The whole state of Mississippi, from Holly Springs in the north to Pass Christian in the south; also in Tennessee and Alabama

Reservations Phone: 601/482-5483 for information, or toll free 800/633-MISS for reservations

Phone Hours: 9am to 5pm Monday through Friday (answering service on weekends)

Price Range of Homes: $45 to $150 single, $55 to $165 double

Breakfast Included in Price: Full American (juice, eggs, bacon, toast, coffee), served simply or elegantly according to guest's preference

Brochure Available: Free; host list available for $3.50

Reservations Should Be Made: One or two weeks in advance (no last-minute reservations accepted)

Attractions Near the B&B Homes: National Civil War Park and historic homes in Vicksburg, Natchez, Jackson State Capitol, Columbus Pilgrimage, Holly Springs Pilgrimage, William Faulkner home in Oxford, Jimmie Rodgers Festival, Meridian, Natchez Trace Parkway

Major Schools, Universities Near the B&B Homes: U. of Mississippi at Oxford, Mississippi State, Millsaps, Mississippi College, Mississippi U. for Women, Belhaven

Best B&Bs

■ Beautiful B&B home in Meridian, Mississippi, set among flowering shrubs and dogwood trees. The host has been active in preservation, civic, and cultural activities and will direct you to the historic sites in the region. The home is furnished with family antiques. During the warmer months, enjoy a full Mississippi breakfast on the brick patio in the midst of huge oak trees. (Top 100.)

■ Guest cottage overlooking a Southern courtyard in Como, Mississippi (between Memphis and Jackson). A full breakfast is served when you walk next door to the main house. This is a good location if you plan on attending "Ole Miss" football games at nearby Oxford.

■ Victorian-style home in Meridian, Mississippi. This home is decorated with antiques from around the world. Both hosts are noted gourmet cooks and will include guests for dinner as well as breakfast by prior arrangement. For breakfast, you can expect Southern cheese grits, ham, eggs, homemade muffins, omelets, Mississippi Maucadine Jellies, and much more. You will have plenty of acreage to jog over. There's plenty to do in this area: tour antebellum homes, fish and boat on the lakes, or attend the Jimmie Rodgers Festival every May, the Lively Arts Festival in April, the symphony and Little Theater, and visit the art museum.

■ A Victorian-Greek Revival home in Vicksburg, Mississippi. This area, filled with so much Civil War history, is a pleasant place to visit. The hosts are history buffs and can direct you to some of the most interesting sites. The B&B is filled with the host's personal collection of antiques.

■ Home in Natchez, Mississippi, that is listed on the National Register of Historic Homes. It was built in 1858, high on a bluff overlooking the Mississippi River. It is beautifully furnished in period antiques.

TENNESSEE

—————— B&B Reservation Services ——————

BED & BREAKFAST IN MEMPHIS
P.O. BOX 41621, MEMPHIS, TN 38174

Offers B&B Homes In: Memphis, Nashville, Knoxville, New Orleans, and other areas of the South
Reservations Phone: 901/726-5920
Phone Hours: 9am to 6pm Monday through Friday, 2 to 5pm on Sunday
Price Range of Homes: $45 to $95 and up single or double; weekly and monthly rates available
Breakfast Included in Price: Continental, though a few hosts serve a

full American breakfast; specialties include blueberry muffins, home-made jams, and grits

Brochure Available: Free if you send a stamped, self-addressed no. 10 envelope

Reservations Should Be Made: Two weeks in advance, three weeks or more from April through November (last-minute reservations can sometimes be accepted)

Attractions Near the B&B Homes: Mud Island, famous Beale Street, Victorian Village, Pink Palace Museum of Natural History, Memphis Convention Center, Dixon Gallery and Gardens, Graceland

Major Schools, Universities Near the B&B Homes: Rhodes College, U. of Tennessee Medical School, Memphis State, U. of Mississippi

Best B&Bs

■ One-bedroom B&B in Memphis, Tennessee. This B&B is unhosted. You will have plenty of things to do. The reservation service waxes poetic: "Wake up to the mighty Mississippi. Savor spectacular sunsets from your balcony on the river." The apartment is furnished with elegant country English items. You have a choice of pools indoor and out, and tennis and racquetball courts. You can walk to great restaurants and jazz on highrise. A large efficiency apartment has a dining room/living room with a fully equipped kitchen and full bath. There are parquet floors, high ceiling, and windows in every room. You can retreat to the park next door which is filled with lush trees.

■ Two carriage houses in the Chickasaw Gardens area of Tennessee (your choice). Both have bedrooms with twin beds, galley kitchens, and private baths.

BED AND BREAKFAST HOSPITALITY—TENNESSEE

P.O. BOX 110227, NASHVILLE, TN 37222

Offers B&B Homes In: Throughout Tennessee, including Memphis, Nashville, Knoxville, and Chattanooga

Reservations Phone: 615/331-5244

Phone Hours: 9am to 5pm Monday through Friday (answering machine available other times)

Price Range of Homes: $28 to $75 single, $38 to $120 double

Breakfast Included in Price: Continental plus

Brochure Available: $2

Reservations Should Be Made: Two weeks in advance (for written confirmation); immediately by telephone

Attractions Near the B&B Homes: All the state parks, lakes, and
hunting areas in the state, Opryland
Major Schools, Universities Near the B&B Homes: Vanderbilt, Austin
Peay, Memphis State

Best B&Bs

■ Restored church in West Nashville, Tennessee. A suite is available with
an antique double bed with sitting area and private bath. Another
guestroom offers a Louis XIV double bed with private bath. A contemporary loft can sleep four, and has the added plus of a Jacuzzi.

The Southwest & South Central States

―――――――― **B&B Reservation Services** ――――――――

BED AND BREAKFAST RESERVATION SERVICES AND TOURIST ACCOMMODATIONS
11 SINGLETON, EUREKA SPRINGS, AR 72632

Offers B&B Homes In: Eureka Springs and northwestern Arkansas
Reservations Phone: 501/253-9111
Phone Hours: 24 hours daily
Price Range of Homes: $45 to $125 single or double
Breakfast Included in Price: Continental to full American
Brochure Available: In progress
Reservations Should Be Made: As early as possible (last-minute reservations accepted if possible)

Attractions Near the B&B Homes: The Passion Play, Thorncrown Chapel, Miles Musical Museum, Silver Dollar City
Major Schools, Universities Near the B&B Homes: U. of Arkansas

Best B&Bs ――――――――――――――――――――――――

- Restored Victorian in Eureka Springs, Arkansas. This is described as "an old-fashioned place with a touch of magic." It's located in the historic district, and decorated with a whimsical collection of items. The guestrooms have ceiling fans and handmade quilts on antique brass-and-iron bedsteads. Breakfast is served on the balcony overlooking a garden. *Insider's Tip:* Take a closer look at this garden. It has wildflowers, curious birdhouses, and a lily-filled fish pond.

ARKANSAS & OZARKS BED & BREAKFAST
HC61, BOX 72, CALICO ROCK, AR 72519

Offers B&B Homes In: Batesville, Calico Rock, Des Arc, Eureka Springs, Fayetteville, Fort Smith, Mountain View, Norfork, Rogers, and Yellville (all in Arkansas)
Reservations Phone: 501/297-8211 days, 501/297-8764 evenings

Phone Hours: 9am to 5pm and evenings Monday through Saturday

Price Range of Homes: $28 to $50 single, $30 to $69 double

Breakfast Included in Price: Continental to full American, many serving lavish spreads

Brochure Available: Free if you send a stamped, self-addressed envelope

Reservations Should Be Made: As much in advance as possible; $35 deposit

Attractions Near the B&B Homes: Blanchard Caverns, Ozark National Forest, White River, Ozark Folk Center

Major Schools, Universities Near the B&B Homes: Arkansas College, U. of Arkansas

Best B&Bs

■ Contemporary home in Calico Rock, Arkansas—near some of the best trout fishing in the world. Retreat to a secluded woodland without forsaking some of the civilized comforts. This B&B lets you share a large family room and a games room with satellite TV and a pool table. Later you can relax your muscles in a hot tub in the sun room. Talk with the artist/host about her lovely stained-glass creations and her collectibles from all over the world. Nearby you can sample the folk music and crafts of the Ozarks—or try your hand at trout fishing on the White River (where some close-to-world-record-size trout have been hauled in). All at a super-bargain price. **(Top 100.)**

■ Two-story Colonial mountain home. This B&B in the Ozarks is listed in the National Historic Register and furnished with antiques and wicker. In the morning you can dig your fork into fluffy Belgian waffles—the house specialty—on a glass-enclosed porch. Then drive to nearby Norfolk and Bull Shoals lakes. You are also near a variety of Ozark art and crafts shops as well as music shows, golf, fishing, and swimming.

■ Elegant Victorian home in the Ozarks. Beautifully restored. You have a choice of six rooms and a "honeymoon" suite.

■ Log cabins in Calico Rock, Arkansas. You may feel a little like a pioneer gone soft with modern comforts. Each cabin has a sleeping loft which sleeps two, plus a downstairs area with a hide-a-bed or double bed, kitchen, bath (showers only), and a fireplace or wood stove. You have to fix your own breakfast, but all the fixings—cereal, homemade fruit bread, milk, coffee—are in the cabin. *Insider's Tip:* Save some time just to sit on the front porch. You will have either a panoramic view of the river or of the woods.

■ Colonial Revival home in Des Arc, Arkansas. This unusual home, recorded on the National Register of Historical Places, is halfway between Memphis and Little Rock. Nearby are wildlife management areas and lakes. *Insider's Tip:* Like to talk about science? The host is a retired petroleum engineer; the hostess, a retired science teacher. Even the breakfast is scientific, healthful, and (on request) made to accommodate special dietary needs.

■ Country home in Calico Rock, Arkansas. High on a 200-foot bluff overlooking the spectacular White River. The three-manual organ in the living room is available to musical guests. The host is a retired marine officer who can arrange trout fishing and river float trips.

B&B Inns

THE GREAT SOUTHERN HOTEL
127 W. CEDAR, BRINKLEY, AR 72021

Reservations Phone: 501/734-4955
Description: The three-story brick hotel has 61 rooms with baths, mosaic-tile floors, and pressed-tin patterned ceilings 15 feet tall. Restored in a turn-of-the-century style, the bedrooms have antique double beds and furnishings. The ground-floor rooms have ceiling fans, air conditioning, and cable TV.
Amenities: Full breakfast, exercise room/sauna, award-winning restaurant

Nearby Attractions: Louisiana Purchase Marker State Park, Mississippi Fly Way
Special Services: Airport pickup
Rates: $41 to $47 double

COLORADO

B&B Reservation Services

BED & BREAKFAST COLORADO, LTD.
P.O. BOX 12206 BOULDER, CO 80303

Offers B&B Homes In: Throughout Colorado
Reservations Phone: 303/494-4994
Phone Hours: 8:30am to 5pm Monday through Friday (closed Saturday, Sunday, and major holidays)
Price Range of Homes: $30 to $75 single, $40 to $125 double
Breakfast Included in Price: Continental or full American (juice, eggs, bacon, toast, coffee); breakfasts vary with each home: some may offer Continental during the week with full breakfast on weekends; special diets accommodated
Brochure Available: Statewide directory, $5
Reservations Should Be Made: Two weeks in advance (last-minute reservations accepted if possible, but no placements after sundown); $5 add-on for one-night stays

Best B&Bs

■ The "miner's cabin" just outside of Boulder, Colorado. There you are up at dawn, washing in icy water, preparing to descend into a gold mine in search of streaks of yellow that will make you rich. Well, that's what the first occupants of this 19th-century cabin once did in the bustling Gold Hill Mining District. But today the building has been completely modernized, saving the early charm but adding modern amenities that miners never knew—such as electric heat and color TV. You will have full use of the cabin which includes a full kitchen, living/dining room, and bedroom. Can accommodate up to four people. (Top 100.)

■ Starry Pines Bed and Breakfast in Snowmass Valley, Colorado. Wake up to wonderful views of Mt. Sopris and the Elk Mountain range. Then, time for a Continental breakfast on the deck overlooking a rushing mountain stream. End of the day—sink into a hot tub and watch the sun set. This is the life. Two ground level guestrooms.

■ Marion Place in Central Denver, Colorado. A turn-of-the-century home with fine maple woodwork and period antiques. In summer you will enjoy the private patio. In winter, the three working fireplaces will warm your spirits.

BED & BREAKFAST ROCKY MOUNTAINS
P.O. BOX 804, COLORADO SPRINGS, CO 80901

Offers B&B Homes In: Colorado, New Mexico, Utah
Reservations Phone: 719/630-3433
Phone Hours: 9:30am to 5pm (Mountain Standard Time), Monday through Friday
Price Range of Homes: $30 to $68 single, $35 to $125 double
Breakfast Included in Price: Over half the hosts serve a full breakfast from Western to gourmet, often including homemade delicacies.
Brochure Available: Free; descriptive directory updated quarterly listing 100-plus approved B&B homes and inns costs $4.50; an annual subscription is $10, including the directory, update, and newsletter
Reservations Should Be Made: In advance if possible; MasterCard and VISA accepted or personal check

Attractions Near the B&B Homes: National forests, 30 state parks, skiing, hiking, gold panning, white-water rafting, ballooning, snowmobiling, horseback riding, Jeep tours, sleigh rides, hay rides, fishing, 53 mountain peaks over 24,000 feet high, ghost towns, and mining towns
Major Schools, Universities Near the B&B Homes: Colorado State U., Colorado College, Colorado School of Mines, U. of Colorado, U. of Denver, Colorado Mountain College, U.S. Air Force Academy; and all universities in northern New Mexico and Utah

Best B&Bs
■ Hand-hewn log Onahu Lodge in Grand Lake, Colorado. Have you ever wanted to escape to a remote, beautiful place to write your novel, or paint pictures? You may have found it here overlooking Rocky Mount National Park and the "Never Summer" Mountains. Instead of watching TV, you will watch elk at the salt lick. You can rent a horse nearby, take a hike, go boating, play golf—and come home to a double bedded guestroom or one with twin beds. Your host is interested in Native American art and culture. This B&B is a great bargain. (**Top 100.**)

■ **Prize-winning Victorian home in Denver, Colorado.** This restored 1879 home has won nine awards for excellence and has been recommended in over 100 publications. All rooms have private baths and phones, stereo chamber music, fresh flowers, and private garden views. For icing on this romantic cake, you can also arrange for carriage rides. Your host is active in historic preservation. He is a lecturer on law, travel, and marketing. You are only five blocks from the capitol and mall, but in the quiet residential historic district.

■ **St. Mary's Glacier Bed and Breakfast in Idaho Springs, Colorado,** with a triple-header view—the Continental Divide, a waterfall, and a lake! At night come home to a roaring fire in a wood-burning stove in the living room and a private hot tub. Activities including hiking the glacier—or enjoying the view in a more sedate fashion on the deck.

■ **The Log Cabin in Elk River Valley, Colorado.** A brand new cabin made of logs and river rock. About 15 miles from the Steamboat ski area. The cabin has just about everything you could ask for—including a wood stove, library, microwave, and tiny refrigerator. Your hosts love the outdoors and square dancing.

■ **Snowberry Hill in Dillon, Colorado**—only 10 minutes from the Keystone ski slopes. You will enjoy a complete suite with a private entrance, and a full kitchen.

■ **Country estate in Durango, Colorado.** Swedish immigrants started this home in the early 1900s. Modifications have turned it into a European country-styled estate. The main house has four guestrooms with antiques and fresh flowers. Every room has a view of the mountains and a grazing herd of sheep. *Insider's Tip:* For real privacy, you can rent a separate cabin with three rooms, all furnished in Southwestern style.

■ **Intimate B&B in Santa Fe, New Mexico.** You will know you're in the Southwest as you walk through this home's collection of handpainted furniture, and Native American rugs and art. Two guestrooms in the main house offer you a double brass bed in one and a queen-size four-poster in the other. Both rooms share a 30-foot living room for guest use only—with color cable TV, fireplace, travel information, and reading material. A detached guesthouse is also available. Only three blocks from downtown Santa Fe Plaza.

■ **Adobe B&B in Taos, New Mexico.** This home is a blend of European tradition and Southwestern architecture. It is built around a center flower-filled courtyard. Built by the Spanish over 200 years ago, it has been carefully restored. Your choice of six guestrooms. Fresh European pastries are served during the summer in the afternoon.

BED & BREAKFAST VAIL VALLEY
P.O. 491, VAIL, CO 81658

Offers B&B Homes In: Vail/Beaver Creek, Aspen, Steamboat, Summit County, Breckenridge and Keystone, and Copper Mountain ski areas
Reservations Phone: 303/949-1212
Phone Hours: 9am to 5pm Monday through Friday; answering machine other times
Price Range of Homes: On request
Breakfast Included in Price: Continental or full American, specialties available at most homes
Brochure Available: $2
Reservations Should Be Made: As far in advance as possible, especially for winter holidays (last-minute reservations honored subject to availability)

Attractions Near the B&B Homes: Vail and Beaver Creek ski areas with annual average snowfall of 300 to 350 inches, ten square miles of skiing terrain

Best B&Bs

■ Private home in East Vail, Colorado. The hosts live upstairs in this mountain hideaway known as Cotton Falls. You can join them in the morning for such house specialties as eggs Benedict. You are located on a free bus route that takes you to ski areas. You will enjoy such nice touches as a rock fireplace and a private entrance.

■ Private home in Frisco, Colorado. The amenities include a delightful summer breakfast served by a backyard creek. It should be quite a treat—the host is a local baker. On cold winter days after a day on the ski slopes, you can come home to an inside hot tub in the atrium. The home is on a bike path. A free shuttle bus will take you to the nearby ski areas.

B&B Inns

FIRESIDE INN
114 FRENCH ST. (P.O. BOX 2252), BRECKENRIDGE, CO 80424

Reservations Phone: 303/453-6456
Description: The accommodations at this Victorian inn range from

dormitory space to private rooms and even a private suite. All are tastefully decorated and comfortable

Nearby Attractions: Ski area, hiking, biking, boating
Special Services: Hot tub, free shuttle to town and ski areas
Rates: $18 in a dorm, $56 double, in fall and winter; $10 in a dorm, $35 double, in spring and summer
Innkeeper's Tip: The inn is located two blocks off Main Street in the historic district of a restored Victorian era mining town. The town is surrounded by mountains up to 14,000 feet high. The Breckenridge ski area is only a half mile from the inn.

THE HOME RANCH
P.O. BOX 822FB, CLARK, CO 80428

Reservations Phone: 303/879-1780
Description: This small guest ranch is located in the mountains of northwestern Colorado. The seven cabins range from a studio to a two-bedroom/two-bath with a living room. They are furnished with antiques and original wall hangings, with down comforters on the beds. Outside on the porch stands your own private spa.
Amenities: The full breakfast is served family style in the lodge dining room. Three meals a day are included in the rates.

Nearby Attractions: Mount Zirkel Wilderness Area, Steamboat and Pearl Lakes state parks, Continental Divide, horseback riding (the specialty here, and lots of it), fishing, bathing, boating, hiking
Special Services: Airport pickup; heated pool; hot tub and sauna; coffee maker; and refrigerator stocked with cheeses, crackers, and homemade cookies
Rates: $225 single, $400 double

THE ASPEN LODGE
LONGS PEAK ROUTE, ESTES PARK, CO 80517

Reservations Phone: 303/586-8133, or toll free 800/332-MTNS
Description: This handcrafted log lodge has 36 rooms, individual cabins, and a separate dining facility with three meals a day included in the rate.
Amenities: Breakfast featuring homemade sweet rolls and huevos rancheros

Nearby Attractions: Rocky Mountain National Park, Estes Park, Hidden Valley ski area
Special Services: Racquetball, horseback riding, tennis, skiing, fishing, snowmobiling, heated pool, sleigh and hay rides
Rates: $100 per person per day in summer, $60 to $90 per double room in winter

QUEEN ANNE INN
2147 TREMONT PLACE, DENVER, CO 80205

Reservations Phone: 303/296-6666
Description: Award-winning inn right in downtown Denver. Ten rooms individually designed with period lighting and heirloom antiques and fresh flowers. The owners describe the ambience they were trying to create—"that of visiting the elegant home of a well-to-do beloved aunt."
Amenities: Complimentary beverages, snack bowls, and Continental-plus breakfast; Offstreet parking

Nearby Attractions: All of Denver and the nearby mountains
Special Services: Bikes available
Rates: 1991–92 rates still being determined. Available on request.
Author's Tip: This B&B inn has garnered an amazing amount of rave reviews from the press. For something "really different," request the Aspen Room. The entire room is a painted mural (walls and ceiling) of a Colorado Aspen grove. You have the sense of camping out—with air conditioning.

SAN SOPHIA
P.O. BOX 1825, TELLURIDE, CO 81435

Reservations Phone: 800/537-4781
Description: The two-year-old Victorian-styled inn is situated ½ block from the Oak Street ski lift. The observatory and dining deck afford incredible views of the surrounding 13,000 foot mountains. All rooms have luxurious oversized tubs and brass beds.
Amenities: Complimentary full breakfast and apres ski. Concierge service, gazebo with sunken Jacuzzi, cable TV and VCRs, library/lounge with fireplace, garden, ski lockers and boot dryers, and underground parking.

Nearby Attractions: Downhill and cross-country skiing, trout fishing, biking, hiking, and photography. The San Miguel River is directly in back of the inn.

Rates: $70 to $105 double, summer, $125 to $175 double, winter

Insider's Tip: Located one block from the Historic Telluride Downtown District. Excellent gourmet restaurants, shopping, museum and the first bank from which Butch Cassidy made an early withdrawal. Spectacular views of Bridal Veil and Ingram falls—highest waterfalls in Colorado.

KANSAS

B&B Reservation Services

BED & BREAKFAST KANSAS CITY
P.O. BOX 14781, LENEXA, KS 66215

Offers B&B Homes In: Kansas City, Parkville, Lee's Summit, Lexington, Concordia, Independence, Liberty, Grandview, St. Joseph, Weston, and Warrensburg (in Missouri); Lenexa, Overbrook, Louisburg (in Kansas)

Reservations Phone: 913/888-3636

Phone Hours: daily, evenings and weekends until 11pm

Price Range of Homes: $30 to $95 single, $35 to $135 double

Breakfast Included in Price: All B&Bs serve a full breakfast

Brochure Available: "Homes Directory" for $1 if you send a stamped, self-addressed no. 10 envelope

Reservations Should Be Made: Two weeks in advance (last-minute reservations usually accepted)

Attractions Near the B&B Homes: Truman Library, Worlds of Fun, Crown Center Plaza, Kansas City Zoo, Nelson Art Gallery, Kansas City Museum, American Royal, Country Club Plaza, Stadium, dinner theaters, American Heartland Theater

Major Schools, Universities Near the B&B Homes: U. of Missouri, Avila College, U. of Kansas, Central Missouri State

Best B&Bs

- *Note:* See their "top" selection, Southmoreland, listed in the Kansas City, Missouri, section of this book.

- Horse & carriage house B&B in Independence, Missouri. Right off Independence Square, around the corner from the Truman Home. Built in 1885, it has been carefully restored with oak woodwork, pocket doors, beveled-glass windows, and oak beam ceilings. Two guestrooms available. Complimentary wine and cheese served in the evening.

- Lakeview home in Lee's Summit, Missouri. You can take a four-mile walk around the lake, and swim in the lake or pools. Local fish are blue gill and catfish.

- 1854 antebellum home in Lexington, Missouri. This 24-room Victorian mansion has been completely restored. Six guestrooms. This B&B was built on a hillside, surrounded by 10 acres.

- Spacious English Cotswold home in Independence, Missouri. A terrace overlooks the Missouri River with a good view of the Kansas City skyline.

- Contemporary geodesic dome home near Kansas City, Missouri. Located on nine acres, this B&B has 2,000 square feet of deck. It has been described as a "treehouse in the woods." There are two guestrooms, a hot tub on the deck, and a pool table in the recreation room. Breakfast specialty: Belgian waffles.

LOUISIANA

B&B Reservation Services

SOUTHERN COMFORT BED & BREAKFAST RESERVATION SERVICE

2856 HUNDRED OAKS, BATON ROUGE, LA 70808

Offers B&B Homes In: Louisiana, Mississippi, and Houston, Texas
Reservations Phone: 504/346-1928, or toll free 800/749-1928
Phone Hours: 8am to 8pm daily (no collect calls)
Price Range of Homes: $35 to $125 single, $35 to $160 double
   (depending on the number of additional people)

Breakfast Included in Price: Continental or full American (except in a few unhosted apartments); some homes serve "plantation breakfasts" which can include various meats, grits and gravy, hot breads, and native preserves

Brochure Available: "Directory of Host Homes" for $3.50. General brochure free

Reservations Should Be Made: Two weeks in advance (last-minute reservations accepted if possible)

Attractions Near the B&B Homes: National parks and forests, swamp tours, New Orleans French Quarter, riverboat cruises, museums, plantation homes, old and new state capitols, naval museum, Vicksburg National Park, bayous, sugarcane and cotton fields, American Rose Society Headquarters, Louisiana Passion Play, Mississippi Gulf Coast, U.S. Army's Fort Polk & Military Museum, music, and food

Major Schools, Universities Near the B&B Homes: Louisiana State, Southern U., Tulane, Loyola, Xavier, Dillard, U. of Mississippi, Mississippi Southern

Best B&Bs

■ Antebellum Acadian raised mansion in Lafayette, Louisiana, in the heart of Cajun country. Listed on the National Register of Historic Homes, this B&B has two fully restored Victorian carriage houses on the grounds where guests can stay in three bedrooms and a suite, all with private baths. The rooms are decorated with a collection of antique furniture of native woods. Breakfast is a Cajun treat featuring pain perdu (try it!) and other delicacies, served on a glassed-in porch overlooking a New Orleans–style courtyard. In winter, breakfast is served by the fireplace. The host is a petroleum geologist who collects guns and Samurai swords. The other host loves to weave, and deals in antiques. The quarters are wheelchair accessible. The hosts can arrange fishing or duck hunting trips or a fantastic swamp tour. **(Top 100.)**

■ Guesthouse on the grounds of a restored plantation home south of Alexandria, Louisiana. You will be a guest on a working plantation that raises cotton, corn, and horses, and enjoy such civilized comforts as a swimming pool and barbecue patio. The cottage is complete with a full kitchen, working fireplace, and queen sofa sleeper in the living room, plus two bedrooms with double beds and a shared bath. Will accommodate a normal size wheelchair. You make your own breakfast with fresh fixings in the refrigerator. Good central location for touring historic homes and antiques shops.

■ Contemporary B&B in Slidell, Louisiana, on Lake Pontchartrain's North Shore. About 45 minutes to downtown New Orleans. This home overlooks the Pearl River. One bedroom has a king-size bed and private bath with tub and shower. The other has a queen-size bed, also with private bath.

■ 140-year-old Greek Revival mansion with a "friendly ghost," near Natchez/Vicksburg, Mississippi. An elegant home with antiques, rural grounds, and a swimming pool and fishing pond. A plantation breakfast is served. A competent baby-sitter is available (not the ghost).

■ Quiet country home in the piney woods of Lake Pontchartrain's North Shore, Louisiana. Separate apartment in the owner's home has a private entrance, a great room, two bedrooms and a bath, wood-burning fireplace, and country antique furnishings.

■ Antebellum home in Washington, Louisiana. What! You've never been to Washington? This was once a booming little city, the largest steam-boat port between New Orleans and St. Louis. Now it's turned quiet and sedate with many 19th-century homes to tour and excellent Cajun restaurants and crafts shops to visit. This house was built in 1825 and was recently restored especially to accommodate B&B guests. Breakfast may include hot biscuits and fig preserves.

■ National Historic Landmark is now a B&B in Natchez, Mississippi. This home was once the residence of a famous general who later became a Mississippi governor and member of congress. It has been restored with all modern conveniences and welcomes you to 26 acres of grounds. Rooms and suites all have private baths. Garden cottages and a restored carriage house also offer B&B accommodations. *Insider's Tip:* A formal five-course dinner by candlelight in the formal dining room can be arranged in advance.

■ Queen Anne Victorian B&B in a historic district of Houston, Texas. There are five guest bedrooms in the house and carriage house. This home faces a boulevard with an esplanade ideal for walking or biking. The host shares laundry facilities, a tandem bicycle, and rowing machine with guests. There is a wheelchair ramp at the front entrance.

BED & BREAKFAST, INC., RESERVATION SERVICE

1360 MOSS ST. (P.O. BOX 52257), NEW ORLEANS, LA 70152-2257

Offers B&B Homes In: New Orleans and surrounding areas
Reservations Phone: 504/525-4640, or toll free 800/749-4640
Phone Hours: 24 hours daily
Price Range of Homes: $25 to $225 single, $35 to $225 double
   (some rates may go up seasonally)

Breakfast Included in Price: Continental (juice, roll or toast, coffee or tea)

Brochure Available: Free

Reservations Should Be Made: Anytime (last-minute reservations accepted if possible)

Attractions Near the B&B Homes: French Quarter, Mississippi River, Superdome, Audubon Zoo, New Orleans Museum of Art, jazz halls, world-famous restaurants, antiques stores, historic St. Charles Avenue streetcar, Jackson Square artists

Major Schools, Universities Near the B&B Homes: Tulane, Loyola, U. of New Orleans, Dominican College, Tulane Medical School, LSU Dental School

Best B&Bs

■ Quaint guest cottages in New Orleans, Louisiana. Three private guest cottages sit behind an 1876 home. They have wonderful decorative touches: leaded-glass windows, French doors, cypress staircases, and a brick courtyard. Guests are only minutes away from major New Orleans attractions, including the French Quarter, the Superdome, and the Mississippi River. Each cottage has a telephone, tea and coffee pot, TV, stereo, queen-size and/or twin bed. *Insider's Tip:* These cottages have many repeat guests. The staff of CNN (Cable Network News) stayed here during the Republican National Convention. **(Top 100.)**

■ Queen Anne Victorian home in New Orleans, Louisiana. Right in the Garden District, this home typifies past life in the Deep South with its wide veranda, tall French windows, high ceilings, and detailed woodwork. The home is decorated with original artwork. At the corner the St. Charles Avenue streetcar can take you to the downtown convention center and the French Quarter. The hosts are music and food enthusiasts.

■ The Lanaux House next to the French Quarter in New Orleans, Louisiana, is a historic Italianate gem favored by movie makers. They love to shoot this house in the background of their scenes. You will have a private suite with living room, bedroom with an antique double bed, and bath. You can stroll to all of the attractions of the French Quarter, including Jackson Square's street performers/artists.

■ The Napoleon Avenue home in New Orleans, Louisiana. You really get a sense of New Orleans in the early 1900s as you relax on the front veranda overlooking an oak-lined boulevard. Inside antiques are everywhere. Don't worry about staying out late. The hosts' sleeping quarters are apart from the guest bedrooms.

■ A Greek Revival home in the historic district of Algiers Point. You can walk three blocks to catch a ferry to the foot of Canal Street and the edge of the French Quarter. The guest suite has a bedroom with queen-size bed, sitting room, and private hall bath.

PEGGY LINDSAY ENTERPRISES
1435 PLEASANT ST., NEW ORLEANS, LA 70115

Offers B&B Homes In: New Orleans area
Reservations Phone: 504/897-3867
Phone Hours: 7am to 11pm Monday through Friday (accept calls on weekends)
Price Range of Homes: $40 single, $50 to $75 double (rates 20% more during Mardi Gras and Super Bowl periods, and about 20% less during the summer)
Breakfast Included in Price: Continental (juice, roll or toast, coffee)
Brochure Available: Free
Reservations Should Be Made: Two weeks in advance (last-minute reservations accepted when possible)

Attractions Near the B&B Homes: Historic areas (French Quarter, Garden District), St. Charles Avenue streetcar, Audubon Zoo, battle-fields, many five-star restaurants
Major Schools, Universities Near the B&B Homes: Tulane, Loyola

Best B&Bs
■ Tudor mansion in New Orleans, Louisiana. Located right on glamor-ous oak-lined St. Charles Avenue. This home has large guestrooms with 13-foot-high ceilings. You can walk to several fine restaurants or take the trolley to the French Quarter. You can have breakfast in your room or on the patio. (Top 100.)

■ One-bedroom apartment in New Orleans, Louisiana. Located in the beautiful Garden District of the city. Two couples could share this apartment, which has a newly renovated living-dining area with a complete kitchen.

■ Guesthouse on St. Charles Avenue in New Orleans, Louisiana. You may have seen this house in the movies. Here are some clues. It was the setting for a movie filmed by an internationally known film director. It marked the controversial film debut of a major new young star. The trolley right outside will take you to the central business district and the French Quarter in just 15 minutes.

■ Live in the midst of six antiques stores in a one-bedroom apartment in New Orleans, Louisiana, located right behind an antique furniture store. You can shop all day. Or take the Magazine bus to the French Quarter.

NEW ORLEANS BED & BREAKFAST

P.O. BOX 8163, NEW ORLEANS, LA 70182

Offers B&B Homes In: New Orleans and surrounding area, "Cajun country," plantations
Reservations Phone: 304/838-0071 or 304/838-0072
Phone Hours: 8am to 5pm daily
Price Range of Homes: $35 to $150 single, $45 to $150 double (prices higher during special-event weeks)
Breakfast Included in Price: Continental (juice, roll or toast, coffee)
Brochure Available: Free
Reservations Should Be Made: As early as possible for special events and best selection (last-minute reservations accepted if available)

Attractions Near the B&B Homes: Historic homes, Audubon Park Zoo, plantation tours and river cruises, Cajun bayou tours, Gulf Coast, Acadian Country, French Quarter, New Orleans nightlife, Longvue Gardens, Magazine Street antiques shops, West End Yacht Club and restaurants on Lake Pontchartrain
Major Schools, Universities Near the B&B Homes: Tulane, Loyola, U. of New Orleans, Dillard, New Orleans Baptist Seminary

Best B&Bs

■ A cottage built for two in New Orleans, Louisiana. If Paris is out this year for your honeymoon or anniversary, how about a view of the rooftops and gardens of New Orleans? That is the view you will have from a balcony of your own private guesthouse. You are close to many of the best restaurants, shops, museums, and historical sites. The host is a whiz at providing you with local information. Accommodations are also available in the main house nearby for one or two couples. **(Top 100.)**

■ Stately old family home on St. Charles Avenue in New Orleans, Louisiana. We're talking old elegance: glass entry doors, antiques, stained-glass window. Two-bedroom suite upstairs. Step right out the door to catch the trolley to the French Quarter (a 15-minute ride).

■ 1920s brick home in New Orleans, Louisiana, on an oak-lined boulevard. You will stay behind the main house in a garden apartment with twin beds, a trundle bed, living area, kitchen, and bath. Plenty of offstreet parking. All this room is perfect for a large family traveling together.

■ A beautifully restored Victorian home in New Orleans, Louisiana, close to the trolley line and Audubon Park. Choose from several guestrooms with private baths and a large common room where guests can meet each other or watch TV.

B&B Inns

TEZCUCO
3138 HWY. 44, DARROW, LA 70725

Reservations Phone: 504/562-3929
Description: This 1855 Greek Revival plantation house is set beneath majestic live oaks. It has individual cottages with bedroom, sitting room, and bath, plus formal gardens, a chapel, dollhouse, black-smith shop, carriage house, and a commissary.
Amenities: Country creole breakfast served in your cottage on a silver tray consists of juice, eggs, grits, sausage or bacon, biscuits, jellies, coffee or tea

Nearby Attractions: Center of plantation country on a historic Missis-sippi road
Special Services: Complimentary wine, tour of the plantation
Rates: $60 to $185 double

NINE-O-FIVE ROYAL HOTEL
905 ROYAL ST., NEW ORLEANS, LA 70116

Reservations Phone: 504/523-0219
Description: This quaint European-style hotel built in the 1980s is located in the heart of the French Quarter. The rooms are furnished with kitchenettes and balconies overlooking Royal Street.

Nearby Attractions: The French Market, Jackson Square, riverboat rides, famous restaurants
Special Services: Color TV, daily maid service
Rates: $55 single, $65 double. Higher rates for suites, king-size beds and special events

MARQUETTE HOUSE HOSTEL
2253 CARONDELET ST., NEW ORLEANS, LA 70130

Reservations Phone: 504/523-3014
Description: You'll find clean, simple, basic accommodation for the
budget traveler in this 100-year-old antebellum home located a block
off the historic St. Charles Avenue streetcar line next to the Garden
District, 22 blocks from the French Quarter. All rooms are with hall
bath.

Nearby Attractions: Chalmette National Historic Site commemorating
the Battle of New Orleans, the Mississippi River with its steamboats,
Jean Lafitte National Park
Special Services: Guest kitchen, garden patio, picnic tables, arrangements for tours
Rates: $21 single, $25 double, $9.50 to $12.50 in dormitories. Private
rooms also available, $39 to $59 double

MISSOURI

B&B Reservation Services

OZARK MOUNTAIN COUNTRY BED & BREAKFAST
P.O. BOX 295, BRANSON, MO 65616

Offers B&B Homes In: Southwest Missouri, Northwest Arkansas, and
Northeast Oklahoma
Reservations Phone: 417/334-4720 or toll free 800/321-8594
Phone Hours: Anytime, daily
Price Range of Homes: $35 to $80 single, $35 to $85 double
Breakfast Included in Price: Continental (juice, roll or toast, coffee);
most homes also offer gourmet or hearty country breakfasts
Brochure Available: Free if you send a stamped, self-addressed no.
10 envelope
Reservations Should Be Made: Two weeks in advance (last-minute
reservations accepted if possible)

Attractions Near the B&B Homes: Mountain Music Shows, Shepherd
of the Hills, Silver Dollar City, White Water Fun Park, fishing in
Taneycomo and Table Rock lakes

Best B&Bs

- Branson, Missouri, B&B in a contemporary home with four guest-rooms. Branson is the setting for the famous novel, *The Shepherd of the Hills*. You can make this home your headquarters for touring all of the great fishing spots and water recreation areas of Table Rock Lake. Stay in a guestroom on the patio level with a king-size bed, or choose a room on the ground floor with a double bed. You are welcome to use the charcoal grill, picnic table, microwave, refrigerator, and wet bar. You can also dip into the swimming pool or the Jacuzzi spa. **(Top 100.)**

- Lakeview, Missouri, B&B just three miles from Silver Dollar City theme park. Choice of three guestrooms. Come home to a great room with a fireplace.

- Lakeview, Missouri, guest cottage in the Indian Point area. Real privacy with many amenities—including a paddle boat for guest use, private fishing, and swimming from the dock.

- Farm home near Lampe, Missouri (halfway between Silver Dollar City and Eureka Springs, Arkansas). A honeymoon suite is available with a king-size bed, private bath, Jacuzzi, and garden room. *Insider's Tip:* Take a hike to the ever-flowing spring.

- Lake Taneycomo B&B. Right across the lake from Branson, Missouri. The rooms are furnished with antiques. One three-room suite has a Jacuzzi and steam shower. Two queen-size beds are available in separate rooms.

- Victorian home in Hartville, Missouri. This area was a Civil War battle site, and is the crossroads of scenic routes and Rtes. 5 and 38 (transcontinental bicycle route). It's close to Mansfield (Laura Ingalls Wilder home and museum). The home is decorated with antiques of the Victorian era.

Nominated by the author and Bed & Breakfast Kansas City:
Southmoreland in the Country Club Plaza area of Kansas City, Missouri. This B&B is just about perfect. The owners and managers Penni Johnson and Susan Moehl spent years looking for unusual touches for this totally restored great old house with twelve guest-rooms. Each of the rooms is named after a famous Kansas City resident and decorated accordingly. For example in the William Rockhill Nelson room (he was founder of the Kansas City *Star*) you will find a king-size canopy bed, a working fireplace, and Chippendale furniture with Irish hunt prints on the wall. In the Kersey Coates room (Mr. Coates was a Shaker), you will find simple, beautiful Shaker furniture, a full-size pencil post bed, and a private deck. For breakfast Penni and Susan have dreamed up something really unusual

—they duplicate menus from famous inns around the country. For example, one morning they feature items served in New Mexico— zucchini egg ramekins with cheese sauce, and cheddar cheese muffins. Southmoreland is great for business travelers with telephones and FAX. You can walk to the Country Club Place with its 300 specialty shops and restaurants. Our congratulations to Penni and Susan for doing everything right, as well as being such pleasant hosts. (Top 100.)

Rates: $95 to $125 single, $105 to $135 double.

For reservations: Call 913/888-3636 or 816/531-7979. See Bed & Breakfast Kansas City in the Kansas section for all of their Missouri and Kansas listings.

B&B Inns

GARTH WOODSIDE MANSION

R.R. #1 HANNIBAL, MO 63401

Reservations Phone: 314/221-2789

Description: Mark Twain once stayed in this eight-room inn (in what is now called—appropriately enough—the Clemens Room). The mansion is located amidst 39 acres of meadows and woodlands.

Amenities: Turn-down service at night, nightshirts provided for guests

Nearby Attractions: Mark Twain Home & Museum, Mark Twain Cave, Wax Museum

Rates: $58 to $80 double.

SAINT CHARLES HOUSE

338 S. MAIN, ST. CHARLES, MO 63301

Reservations Phone: 314/946-6221

Description: Located in the heart of historic St. Charles, Missouri, this elegant inn is furnished with antiques and features an old-fashioned back porch with rockers and a swing.

Amenities: Refrigerators, breakfast served in room

Nearby Attractions: 30 minutes from St. Louis and the art museum, zoo, Union Station, and the arch. Shops, restaurants, and a free trolley near the inn.

Rates: $75 to $105 double

Inkeeper's Tip: "St. Charles loves festivals and celebrates with one each month from early spring through autumn and into Christmas."

NEW MEXICO

B&B Reservation Services

BED & BREAKFAST OF NEW MEXICO
P.O. BOX 2805, SANTA FE, NM 87504

Offers B&B Homes In: New Mexico
Reservations Phone: 505/982-3332
Phone Hours: 9am to 5pm
Price Range of Homes: $50 to $121 double
Breakfast Included in Price: Continental
Reservations Should Be Made: Two weeks in advance (last-minute reservations accepted if possible)

Attractions Near the B&B Homes: Annual Indian Market (third week of August), cliff dwellings, pueblo and Spanish church ruins, colorful adobe architecture, major art center, ski basin, opera, Chamber Music Festival, arts festival

---

■ Restored old fort in Santa Cruz, New Mexico, 30 minutes north of Santa Fe and 30 minutes south of Taos. Imagine if you were bouncing down old dirt roads in a stagecoach some 200 years ago. Up ahead you'd see an adobe fort, with walls a comforting two feet thick to resist Native American attacks, your rest stop for the night. Modern travelers can experience this same welcoming sight because the fort/stagecoach stop still exists, now reincarnated as a B&B. You'll have a choice of two rooms with private baths and a room with fireplace, or one of two twin-bedded rooms that share a bath. Walk the three acres, which are unusually green and have a beautiful weeping willow and a lilac tree. Then take a dip in the private swimming pool. Full breakfast is served, often including baked egg specialties with homemade bread. *Insider's Tip:* Ask for one of the three rooms that open on a Spanish-style courtyard with a spouting fountain. Three ski areas are near at hand. In summer go shopping for the wonderful woven products by the Chimayo tribal weavers. (Top 100.)

■ B&B suites near Taos Pueblo, New Mexico, and 25 minutes from Taos Ski. The "Virgil Suite" is ideal for a traveling family or two couples traveling together. It offers two large bedrooms and a private living room with open-beam ceilings and a kiva fireplace, with a private entrance. The "Truchas Suite" has a large bedroom with a queen-size bed, sculpted adobe walls, a kiva fireplace, and a private entrance.

■ Mountaintop home close to Alamogordo, New Mexico, and the Space Museum. The home is surrounded by tall pine trees and has wonderful views of the surrounding countryside. Guests "have full use of the home, including kitchen, washer and dryer, dishwasher, etc."

■ Old adobe home in the heart of the Historic District of Santa Fe, New Mexico. Right after the Civil War, this building came to life as the Santa Fe Meat & Livestock Headquarters. But has it ever changed. Today there is a grand piano in the parlor (available to guests). You really can relive the past, in a home with walls up to 30 inches thick.

■ Adobe-style home in the most fashionable section of Santa Fe, New Mexico, close to downtown. Located atop a ridge, the home provides beautiful sunset views from the extensive decks. On cool days a kiva fireplace offers warm comfort. A glass-enclosed hot tub is available to guests. Breakfast consists of a variety of homemade breads. You may be a little surprised by the contrasting accents in this B&B. The host is from Texas, the hostess from England.

B&B Inns

CASA DE PATRON
LINCOLN, NM 88338

Reservations Phone: 505/653-4676

Reader Recommendation: Lionel Lipman of San Antonio, Texas, writes, "It is no small feat to take three 'flat land touristers' from Texas and make them feel completely comfortable and secure in a town of 65 people without stores or gas stations. This, however, is what Cleis and Jeremy Jordan accomplished when we arrived at the Casa de Patron in Lincoln last Christmas. Not only did we feel comfortable and secure, but we felt as though we had come home after a long absence to celebrate Christmas with our family and friends."

Author's Note: We received a great number of reader recommenda-tions about the Casa de Patron. Many arrived in identical envelopes bearing the same type of stamp, suggesting that this enterprising B&B had passed out the forms to visiting guests. Nothing wrong with that. The important thing is that so many people took the time to respond with such enthusiasm.

PRESTON HOUSE
106 FAITHWAY ST., SANTA FE, NM 87501

Reservations Phone: 505/982-3465
Description: This Queen Anne–style building was built in 1886 and is listed on the National Historic Register. It provides the comfort of the present in a turn-of-the-century setting. All rooms have private baths and fireplaces. Newly opened adobe compound is furnished in South-western style with fireplaces and antiques.

Nearby Attractions: Skiing, museums, art galleries, hiking, fishing, opera, Native American pueblos
Special Services: Afternoon refreshments, help with trip planning
Rates: $55 to $125 double

TEXAS

B&B Reservation Services

SAND DOLLAR HOSPITALITY/BED & BREAKFAST
3605 MENDENHALL, CORPUS CHRISTI, TX 78415

Offers B&B Homes In: Texas Coastal Bend, primarily Corpus Christi
Reservations Phone: 512/853-1222
Phone Hours: 8am to 8pm daily
Price Range of Homes: $39 to $54 single, $42 to $60 double
Breakfast Included in Price: Continental or full American, depending on individual home, plus some Mexican specialties, such as breakfast taquitos and Mexican sweet breads
Brochure Available: Free

Reservations Should Be Made: Three days in advance preferred (last-minute reservations accepted if possible)

Attractions Near the B&B Homes: Padre Island, King Ranch, Aransas Wildlife Refuge (home of the whooping crane), Rockport Art Colony, Japanese Art Museum, Corpus Christi Art Museum, Natural History Museum, Texas State Aquarium

Major Schools, Universities Near the B&B Homes: Corpus Christi State, Del Mar Jr. College

Best B&Bs

■ Home in Corpus Christi, Texas. Your choice of two bedrooms, one with a double bed, the other with a queen-size bed. The rooms share a full bath. In fair weather you can have your morning coffee on a covered patio. Well-behaved pets are acceptable.

■ Home near downtown Corpus Christi, Texas. Close to town but still only a block from the water. This B&B, Blue Heron, has two guestrooms with king-size beds and a backyard pool, plus a new paneled indoor hot tub.

BED & BREAKFAST TEXAS STYLE, INC.
4224 W. RED BIRD LANE, DALLAS, TX 75237

Offers B&B Homes In: Austin, Arlington, Amarillo, Aledo, Belton, Big Sandy, Brownsville, Burnet, Burton-Brenham, Canyon, Cedar Creek Lake, Center, Chappell Hill, Cleburne, Dallas, El Paso, Fort Worth, Fredericksburg, Fort Stockton, Galveston, Garland, Georgetown, Houston, Jacksonville, Jefferson, Lake Ray Hubbard, Midland, Marshall, Waco

Reservations Phone: 214/298-8586 or 214/298-5433

Phone Hours: 8:30am to 5:30pm Monday through Friday; answering machine other hours

Price Range of Homes: $30 to $60 single, $40 to $85 double; some higher

Breakfast Included in Price: Continental to full American, but sometimes left in the refrigerator for unhosted accommodations

Brochure Available: Free; special directory for $3.50

Reservations Should Be Made: One week in advance preferred, but last-minute reservations accepted

Attractions Near the B&B Homes: Rivers, state fairs, Six Flags,

Ranger Games, Gulf of Mexico, Oil Museum in Midland, Kimball
Museum
Major Schools, Universities Near the B&B Homes: SMU, U. of
Texas, Rice, U. of Houston, Baylor, Texas Christian U., U. of Texas
at Arlington, Midwestern U.

BED & BREAKFAST OF FREDERICKSBURG
102 S. CHERRY, FREDERICKSBURG, TX 78624

Offers B&B Homes In: Fredericksburg area
Reservations Phone: 512/997-4712
Phone Hours: 9am to 7pm daily
Price Range of Homes: $55 to $75 double
Breakfast Included in Price: Continental to full American
Brochure Available: Free
Reservations Should Be Made: One week to two or three months in
   advance, depending on event

Attractions Near the B&B Homes: Admiral Nimitz State Historical
Park; Pioneer Museum; Enchanted Rock State Park; LBJ Ranch

Best B&Bs

■ The Blackburn House in the Texas Hill country. This house was restored by a Houston couple as their vacation home. And what a
vacation for the eyes it provides—with exposed beams, wood floors,
skylighted bath, and staircase. It is furnished with antiques, including
oak and Texas pine pieces. This country-style home has a guestroom
downstairs with a full bath. Upstairs, a large loft-style room with two
¾-size beds and a half bath. After breakfast you can sit on the porch,
watching your kids play in a large yard. You make your own breakfast
with fixings in the refrigerator. **(Top 100.)**

■ The Vogel House in Fredericksburg, Texas. This is a restored "Sunday
house" built in the 1880s—a block off Main Street. The owner is an
interior decorator, relocated from Houston. The home has been
awarded a Historical Plaque as a representative of one of the older
homes in the area. You have a choice of three bedrooms downstairs
with king-size beds, and full private baths. Two bedrooms upstairs with
double beds. The house is described as "ideally equipped for small

families traveling together, having full kitchen facilities and dining room. In the fall, guests may enjoy the wood-burning stove in the living room, and a hot tub on the back porch year round."

■ Country living on a 450-acre ranch north of Fredericksburg, Texas. The ranch house is over 50 years old, with two guestrooms—one with a queen-size bed, the other with a double bed. The living room has a wood-burning stove.

■ "The Corner House" in Fredericksburg, Texas, right off Main Street. This house has high ceilings in the living and dining rooms, and is furnished with antiques and modern items. The two bedrooms have queen-size beds and share a bath (tub only).

■ The Morgan House in Fredericksburg, Texas, is a restored frame house that dates back to the early 1900s. The rear of the yard slopes down to Baron's Creek. All rooms are decorated with antiques. Cable TV is available in the living room and there are ceiling fans throughout the house.

■ Two-story guest cottage in Fredericksburg, Texas. Located in a rural area, this cottage offers guests a large room with two twin beds, a fully equipped kitchen area, and one of those wonderful old clawfoot bathtubs. Breakfast is German style, and "fix your own" with ingredients from the refrigerator.

BED & BREAKFAST HOSTS OF SAN ANTONIO
166 ROCKHILL, SAN ANTONIO, TX 78209

Offers B&B Homes In: San Antonio and outlying area
Reservations Phone: 512/824-8036
Phone Hours: 9am to 5pm weekdays
Price Range of Homes: $36.50 to $94 per room, tax included
Breakfast Included in Price: Continental to full American
Brochure Available: Free
Reservations Should Be Made: As early as possible; last-minute reservations may be made at inns

Attractions Near the B&B Homes: Sea World, the Alamo, the Missions, the Riverwalk, Mexican Market, zoo, Botanical Gardens, museums, historic King William District, La Villita
Major Schools, Universities Near the B&B Homes: U. of Texas at San Antonio, Trinity U., Our Lady of the Lake, U.T. Health Science Center Medical and Dental Schools

Best B&Bs

■ Terrell Castle in San Antonio, Texas. A rock built in 1894 for $16,500 and worth hundreds of thousands of dollars today. Your choice of unique rooms, such as the Yellow Rose Room, "furnished with a high antique double bed with a lace canopy." The Giles Suite has a king-size bed under a canopy, TV, fireplace, wet bar, and private bath. *Insider's Tip:* Be sure to visit the library, a beautiful room with a molded-brick fireplace. Then take a complete tour of this beautiful "castle." **(Top 100.)**

■ A Cape Cod guesthouse in Alamo Heights, San Antonio, Texas. This home offers comfortable rooms furnished with many antiques. The cathedral ceilings and fireplace add to the charm. A large sundeck looks out over a swimming pool. *Insider's Tip:* Musicians can try the grand piano in the Music Room.

■ The Bonner Garden in San Antonio, Texas. Imagine an Italian villa in Texas with a 360-degree view of San Antonio from a garden on the roof. Imagine coming home from a day of sightseeing and slipping into a pool surrounded by flowering shrubs. Then going to your room furnished with antiques and Batenburg lace draperies. *Insider's Tip:* For extra privacy, choose the Southwestern-style studio which is separated from the main house but offers the same wonderful outdoor amenities.

■ Falling Pines Bed and Breakfast in San Antonio, Texas. This mansion was built in 1911 by a cotton speculator who bet wrong on the swings in the market. But before he lost his money, he lavished care and money on this 9,000 square foot home. It was restored in 1979 and furnished with antiques. You have a choice of second floor bedrooms with double beds and private baths or two other bedrooms with an adjoining private bath. A Continental breakfast is served in the sun room.

■ Restored carriage house guest apartment in San Antonio, Texas. There's something about a cathedral ceiling that lends a touch of architectural grace to a bedroom, especially one with a queen-size bed and white wicker furnishings with blue and coral chintz. You can use the kitchenette for lunch and dinner, and breakfast in the kitchen with a full Continental breakfast. Nonsmokers.

■ "Marmie's" 100-year-old Victorian home in San Antonio, Texas. Not every B&B puts out the welcome mat for young children, but they are certainly welcome here. You and your spouse can stay in the polished guest bedroom with double bed and private bath. Your children can share a queen sofa bed in the TV room. You are within walking distance of the famous River Walk and the Ten Cent Trolley is nearby. At night there are refreshments for adults and snacks for the children. Didn't we tell you that Marmie likes kids.

———————————— B&B Inns ————————————

BULLIS HOUSE INN
621 PIERCE ST. (P.O. BOX 8059), SAN ANTONIO, TX 78208

Reservations Phone: 512/223-9426

Description: This historic white mansion is only minutes from the Alamo, River Walk, and downtown. The interior is decorated with chandeliers, fireplaces, 14-foot ceilings, and geometrically patterned floors of fine woods. All guest rooms are individually decorated. Built in 1906 for Gen. John Bullis, a noted cavalry officer famous for his efforts in taming the Texas frontier, it's a registered Texas Historic Landmark.

Amenities: Continental breakfast with a variety of muffins, swimming pool, badminton, volleyball, and other lawn games

Nearby Attractions: Fort Sam Houston and Old Army Museum, Botanical Gardens and Brackenridge Park and Zoo, Institute of Texas Culture, San Antonio Art Museum, Spanish Missions National Park, McNay Art Museum, Sea World

Rates: $29 to $78 single, $36 to $79 double

Innkeeper's Tip: "On the 4th of July our guests on our wide veranda can witness a beautiful fireworks display across the street at Fort Sam. In December, come for lovely music, parades, and the Christmas lights that dot the trees along the River Walk."

California & the West

ARIZONA

―――――― **B&B Reservation Services** ――――――

BED & BREAKFAST IN ARIZONA
P.O. BOX 8628, SCOTTSDALE, AZ 85252

Offers B&B Homes In: Arizona (homes, ranches, guesthouses, and inns)
Reservations Phone: 602/995-2831 or toll free 800/266-STAY (7829)
Phone Hours: 10am to 1pm and 2pm to 6pm Monday through Friday and 10am to 2pm on Saturday and Sunday (no holidays)
Price Range of Homes: $35 to $75 single, $45 to $150 double
Breakfast Included in Price: Continental or full American; many hosts are gourmet cooks.
Brochure Available: Free if you phone in; directory available for $2
Reservations Should Be Made: Two weeks' advance notice preferred, but will attempt late reservations up to 24 hours in advance; VISA, MasterCard, and American Express accepted

Attractions Near the B&B Homes: Grand Canyon, Native American monuments, Phoenix and Tucson zoos, Zane Grey home, national forests, 19 state parks, Lake Havasu, Lake Powell, Lowell Observatory, Kitt Peak Observatory, botanical gardens, and art museums
Major Schools, Universities Near the B&B Homes: American Graduate School of Business, U. of Arizona at Tucson, Northern Arizona U. at Flagstaff, Arizona State U. at Tempe, Orme and Judson private schools

Best B&Bs
■ In Sedona, Arizona, an artists' and photographers' favorite. Half-century old historic ranch estate with magnificent red rock views was featured in films of the Old West. There are beautiful gardens with a spa and pool; deer are on the property. The host serves a lavish Continental breakfast with lots of fruit, homemade muffins, breads, and jams. There are late afternoon refreshments and a homemade goody with turn-down. Warm, friendly hosts are most helpful with orienting guests to the area. Romantic, five-star accommodations with a private antique-filled parlor for guests. "View Suite" has great views, a canopied queen-size bed, rock fireplace, dressing room, and private bath.

"Rose Garden Room" has king-size or twin beds, marble-topped nightstands, cozy rock fireplace, private bath, and French doors opening on to a walled rose garden. From May through October, you can stay in "The Bunkhouse", a cozy hideaway with queen-size bed, flagstone floor, and fireplace in the old bunkhouse building, with private bath a short walk to the main house. Two small resident dogs; guest areas are off-limits to them. Two night minimum stay. (Top 100.)

■ Charming multi-story Victorian private home on the National Historic Register in Prescott, Arizona. The two bedrooms upstairs, one with double bed, the other with twins, share a hall bath. The whole house is decorated with authentic antiques, including 1920s-era kitchen appliances. Ruffled curtains and handmade quilts are all done by the host. Crackling fires in the fireplaces warm you in the winter. In the summer you can relax on the porch swing, or walk to the courthouse square . . . and back through the years. Resident cats.

■ Home in Lakeside, Arizona. The very friendly host is a dynamo who has done every piece of needlework, every piece of ceramic craft work in the house, and cooks a breakfast that simply won't quit. Biscuits and two kinds of muffins cooked from scratch, with sausage gravy, three kinds of breakfast meats, eggs cooked to your order, fruit compote with cream sauce, etc., etc. Each bed has an electric blanket with individual controls: your partner can stay cool while you roast, or vice versa. This B&B is on the Fort Apache Reservation boundary, and a half mile from Zane Grey's famous Mogollon rim. Hiking and cross-country ski trails are right out the door. The ski slopes of Sunrise are 30 miles away. Queen-size bed room with private connecting bath. Double- and queen-size beds in rooms with shared bath. Note: A guest cottage (breakfast available at additional cost) is available for large parties or families. Children accepted in all accommodations.

■ Apache Junction, Arizona: a ranch family used this guest ranch as the main headquarters for their cattle operation in the White Mountains. These are hospitable country folk who have been written about even in Europe, and they know how to provide true hospitality. There are individual cabins with private baths; enjoy breakfast in the main house. Parties up to 22 people can be accommodated with advance notice. This property is on the National Forest fence line, in the shadows of the famous Superstition Mountains. Horseback riding can be arranged nearby. Smoking permitted.

■ A quiet Phoenix, Arizona, suburban tract-house. Inside this is a never-never-land filled with stained glass and antiques, featured in a number of national and local articles on interior design and B&B. The warm, gracious host is a docent (tour guide) at the Phoenix Art Museum, and a gourmet chef; your other host creates stained-glass windows. Breakfast of choice. Backyard with gazebo, open-pit fire-place, and Jacuzzi is an oasis in the midst of the urban crush. Strategically located between the downtown area (Civic Plaza, museums, etc.) and Biltmore area. There is a double bed room with private hall bath. Child with single parent welcome.

■ A private residence on the edge of Paradise Valley, Phoenix, Arizona. Each room is filled with objets d'art and the little touches that make B&B a special experience: potpourris from the host's garden; robes, beach towels, and sun hats; turn-down of beds with treat; complimentary refreshments in the evening, laundry privileges, and more. Breakfast is served on patio tables—overlooking a croquet lawn, putting green, and a view of the mountains—next to the pool with plenty of chaise longues and an airy gazebo. The family room has a fireplace, library, and VCR. All rooms have private connecting baths, TVs, ceiling fans, walk-in closets, and in-room phone. "Poolside" room has a private door to the patio and pool, king-size bed, and dressing room with sit-down vanity. "The Suite" has two bedrooms with connecting bath, one room with a king-size bed, and the second with three twin beds (often used as a sitting room). Clubhouse, golf course, and tennis courts are nearby.

■ A 1920s era private home on the slopes of Camelback Mountain in Phoenix, Arizona, a classic adobe hacienda. Sunset vistas from the roof/deck next to the Phoenician Resort. Visit nearby downtown Scottsdale and the many local golf courses. The two-story living room with fireplace and unusual hacienda architecture is a perfect setting for an elegant wedding. Continental breakfast is served weekdays and full breakfast on weekends. One bedroom has twin antique hand-carved Mexican bedsteads and private connecting half-bath. Shares tub/shower with second queen-size bed room which also has a private connecting half-bath. Children eight and older are welcome.

■ Handcrafted Southwestern adobe home on two acres of landscaped desert with cactus garden, located in the prestigious Pinnacle Peak area of Scottsdale, Arizona. Twin adjustable electric beds in a room with private entrance overlooking the pool; private hall bath with tub and shower. The hand craftsmanship in this mini-oasis must be seen to be believed. There are desert vistas from your bedroom window or next to the pool under a covered patio with table and chairs. Enjoy a gourmet breakfast with this host couple, 15 minutes from the Mayo Clinic or downtown Scottsdale; near Princess Resort, Rawhide, Troon golf course, Carefree/Cave Creek, and Horseworld.

BED & BREAKFAST SCOTTSDALE AND THE WEST

P.O. BOX 3999, PRESCOTT, AZ 86302

Offers B&B Homes In: Scottsdale and throughout Arizona. "We also network with other reservation services in other Western states to get you a room."

Reservations Phone: 602/776-1102

Phone Hours: 9am to 6pm daily

Price Range of Homes: $40 to $125 single, $65 to $125 double

Breakfast Included in Price: Continental (juice, roll or toast, coffee), and full American with specialties (pecan rolls, chili and eggs); pick your own breakfast fruit from some hosts' orchards.

Brochure Available: Free; also free home list and map.

Reservations Should Be Made: Two to three weeks in advance, one month in advance for February reservations (last-minute reservations accepted when possible)

Attractions Near the B&B Homes: Architect Frank Lloyd Wright's Taliesin West (Scottsdale), Rawhide Western Town (Scottsdale), San Francisco Mountains, Arizona Ski Bowl and the prehistoric ruins of Wupatki National Monument and Walnut Canyon (Flagstaff), Red Rock Country, Oak Creek Canyon and the historic mining town of Jerome (Sedona), Native American cliff dwellings of Montezuma's Castle, ruins of Tuzigoot National Monument and Fort Verde (Prescott), and the magnificent Organ Pipe Catus National Monument (Ajo).

Major Schools, Universities Near the B&B Homes: Scottsdale Artists School, New Mayo Clinic and Research Center, Arizona State U. at Tempe, U. of Arizona at Tucson, American Graduate School of International Management in Phoenix.

Best B&Bs

■ Spanish contemporary in Paradise Valley, Scottsdale, Arizona. This B&B is located cheek-by-jowl to the magnificent Camelback Country Club. Wake up in the morning and slip into something cool, a patio pool with gazebo. A separate lawn area has been desert landscaped. You have a choice of three guest suites, each with private bath, dressing area, TV, and telephone. One visiting Minnesota executive gushed, "I haven't been able to think of a superlative appropriate for how outstanding this B&B is. How can one improve on perfection?" **(Top 100.)**

■ Spanish contemporary in Fountain Hills, Scottsdale, Arizona. Calling all sports! This three-story, 6,500-square-foot home built in 1896 offers two large suites (one with a fireplace), a 30-foot tropical pool, and a championship tennis court. Want to sit this one out? Retreat to the library in the view loft (choice of books and videos).

■ B&B in Cave Creek, Arizona. Located on 10 acres of cacti- and tree-covered desert. Hike through desert flora and fauna to old Native American sites. The host is an archeologist and jewelry designer.

■ Modern executive home on the outskirts of Phoenix, Arizona. By the time you get to Phoenix, you'll be ready for this national award-winning B&B located on one acre in a quiet residential area. Rooms and suites available. Private home limousine available for airport pick-up. Golf privileges at the nearby country club.

■ Modern two-story B&B in North Scottsdale, Arizona. Upstairs area has a private entrance. Two rooms with private bath. A private deck overlooks the swimming pool.

■ A refurbished 1929 Santa Fe—style adobe home located near the historic district of Tucson, Arizona. Gourmet breakfasts and afternoon tea.

MI CASA SU CASA
P.O. BOX 950, TEMPE, AZ 85280-0950

Offers B&B Homes In: Almost all regions of Arizona plus New Mexico and Utah
Reservations Phone: 602/990-0682 for information; toll free 800/456-0682 for reservations
Phone Hours: 8am to 8pm
Price Range of Homes: $30 to $125 single, $35 to $125 double
Breakfast Included in Price: Continental or full
Brochure Available: Free; comprehensive directory, $5.

Attractions Near the B&B Homes: Grand Canyon, Canyon de Chelly, Petrified Forest, White Mountains, and all of the other major attractions of this region.

Best B&Bs
■ Luxurious Spanish Colonial home in Sedona, Arizona. The reservation service owner describes this B&B as "glorious!" It has Mexican tile floors, Oriental rugs, a landscaped desert front yard, and a tropical backyard with Mummy Mountain in the distance. The pool is heated and is surrounded by roses, palm trees, and a putting green lawn. One guestroom has glass doors opening to a large patio and pool. The second room is a suite with full bath between two rooms. The third guestroom has king and twin beds with a connecting full bath and an exit to the pool and patio. Each room has cable TV and phones. The

host speaks Italian, Spanish, and French—and she enjoys art, golf, and tennis. The rates are amazingly reasonable for all of this desert luxury. (Top 100.)

■ A tri-level home in Flagstaff, Arizona. The house has the feeling of being deep in the forest with many trees and views of Mt. Elden and all the peaks. Guests may enjoy the family room with a wet bar, microwave, refrigerator, TV, VCR, and a wood-burning stove. The home is decorated with many photos and paintings of the Grand Canyon. Want to know more about how the nearby Grand Canyon was formed? The host holds a master's degree in geology. The other host has been a commercial river guide for over ten years on the Colorado River.

■ B&B in Sedona, Arizona. Your hosts, a couple from Germany, welcome you to a home with a pool in summer, and a fireplace in the common room in the winter.

■ Greyfire Farm eight miles south of Sedona, Arizona. Two acres of high desert provide beautiful views of the red rocks and mesas of Sedona. Full breakfast is served and includes homemade breads or muffins. Pets are welcome. Hey, you can even bring a small horse (for a small extra fee). Nearby are bridle and hiking trails through National Forest Service land.

■ Adobe mansion in downtown Tucson, Arizona, close to shops, theaters, museums, and restaurants (nouvelle French to authentic Mexican). This unusual structure was built in 1886 amidst other historic mansions, and you may have seen its pictures in books and articles. The private courtyards have fountains and lush gardens. Guest accommodations include a secluded carriage house apartment. In the main house you can settle into a gatehouse suite with a private entrance to the courtyard, and a sitting room/bedroom with a queen-size bed. The host is from Virginia and loves historic houses. It shows all through this house.

■ B&B in Tucson, Arizona, in a quiet residential area. Two guestrooms share a large recreation room with pool table, VCR (with a movie library), and a full bath. Minutes to the Mayo Clinic, golf courses, and jogging trail through the Indian Bend green belt.

OLD PUEBLO HOMESTAYS (FORMERLY BARBARA BED AND BREAKFAST)
P.O. BOX 13603, TUCSON, AZ 85732

Offers B&B Homes In: The Tucson area
Reservations Phone: 602/790-2399

Phone Hours: 24-hour answering machine
Price Range of Homes: $30 to $85 single, $40 to $95 double
Breakfast Included in Price: Continental or full American
Brochure Available: Free if you send a stamped, self-addressed no.
  10 envelope
Reservations Should Be Made: Two weeks in advance (last-minute
  reservations accepted when possible)

Attractions Near the B&B Homes: Arizona Sonora Desert Museum,
  Saguaro National Monument, Sabino Canyon, San Xavier Mission,
  Nogales, Mexico, Old Tucson (movie location and amusement park)
Major Schools, Universities Near the B&B Homes: U. of Arizona

Best B&Bs

■ Rimrock West is a Southwestern hacienda B&B in the foothills of the
Santa Catalina Mountains, two miles from the city limits of Tucson,
Arizona. Your hosts are two talented artists. You can stay in one of two
guestrooms in the main house with queen-size or twin beds and a
private bath. The home opens into a courtyard with a fountain. There is
a separate adobe guesthouse near the pool with a living room, full
kitchen, and a bedroom with a queen-size bed. This house also offers a
fireplace, TV, and great mountain views. Breakfast is informal and
includes fresh baked muffins and conversation with your hosts about the
arts of Tucson. Afterwards you can walk over 20 acres filled with desert
plants, flowers, and birds. Come home in time to watch the sunset and
the lights coming on in Tucson in the distance. **(Top 100.)**

■ New Santa Fe, Arizona, home in the Tucson Mountains. Another spot
to watch the city lights and enjoy superb mountain views. The guest
bedroom is large, with flowers, a fruit basket, and interesting Mexican
decor. There is a queen-size bed and private bath and entrance (with
your own patio). Later in the day you can soak in a Jacuzzi.

■ The "Desert Yankee" is a family residence built in 1955 around a
courtyard, three miles from the downtown Tucson, Arizona, business
district. Choice of four rooms with twin, double, or queen-size beds, all
with private baths. Guests can dip into the pool. The Continental-plus
breakfast is served in the courtyard.

■ Timrod, Arizona, B&B is a home set in an attractive rural area with
mountain views. You can stay in a self-contained four-room suite with a
king-size bed, private bath, full kitchen, and a separate entrance. This
is a fix-your-own breakfast with ingredients supplied by your host. The
second suite has two bedrooms with double beds and bath. *Insider's
Tip:* Want to know more about how to make pottery? The host is a
potter and will give lessons.

■ Famous B&B in Tucson, Arizona. This home is in the historic district, and was featured in the book *Desert Southwest* and in many magazine articles. You can stay in a carriage house suite with a queen-size bed, private bath, and a kitchenette stocked with complimentary wine and snacks. The living room of this suite is furnished with period antiques. Or you could choose a gatehouse suite with sitting/bedroom and a queen-size bed. The kitchenette also has a stocked refrigerator. Or a Victorian room with a queen-size bed and antiques.

CALIFORNIA

_____ **B&B Reservation Services** _____

EYE OPENERS BED & BREAKFAST RESERVATIONS
P.O. BOX 694, ALTADENA, CA 91001

Offers B&B Homes In: California, from San Diego to San Francisco
Reservations Phone: 213/684-4428 or 818/797-2055
Phone Hours: 8am to 6pm Monday to Saturday
Price Range of Homes: $30 to $100 single, $35 to $125 double
Breakfast Included in Price: Continental or full American (juice, eggs, bacon, toast, coffee) and regional specialties
Brochure Available: Free if you send a stamped, self-addressed no. 10 envelope; $1 for home descriptions
Reservations Should Be Made: Two weeks in advance (last-minute reservations accepted if possible)

Attractions Near the B&B Homes: Angeles National Forest, Huntington Library and Gardens, San Diego and Los Angeles zoos, Universal Studios, Rose Bowl, Norton Simon Museum, Asia Pacific Museum, Dodger Stadium, Santa Anita Race Track, NBC-TV Studios, Yosemite, Balboa, Golden Gate Park, California coastline and desert
Major Schools, Universities Near the B&B Homes: California Institute of Technology, Art Center College of Design, Fuller Theological Seminary, UCLA, USC, the Claremont Colleges, San Francisco State, UC San Diego

Best B&Bs _____
■ Maestro's Manor, a sprawling colonial ranch-style home located in old Pasadena, California. Has a very large living room, book-lined

library, each with a fireplace, and two large guestrooms. Enjoy a full breakfast on the sunny patio or in the formal dining room. The host is a concert pianist, organist, and harpsichordist. This B&B is one mile from the Huntington Library and Gardens, museums, numerous good restaurants, and just 15 miles northeast of Los Angeles as well as close to many tourist attractions. (Top 100.)

- San Francisco, California, hilltop home with three guestrooms features two-story windows with glorious views of the bay. Enjoy a full breakfast with the view. The hosts are long-time residents of San Francisco and provide helpful maps and directions. Parking provided and public transportation is available.

- A crow's nest with a 360-degree view tops this tri-level Newport Beach, California, home. The third level is a large guest deck with a barbecue and refrigerator. Stained glass is featured throughout the house. Perfectly located for beach and bay activities; bicycles and beach chairs are available. Full or Continental breakfast and afternoon refreshments are served.

- Get away to this large Yosemite area A-frame home with open-beamed ceilings on a tree-filled hillside above a private lake. Swimming, boating, golf, tennis, fishing, and picnicking are available in this private community. A full breakfast is served in the gazebo with a view of the Yosemite Mountains.

- A converted trolley car is now a very private B&B in San Diego, California, with living room, dining area, small kitchen, and bedroom. Decorated with antiques and memorabilia, this charming B&B overlooks a ravine with marvelous wildlife, yet is centrally located to most San Diego tourist attractions. Also available across a grassy yard is a beautifully decorated very private antique appointed four-room cottage.

- Two-story art deco—style architect-designed B&B nestled in the Los Feliz Hills of Los Angeles, California, near Griffith Park and the Greek Theatre. Offers a quiet, comfortable setting convenient to fine restaurants, entertainment, and tourist attractions. Public transportation is available.

- Beachfront B&B south of Los Angeles, California, offers the entire first floor. Step out onto the strand from your private entrance, walk to good restaurants, bike to adjacent beaches, and sun on large sandy beaches. This B&B has a living room with fireplace and wet bar, dining area, and two guestrooms.

HOSPITALITY PLUS
P.O. BOX 336, DANA POINT, CA 92629

Offers B&B Homes In: 80 cities throughout California
Reservations Phone: 714/496-7050
Phone Hours: 9am to 5pm Monday through Friday, plus Saturday and Sunday evenings
Price Range of Homes: $15 to $40 single, $20 to $55 double
Breakfast Included in Price: About 20% of homes serve Continental; others serve full breakfasts with specialties such as Swedish round pancakes, Ortega omelets, and cinnamon rolls
Brochure Available: For 50¢
Reservations Should Be Made: Two weeks in advance (last-minute reservations accepted if possible); phone reservations preferred

Attractions Near the B&B Homes: Disneyland, Sequoia National Park, Yosemite, San Diego Zoo, Wild Animal Park, Lion Country Safari, Amtrak to Missions of California, Pageant of the Masters, Pacific Ocean, Lake Tahoe, redwoods
Major Schools, Universities Near the B&B Homes: Stanford, UCLA, UC Berkeley, plus other U. of California campuses, USC

Best B&Bs _____

■ Pelican Rock at Laguna Beach, California. The only oceanfront B&B in town.

■ Monarch Pacific at Laguna, California. Beautiful four-acre setting with great sunsets and ocean views. Private bath.

■ Hideaway cottage in San Francisco, California. Your whole family can stay in this secluded cottage behind a Victorian house. It has a bedroom, kitchen, and living room. And you are within walking distance of the trolley.

BED & BREAKFAST RENT-A-ROOM
11531 VARNA ST., GARDEN GROVE, CA 92640

Offers B&B Homes In: Los Angeles, Disneyland, San Diego, Huntington Beach, Laguna Beach, Lake Arrowhead, and along the coast
Reservations Phone: 714/638-1406
Phone Hours: 8am to 10pm daily
Price Range of Homes: $35 to $60 single, $40 to $80 double
Breakfast Included in Price: Continental (some hosts serve a different

Continental breakfast every day, with crêpes, French toast, etc.), and some full American

Brochure Available: Free if you send a stamped, self-addressed no. 10 envelope

Reservations Should Be Made: Two weeks in advance (last-minute reservations accepted if possible)

Attractions Near the B&B Homes: Hollywood, Universal City, Marineland, ports o' call, *Queen Mary,* Disneyland, Getty Museum, Knott's Berry Farm, Lion Country Safari, San Diego Zoo, Wild Animal Park, Sea World, Tijuana (Mexico), missions in San Diego, San Juan Capistrano

Major Schools, Universities Near the B&B Homes: UCLA, USC, Long Beach State, Fullerton State, UC Irvine, U. of San Diego, San Diego State

Best B&Bs

■ Colonial ranch-style home on a private beach at Rancho Palos Verdes. Located in a cove called Portuguese Bend (which was once a whaling station), this exceptional B&B welcomes you with lit candles in the windows and unusual antique accessories, including some furnishings over 200 years old. You can choose a guestroom decorated in the Colonial style with a writing desk, color TV, and two large closets. The second is decorated in a Spanish motif and also provides a color TV. Breakfast is wonderful: quiche; pancakes; waffles; or French toast with ham, sausage, or freshly squeezed orange juice. Says the RSO, "The host is very attentive to her guests' privacy. Many honeymooners have returned here to celebrate wedding anniversaries because of the serenity of the area and the moonlight walks along the ocean." *Insider's Tip:* Your host can provide discount tickets for all major California tourist attractions and direct you to the area's *free* tennis courts and golf courses. (Top 100.)

■ Two-story home in Garden Grove, California, only 10 minutes from Disneyland. Also close to major beaches. This B&B offers large rooms with king-size and queen-size beds. Breakfast includes fresh fruit picked minutes before from the host's fruit trees. Coffee and tea are available all day. The other host is an artist-weaver. She will be pleased to demonstrate the art of weaving on a loom.

■ Los Angeles, California, B&B near Wilshire and LaBrea. This Italianate home, built in the 1920s heydays of Hollywood, is furnished with antiques and has two stained-glass ceilings. Located in the Hancock Park area, comparable to posh Beverly Hills. The host is certainly an interesting person with degrees in languages and international relations and well-rounded by trips to over 100 countries.

■ Anaheim, California, B&B one block from Disneyland. Why you can almost hear Donald Duck quacking from this town house. Your choice of two upstairs bedrooms, each with twin beds. No children under 12 (which is a little disappointing because of this home's proximity to Disneyland). *Insider's Tip:* Don't take an expensive taxi if you're arriving at the LAX airport. Take an Airporter Cruise to the Disneyland Hotel. You can arrange for the B&B hosts to meet you there and help with luggage.

■ Stucco home in Rancho Bernardo, California. If you love golf, this could be paradise. The town boasts 13 golf courses. B&B guests can use the Swim and Tennis Club which has three swimming pools. Close to the San Diego Zoo, Sea World, and the other attractions of San Diego. Child care is available and guests can use the kitchen and laundry.

■ Town house in San Diego, California. A quiet neighborhood only five minutes from Sea World. One whole floor is reserved for B&B guests. Hosts will meet guests at the airport and suggest some good local restaurants.

■ B&B facing Mission Bay, California, with a wonderful skyline view of San Diego at night. Two miles to Sea World and seven to the San Diego Zoo. Two guestrooms downstairs and accommodations upstairs that can accommodate a family of five to six people.

■ B&B in Anaheim, California, four miles from Disneyland and Knott's Berry Farm. This large home is located in a quiet residential area. A complete private suite features a bedroom with a queen-size bed and light cooking facilities. There is an adjoining living room with fireplace and color TV. Guests are welcome to relax in a downstairs family room with fireplace, TV, patio, and spa. The RSO says, "Especially good for families with children or for parties requiring three or four rooms." Rates very reasonable.

WINE COUNTRY RESERVATIONS
P.O. BOX 5059, NAPA, CA 94581-0059

Offers B&B Homes In: The Napa Valley
Reservations Phone: 707/257-7757, 707/944-1222, or 707/944-1109; FAX 707/257-7844
Price Range of Homes: $66 to $400, single or double
Breakfast Included in Price: Continental (juice, roll or toast, coffee), which may include muffins, home-baked breads, fruit, cheese, coffee, teas, and juices; some have full breakfast.
Brochure Available: Napa Valley Guide, $7

Reservations Should Be Made: Three to four weeks in advance (last-minute reservations accepted if possible); two nights required on weekends

Attractions Near the B&B Homes: 150 premium wineries, ballooning, hiking, bike trails, Calistoga mud and mineral baths, walking tours of old homes

Major Schools, Universities Near the B&B Homes: Napa Jr. College, Pacific Union College

Best B&Bs

■ Two-story Victorian house in Napa Valley, California, built in 1852. This B&B shows its age beautifully. Every room is furnished in European and American antiques. Consider the luxury you will experience here—down comforters, personal terry robes, a Napa Valley wine served with cheese and fruit in the late afternoon in the parlor. You can enjoy all this and a swimming pool, Jacuzzi, and loaner bicycles. The Continental breakfast is served in the family room or on the patio and features homemade fruit bread, freshly squeezed orange juice, fresh ground coffee, and croissants. Typical comment by recent guests: "We had a wonderful stay." (Top 100.)

■ A 1930s farmhouse right in the heart of wine country. This B&B in Napa Valley, California, overlooks Three Palms Vineyards with the Sterling Winery in the background. Each suite has a private bath and private entrance, a double bed, kitchen, and air conditioning. It is decorated with country-style quilts, antiques, and calicos. Fresh home-baked bread and breakfast fixings are stored in the suite—breakfast when you like. Complimentary wine; this is the Napa Valley, after all.

■ Queen Anne Victorian home in Napa Valley, California. The Victorian theme is carried throughout this B&B, with the furnishings and other antiques. Each room has a queen-size bed, sitting area, and a private bath. You can walk to parks and gourmet restaurants.

■ New Victorian Sybron house in Wine Country, a mile north of Yountville, California. This home, high on a hill, provides wonderful views of Napa Valley. Other nice extras include a wet bar stocked with wine, cheese and crackers, as well as a tennis court and a spa.

■ French country-style B&B in Napa Valley, California. This all-stone structure is secluded within a 300-acre vineyard. You have your choice of three suites with Italian marble fireplaces, vaulted ceilings, king-size brass beds and private entrances. You're only a two-minute walk from the Napa River and only five minutes from a dozen top wineries.

■ A cottage named Vigne del Uomo Felice on the west side of Napa Valley, California, in the middle of a vineyard. This stone B&B has a bedroom, private bath, fireplace, and small kitchen area. Chilled, complimentary wine greets you when you arrive. What does that cottage name mean? "Ranch of the Happy Man."

■ Country home in Napa Valley, California. The Stahlecker B&B is surrounded by 1½ acres of country charm. Three guestrooms are available: Amy's Blue Rose Room, Royal Oak Room, and the Emerald Tool Room (they don't have names like those in your typical motel!). Each room has a queen-size bath and is beautifully decorated. Guests are invited to share the front room with its fireplace and the television room with a large corner brick fireplace. Afterward, take a stroll through the rose garden or sit by a creek under old oaks and laurel trees. *Insider's Tip:* This B&B follows an Irish tradition of serving complimentary tea at 4pm

EL CAMINO REAL BED & BREAKFAST
P.O. BOX 7155, NORTHRIDGE, CA 91327

Offers B&B Homes In: Southern California
Reservations Phone: 818/363-6753
Phone Hours: Evenings (answering machine 24 hours)
Price Range of Homes: $40 to $45 single, $50 to $115 double
Breakfast Included in Price: Continental to full American, except in dormitory accommodations and apartments
Brochure Available: Free with stamped, self-addressed no. 10 envelope
Reservations Should Be Made: As far in advance as possible

Attractions Near the B&B Homes: Pacific Ocean, all southern California attractions including Universal Studios and Disneyland
Major Schools, Universities Near the B&B Homes: UCLA, USC

Best B&Bs
■ Beautiful home in La Jolla, California, just a block from the ocean. You have a choice of: La Jolla Room with apricot and white colors and a king-size bed, the Imperial Room decorated in modern Asian with a queen-size bed, Paradise Island with a hand-painted Mexican tropical decor in mint green and raspberry pink and a queen-size bed. The host serves an expanded Continental breakfast. If you're around in the afternoon, join her for a snack in the dining room. (Top 100.)

▪ Home in Malibu, California. Located high on a hill, this B&B provides a panoramic view of the Pacific Ocean. The home is filled with artwork. *Insider's Tip:* This is a particularly good place to stay if you want to spend some time at the famous Getty Museum, which is nearby. The host is very knowledgeable about fine local restaurants.

▪ House at Seal Beach, California. The B&B offers attractive accommodations with a garden, right on the beach. One guestroom has a king-size bed; the other, twins. Walk out the back door through the garden and you're at the ocean. Hot tub available.

AMERICAN FAMILY INN/BED & BREAKFAST SAN FRANCISCO

P.O. BOX 349, SAN FRANCISCO, CA 94101

Offers B&B Homes In: San Francisco, Marin County, Monterey/ Carmel, and the California Wine Country
Reservations Phone: 415/931-3083; FAX 415/921-BBSF
Phone Hours: 9:30am to 5pm Monday through Friday (answering machine all other hours)
Price Range of Homes: $45 to $125 single, $55 to $125 double, $70 to $100 for family accommodations, $100 and up for boats
Breakfast Included in Price: Full hearty American
Brochure Available: Free
Reservations Should Be Made: By phone, when you know the exact dates (last-minute reservations accepted if space allows)

Attractions Near the B&B Homes: San Francisco cable cars, Fisherman's Wharf, Chinatown, Moscone Convention Center, Golden Gate Park
Major Schools, Universities Near the B&B Homes: UC Medical Center, San Francisco State

Best B&Bs

▪ Contemporary home in San Francisco, California. The reservation service says, "The best view of San Francisco!" This home combines modern architecture and classic antiques. The large bedroom has a panoramic view of the city. For extra creature comforts: a king-size bed, Jacuzzi, and fireplace in the room. The small bedroom has a view of the bay and a queen-size bed. Close to public transportation. The host is an architect.

■ Private cottage in San Francisco, California. This B&B is located on the famous crooked Lombard Street on Russian Hill (you've probably seen this street in dozens of photographs and movies). The tastefully decorated living room has a view of the bay and bay bridge, a fireplace, and a TV.

■ Modern home in San Francisco, California. This three-level home is high on a San Francisco hill with great views of the city and nearby Glen Canyon. It's near all the sights. *Insider's Tip:* Don't skip breakfast. The host serves Swedish pancakes with homemade orange syrup, fancy omelets, and other breakfast specialties. A number of her recipes have been published.

■ This reservation service can also book you on a most unusual B&B: a yacht or a houseboat on San Francisco Bay.

BED & BREAKFAST SAN FRANCISCO
P.O. BOX 349, SAN FRANCISCO, CA 94101

Offers B&B Homes In: San Francisco and the surrounding areas of Marin County, Carmel, Monterey, and the Wine and Gold countries.

Attractions Near the B&B Homes: Fisherman's Wharf and Nob Hill.
Reservations Phone: 415/931-3083; FAX 415/921-2273
Price Range of Homes: $45 to $75 single, $55 to $155 double
Breakfast Included in Price: Continental to full American

Best B&Bs _____
■ The Coddington Suite on top of famous Nob Hill in San Francisco, California. You can choose from two romantic Victorian suites, filled with Victorian antiques. The bedrooms have queen-size beds and the living rooms have fireplaces. Each suite has a small kitchen. People attending conventions can walk to the Fairmont and Mark Hopkins hotels. **(Top 100.)**

■ B&B overlooking Glen Canyon Park in San Francisco, California. You can stay in any of three guestrooms, each facing west for a view of the setting sun, a beautiful eucalyptus grove, and Mt. Davidson (highest point in the city). Don't miss breakfast. The host is a gourmet and loves to cook. You may even meet her husband over coffee, a locally famous attorney who is credited with "saving the San Francisco cable cars" from going out of business forever.

- "No name" Victorian B&B located in one of the most photographed areas of San Francisco, California—the historic district of Alamo Square. You will be close to the Civic Center, Opera House, Union Square, and Davies Symphony Hall. Three of the five guestrooms have fireplaces and private baths. You can dip into an outdoor hot tub but don't be startled if a neighborhood racoon named "Nosey" comes to watch.

- Country cottage in San Francisco, California. Four guestrooms are available, each with a private entrance and furnished with antiques and brass beds. Located on a quiet street with a country feeling. A full breakfast is served in the morning.

- Home on Russian Hill in San Francisco, California. Russian Hill is considered to be one of the city's most beautiful neighborhoods. Cable cars are just a block away. And you can walk to Fisherman's Wharf and North Beach.

- B&B in the Fisherman's Wharf area of San Francisco, California. One room is available, with a fireplace and fresh flowers. Breakfast is served by the bay window. The second room has an antique double bed. Fisherman's Wharf is a short two blocks away.

WINE COUNTRY BED & BREAKFAST
P.O. BOX 3211, SANTA ROSA, CA 95403

Offers B&B Homes In: Santa Rosa and approximately 35-mile radius, including Healdsburg, Sebastopol, Sonoma, St. Helena, and Calistoga
Reservations Phone: 707/578-1661
Phone Hours: 10am to 8pm daily
Price Range of Homes: $70 to $90 double
Breakfast Included in Price: Full American (juice, eggs, bacon, toast, coffee)
Brochure Available: Free if you send a stamped, self-addressed no. 10 envelope
Reservations Should Be Made: Two weeks in advance (no last-minute reservations, but will accept one week ahead if deposit is sent)

Attractions Near the B&B Homes: Over 24 world-famous wineries and vineyards, Redwood Forest in Armstrong State Park, Bodega Bay, Sonoma Old Spanish Mission, Jack London House and Museum, Russian River resorts, historic Russian settlement at Fort Ross, Luther Burbank Gardens

Major Schools, Universities Near the B&B Homes: Sonoma State, Santa Rosa Jr. College

Best B&Bs

■ Redwood country home in the outskirts of Santa Rosa, California. You're surrounded by trees and garden, yet only minutes from the center of town. After a day of exploring the Napa Valley and the town of Sonoma, the Valley of the Moon, and Jack London Park, you'll come home at night to a large bedroom with a king-size bed and private bathroom. The host serves big country-style breakfasts. (Top 100.)

■ Historic home in Healdsburg, California. Located close to the Napa Valley and Alexander Valley and the coast, this B&B offers a bedroom with a double bed, private sitting room, TV, and private bath. The host serves a full breakfast. *Insider's Tip:* Take a picture of yourself in front of the home and its whimsical Queen Anne tower.

CALIFORNIA HOUSEGUESTS INTERNATIONAL, INC.
P.O. BOX 570-643, TARZANA, CA 91357-0643

Offers B&B Homes In: California (statewide), including the Los Angeles area, Carmel, Monterey, Santa Barbara, San Francisco, San Diego, Wine Country (also throughout the U.S., France, Britain, Canada)
Reservations Phone: 818/344-7878
Phone Hours: 7am to 5pm daily (answering machine for off-hours with callback in U.S.; collect out of U.S.)
Price Range of Homes: $40 to $80 single, $45 to $160 and up double
Breakfast Included in Price: Special Continental (croissants, cheese, hot beverage, preserves, fresh fruit, with a flower), or full in selected locations
Brochure Available: Free if you send a stamped, self-addressed no. 10 envelope
Reservations Should Be Made: As early as possible (last-minute reservations accepted if possible)

Best B&Bs

■ Modern beachside home in Hermosa Beach, California. Exceptional decor and art throughout, including a white leather sectional in a sunken living room, a black lacquer grand piano, and a magnificent stained-glass door to the beachfront patio. The private room has a queen-size bed and a private bath.

■ Modern home in Los Angeles, California. Has a pool and well-tended garden. This B&B is near Universal Studios (be sure to take the studio tour). The private guest suite is decorated with Laura Ashley wallpapers and has a queen-size bed, private bath, and a sitting room with a queen-size sofa bed, TV, microwave, and refrigerator. *Insider's Tip:* A baby-sitter is available.

■ Tolucal Lake, California, Mexican hacienda. This B&B sports Spanish tiles, arches, verandas, and courtyard—welcome to old Mexico. And you're close to Hollywood. Choice of two rooms with private bath. A large redwood deck overlooks the pool and gardens.

■ Elegant Tudor home in San Francisco, California. Only 10 to 15 minutes from the center of town but surrounded by lush trees in a most prestigious area. Guests have double rooms, all done in peach decor, with private bath which has a large Jacuzzi and shower.

■ Honeymoon special in Santa Monica, California, near Ocean Avenue. This B&B is a beautifully furnished flat in a secured building. The bedroom is decorated in white and blue with a brass canopy bed and luxurious feather bedding. The host offers a gourmet breakfast and afternoon sherry or tea.

■ Carmel Valley, California, B&B. You'll have your own private suite with deck and hot tub overlooking the valley. The room is done in Southwest style, with a log four-poster bed, fireplace, and private bath. The hosts in the main house bring full breakfast on a tray (why not have breakfast in bed—it's your vacation).

BED AND BREAKFAST OF LOS ANGELES

32074 WATERSIDE LANE, WESTLAKE VILLAGE, CA 91361

Offers B&B Homes In: Los Angeles, Ventura, and Orange Counties; also along the California coast (San Diego to San Francisco)
Reservations Phone: 818/889-8870 or 805/494-9622
Phone Hours: 9am to 9pm Monday through Friday
Price Range of Homes: $30 to $50 and up single, $35 to $85 and up double
Breakfast Included in Price: Continental or full American (juice, eggs, bacon, toast, coffee), with some homes serving regional specialties
Brochure Available: For $2 with a legal-sized stamped, self-addressed envelope
Reservations Should Be Made: One month in advance (last-minute reservations accepted if possible)

Attractions Near the B&B Homes: All Southern California tourist attractions

Major Schools, Universities Near the B&B Homes: USC, UC Occidental, Pepperdine, Marymount, Loyola, Whittier, Cal College Long Beach, Northridge, Saddleback, Domingas Hills, Los Angeles, Fullerton, Polytech at Pomona, and UC Riverside

Best B&Bs

■ Attractive older home in quiet neighborhood of Garden Grove, California. Two upstairs guestrooms with king-size beds and private baths. If you're in a romantic mood, choose the one with a fireplace. If you want to keep up on the news, choose the one with a TV. The host is a doll collector and weaver. Crib is available.

■ Spacious home in Anaheim, California. There are two downstairs guestrooms sharing a bath in the hall. Upstairs is a suite with a living room, fireplace, and private bath. Spa in the yard.

■ Garden home in the Pacific Palisades, California. This is a traditional home in an exclusive neighborhood. Two guestrooms with shared bath. The beach is one-half a downhill mile away. Of course, you have to walk back up.

■ Malibu, California, guesthouse, in the hills. You'll stay in a cottage behind the garage. You can see the ocean through the canyon. Sorry, you must have a car to be able to stay here.

■ Canyon Cottage in Beverly Hills, California. Your host is a writer and the script he has written for your stay features an English country atmosphere and a massive fireplace. A mile from Sunset Boulevard.

■ Country Garden B&B in Sherman Oaks, California. You walk through a garden to your private suite with a sitting room, and a bedroom with twin beds. For an extra son or daughter, you can also open a hide-a-bed in the sitting room. Guests may use the pool, Jacuzzi, patio, and laundry facilities.

■ "The Pink Flamingo" in North Hollywood, California. That's what they call this B&B (you know these Hollywood folk). It has a whimsical decor and a spacious guest wing. You can dip into the pool.

B&B Inns

CARTER HOUSE
1033 3RD ST., EUREKA, CA 95501

Reservations Phone: 707/445-1390

Description: This Victorian mansion has seven rooms for guests, four with private bath. The house has been stylishly restored with antiques and Oriental rugs, yet with modern paintings and ceramics by local artists.

Amenities: Breakfast specialties might include a tart with almond filling, eggs Florentine or Benedict, or kiwi with raspberries. "Best breakfast in California," says the *California Magazine.* Wine and brie in the afternoon, tea, cookies, and cordials at bedtime, can be arranged.

Special Services: Airport pickup with a 1958 Bentley

Rates: $65 to $350 double

Innkeeper's Tip: "Humboldt County is home to more artists per capita than any other county in California. In addition to the area's many flourishing art galleries, museums and fascinating festivals, Humboldt's nightlife is vibrant. Local nightclubs and microbreweries offer excellent music. The local university often hosts symphony concerts or notable dramatic productions. Highly regarded repertory troupes perform year-round in four community theaters." Ask Mark Carter or his staff for more tips when you arrive.

CHALFANT HOUSE

213 ACADEMY ST., BISHOP, CA 93514

Reservations Phone: 619/872-1790

Description: This Victorian home/museum was built in 1898 by P. A. Chalfant, editor and publisher of the first newspaper in the Owens Valley and, for a time, served as a hotel for tungsten miners. The rooms have been restored and furnished with antiques, handmade quilts, and comforters.

Amenities: Gourmet breakfast with homemade jams and breads, old-fashioned ice cream sundaes in the evening

Nearby Attractions: Laws Railroad Museum, lakes for fishing, boating, back-packing, also skiing, golf, hang gliding, Native American petroglyths nearby.

Rates: $60 to $75 double

THE OLD TOWN BED & BREAKFAST INN
1521 3RD ST., EUREKA, CA 95501

Reservations Phone: 707/445-3951
Description: This 1871 Greek Revival Italianate home has five rooms for guests, all individually decorated in soft colors with period furniture; two of the rooms have a shared bath.
Amenities: Full breakfast

Nearby Attractions: Redwoods National Park, Seashore museums, tubing, tennis, golf, racquetball
Rates: $55 to $85 single, $65 to $85 double

CLEONE LODGE INN
24600 N. HWY. 1, FORT BRAGG, CA 95437

Reservations Phone: 707/964-2788
Description: In a quiet setting on three acres of wooded grounds, each unit in the lodge varies in design and decor and may include antiques, wicker furniture, colorful prints, fireplaces, garden views, and kitchens.

Nearby Attractions: Mendocino's rugged coast, redwood groves, wineries, MacKerricher State Park, Lake Cleone, canoeing, trout fishing, horseback riding, bicycling, hiking
Special Services: Outdoor decks and trails.
Rates: $52 to $103 double; MasterCard and VISA accepted

GRAPE LEAF INN
HEALDSBURG, CA 95448

Reservations Phone: 707/433-8140
Description: A 1900 Queen Anne Victorian home converted into a B&B inn with seven guestrooms. The owners describe it as "a very romantic getaway." Four of the guestrooms have Jacuzzis (for two) and four have skylights.
Amenities: Full country breakfast included a baked egg dish, red potatoes, and fresh fruit. Another regular special: blueberry pancakes.

Nearby Attractions: Fifty-five wineries are within a 15 minute radius of the Grape Leaf Inn.

Special Services: First quality Sonoma County wines served in the evening.
Rates: $60 to $125 single or double
Innkeeper's Tip: "Save some time to explore Healdsburg, a very uncommercial small town that provides the restaurants and charm of wine country without the hustle and bustle of some other tourist areas."

DUNBAR HOUSE 1880
271 JONES ST., P.O. BOX 1375, MURPHYS, CA 95247

Reservations Phone: 209/728-2897
Description: Italianate B&B in the heart of gold country. There are comfortable rooms with private baths, wood-burning stoves, and air conditioning. The inn is furnished with country antiques.
Amenities: Complimentary bottle of a local wine and a snack tray is delivered to guests' room. Full country breakfast.

Nearby Attractions: Yosemite, Columbia State Park, Bear Valley ski area.
Rates: $90 single, $95 double.
Innkeeper's Tip: "Several wineries are within walking distance of the inn. Cave explorers can choose from a simple tour to an all-afternoon exploration and rappelling tour."

THE NAPA INN
1137 WARREN ST., NAPA, CA 94559

Reservations Phone: 707/257-1444
Description: This three-story turn-of-the-century home in the quaint preservation area of Napa has five spacious accommodations with baths, and furnished with antiques.
Amenities: Hearty breakfast

Nearby Attractions: Napa Valley wineries, balloon rides, wine train
Special Services: Afternoon refreshments
Rates: $90 to $130 double occupancy

TALL TIMBERS CHALETS
1012 DARMS LANE, NAPA, CA 94558

Reservations Phone: 707/252-7810
Description: The inn's country cottages are sited on two acres. Each
separate cottage is decorated in country style, and contains a bedroom, a living room (with a queen-size sofabed), a breakfast area,
and a bath.
Amenities: Continental breakfast, with fresh fruit in season

Nearby Attractions: Wineries, bike and walking trails, Marine World/
Africa
Special Services: The inn accepts well-behaved children.
Rates: $65 to $125 double, February to October; prices vary Novem-
ber to January.

THE CHATEAU TIVOLI
1057 STEINER ST., SAN FRANCISCO, CA 94115

Reservations Phone: 415/776-5462
Description: This large Victorian town house/arts center was designed
and built in 1892 by architect William H. Armitage. It is furnished
with antiques and art from the estates of Cornelius Vanderbilt,
Charles de Gaulle, J. Paul Getty and the famous Madame Sally
Stanford. Rooms and suites feature canopy beds, marble baths,
balconies, fireplaces, stained glass, handmade quilts, and Oriental
rugs.
Amenities: Complimentary wine upon arrival, breakfast in bed.

Nearby Attractions: Located in the center of San Francisco and part of
the Alamo Square Historic District. Near San Francisco Opera House,
Japan Center, Fisherman's Wharf, Golden Gate Park, Chinatown
Rates: $175 to $200 double
Insider's Tip: Balloon rides over Napa Valley wine country, ferry boat
ride to Sausalito, and brunch on the patio of the Mora Loma Hotel
with grand views of San Francisco.

THE SHERMAN HOUSE
2160 GREEN ST., SAN FRANCISCO, CA 94123

Reservations Phone: 415/563-3600
Description: An 1876 historic landmark converted from a private man-

sion into a 14-room accommodation, the house has been meticulously restored to its original beauty with French Second Empire interiors featuring a splendid three-story music room with gallery salon, a carriage house, formal gardens, a Victorian greenhouse, and a gazebo. Rooms have canopied feather beds and fireplaces.

Nearby Attractions: Historic landmarks, cable cars, Fisherman's Wharf
Special Services: Airport limousine service, courtesy membership in one of San Francisco's best athletic clubs
Rates: $170 to $700 double

PETITE AUBERGE
863 BUSH ST., SAN FRANCISCO, CA 94108

Reservations Phone: 415/928-6000
Description: This French country inn has antiques, fresh flowers, and fireplaces.
Amenities: Fresh fruit, juice, eggs, quiche, or French toast, croissants, muffins, granola, and coffee, tea, or milk

Nearby Attractions: Union Square, Chinatown, cable cars
Special Services: Afternoon tea and hors d'oeuvres
Rates: $105 to $215 double
Author's Tip: If you enjoy your stay in this elegant B&B inn, inquire about the other small inns managed by the same company (Four Sisters Inns) in San Francisco and on the Monterey Peninsula, including the White Swann Inn, The Marina Inn, Gosby House Inn, The Green Gables Inn, and the Cobblestone Inn. The company has just opened its first B&B inn in Southern California, the Blue Lantern Inn of Dana Point in Orange County. A 10% discount is available to travelers 62 or over at any of the Monterey inns, Sunday through Thursday during the winter season.

THE PARSONAGE
1600 OLIVE ST., SANTA BARBARA, CA 93101

Reservations Phone: 805/962-9336
Description: This two-story, restored Queen Anne inn is filled with Oriental rugs and antiques. Features a two-bedroom honeymoon suite with an ocean/mountain view.
Amenities: Fresh-squeezed orange juice, homemade breads and muf-

fins, apple pancakes, and chili cheese soufflé featured on the breakfast menu, served on the sundeck

Nearby Attractions: Santa Barbara Mission, Botanical Gardens, the
Pacific Ocean
Special Services: Complimentary wine offered each evening
Rates: $65 to $125 single, $85 to $155 double

ADOBE INN
1473 MONTEREY ST., SAN LUIS OBISPO, CA 93401

Reservations Phone: 805/549-0321
Description: Southwestern-style inn with 15 guestrooms. Each room has
its own unique features, such as window seats, rocking chairs, etc. All
rooms have color cable TV.
Amenities: Breakfast includes home-baked muffins and breads, seasonal fruits, cereals, yogurt, cottage cheese, orange juice, tea, coffee.
Non-smoking rooms available.

Nearby Attractions: Hearst Castle, Montana d'Oro State Beach and
Park, Edna Valley Wine Country, San Luis Obispo Mission, and
numerous historic homes. Beaches within a 10-mile radius include
Avila Beach, Shell Beach, Pismo Beach, and Morro Bay.
Special Services: Each room is stocked with current magazines. Picnic
lunches available for the beach and wine country for an additional
charge. Reservation services available for Hearst Castle tours, wine
country tours, dinner engagements.
Rates: $49 to $59 single, $59 to $69 double, summer; $45 to $55
single, $49 to $59 double, winter
Innkeeper's Tip: "Every Thursday evening from 6pm until 9pm a
farmer's market is held in downtown San Luis Obispo with live
entertainment, open-air barbecues, fresh fruits and vegetables from
local farms, and lots of fun. Complimentary trolley service is available from the inn to the downtown area on these evenings."

THE BABBLING BROOK INN
1025 LAUREL STREET, SANTA CRUZ, CA 95060

Reservations Phone: 408/427-2437
Description: This secluded inn was built in 1909 on the foundation of
an 1870s tannery, a 1790s grist mill, and a 2,000-year-old Native

American fishing village. Its 12 guestrooms have country French decor, private baths, fireplaces, decks, and two have whirlpool baths.

Amenities: Country breakfast, afternoon wine and cheese buffet.

Nearby Attractions: Beach, wharf, boardwalk, tennis, historic homes tours, golf, shopping.

Rates: $85 to $125 double

Innkeeper's Tip: "Our guests love the cascading waterfalls, pines, redwoods, and acre of gardens that surround our inn. It is a change-of-pace get-away."

UTAH

B&B Inns

PETERSON'S BED & BREAKFAST

95 N. 300 WEST (P.O. BOX 142), MONROE, UT 84754

Reservations Phone: 801/527-4830

Description: Parts of the building are 100 years old, but fit in well with the later additions. The rooms are fitted with king-size, twin, and double beds, sitting areas, kitchens, private baths, and private entrances.

Amenities: Full breakfast with such specialties as country ham, eggs Benedict, Dutch apple pancakes, and homemade coffee cake.

Nearby Attractions: Five national parks, four national forests, Fremont State Park, museum of Native American artifacts, tennis, golf, Monroe Hot Springs

Special Services: Complimentary beverages, cookies, candy, in-room coffee, tea, and cocoa

Rates: $40, single or double; $55 for a suite

BLUFF BED & BREAKFAST
BOX 158, BLUFF, UT 84512

Reservations Phone: 801/672-2220
Description: This is a large Frank Lloyd Wright—style home on 17 desert acres, at the foot of red rock cliffs.
Amenities: Hostess prepares a full breakfast to order—steak and eggs, pancakes, "whatever they like."

Nearby Attractions: Canyon de Chelly, Monument Valley, and many of the West's most famous National Parks are within a two-hour's drive. Close to the San Juan River, one of the last wild rivers in America.
Special Services: The hostess, Rosalie Goodman, is an amatuer geologist and can direct you to some of the more interesting natural formations in the area. She will also pack picnic lunches for guests who want to go exploring some unusual wilderness places.
Rates: $50 to $55 single or double
Innkeeper's Tip: Rosalie Goodman says, "If some of the more adventurous guests would like to experience Navaho life on a indian reservation, I can arrange for them to stay overnight at Will T's hogan (a log-cabin-style indian home). Will T., a Navaho, will also take them on tours. I spent some time with him in Canyon de Chelly recently, and he showed me geological formations I had missed all of my life."

GREENE GATE VILLAGE
76 WEST TABERNACLE ST., ST. GEORGE, UT 84770

Reservations Phone: 801/628-6999
Description: This complex includes nine pioneer homes, restored and decorated with artifacts of the period, as well as a hot tub, old fashioned candy store, and soda fountain.

Nearby Attractions: Six national parks within a 100-mile radius, including Zion, Bryce Canyon, and Grand Canyon. Golf and tennis nearby.
Rates: $50 to $75 double

Alaska & Hawaii

B&B Reservation Services

ALASKA PRIVATE LODGINGS
P.O. BOX 200047-F, ANCHORAGE, AK 99520

Offers B&B Homes In: Anchorage, Seward, Homer, Palmer, Willow,
Talkeetna, Fairbanks, Kenai, Wasilla, Denali Park area
Reservations Phone: 907/258-1717 or 907/248-2292
Phone Hours: 9am to 5pm Monday through Friday
Price Range of Homes: $35 to $55 single, $40 to $80 double
Breakfast Included in Price: Breakfasts vary with each home
Brochure Available: Call or write for free brochure and directory.
Reservations Should Be Made: Advance reservations preferred; one-
night deposit required; VISA and MasterCard accepted

Attractions Near the B&B Homes: Alaska Oil Pipeline; Alaska Railroad; glaciers, gold mines, salmon-spawning waters, mountain
ranges, native wildlife; city, state, and national parks
Major Schools, Universities Near the B&B Homes: U. of Alaska at
Anchorage, Alaska Pacific U.

Best B&Bs

■ Private home in Anchorage, Alaska. This B&B is close to the airport,
and offers three guestrooms, each with private bath. The host serves a
full breakfast. Easy access to public transportation.

■ Log home located only 20 miles north of the entrance to Denali
National Park in Alaska (this park with its grazing grizzlies, elk and
moose, and spectacular Mount McKinley is one of the wonders of the
world). Two guestrooms are available with twin beds and a shared
bath. Full breakfast is served to the guests. *Insider's Tip:* Use the free
bus inside Denali to travel to the various points of interest. In the spring
you'll see grizzlies and their cubs playing on the plains below.

ACCOMMODATIONS ALASKA STYLE—STAY WITH A FRIEND

3605 ARCTIC BLVD., SUITE 173, ANCHORAGE, AK 99503

Offers B&B Homes In: Anchorage, Fairbanks, Juneau, Sitka, Homer, Soldotna, Anchor Point, Valdez, Seward, Palmer, Kena, Wasilla, Willow, Glennallen, Denali Park, Gustavus
Reservations Phone: 907/278-8800
Phone Hours: 8am to 6pm May to September; shorter hours off-season
Price Range of Homes: $40 to $75 single, $50 to $100 double
Breakfast Included in Price: Continental to full American
Brochure Available: $2 for descriptive listing
Reservations Should Be Made: In advance for best selection

Attractions Near the B&B Homes: Denali National Park, Kenai Fjord National Park, Glacier Bay National Park, glaciers, Homer Spit, volcanic mountains, salmon and halibut fishing, kayaking, floating, canoeing, and bicycling
Major Schools, Universities Near the B&B Homes: U. of Alaska, Alaska Pacific U., Sheldon Jackson College

Best B&Bs

■ Home in downtown Anchorage, Alaska. Near a small park and close to the new Anchorage Coastal Trail. The home is large and plainly furnished. Good views of Mount Susitna outside. *Insider's Tip:* Want to know about the early days of Alaska? Talk with your host, a pioneer goldmining engineer. This home was presented with "Wild about Anchorage" award in 1987. (Top 100.)

■ New home on a hillside in Sitka, Alaska. This home offers great views—of Cascade Creek below, and in the distance Sitka Sound, Mount Edgecume, and the Pacific Ocean. On crisp mornings you can take a brisk two-mile walk to downtown Sitka. Rooms are furnished with antiques and reproductions.

■ Downtown Anchorage, Alaska, B&B with a picture-window view of Cook Inlet and the Sleeping Lady (Mt. Susitana). You'll stay in a quiet neighborhood within two blocks of major hotels and restaurants. A barbecue grill and a washer/dryer are available for guest use. The host is a pioneer Alaskan who rides his bike to the airport where he is a propellor specialist. The other host is a pianist. Don't be surprised if she offers an impromptu concert at breakfast.

■ Large split-level family home on the east side of Anchorage, Alaska. This B&B features many unusual collectibles, including Alaskan and African hunting and fishing trophies. There is a great view of the mountains from your breakfast table where you can dine on a full breakfast, including fresh homemade strawberry and raspberry jam. Active hosts are former teachers.

■ Tri-level home in south Anchorage, Alaska, with a private B&B suite decorated with antiques and country collectibles. The sitting room has a wood-burning fireplace and writing nook. There is an outdoor hot tub on a deck overlooking the Chugach State Forest. Hosts are in the legal profession in a home with a real family feeling (two children, two dogs).

■ European-style country home in Palmer, Alaska—with llamas! We're not kidding. You will see friendly llamas right outside your guestroom window. You can even take a llama pack trip into the forests. Your hosts speak English, German, and Dutch.

■ B&B in Anchor Point, Alaska (population 327). If you want to get away from crowds, here's the place. You will stay at Whiskey Gulch in an attractive home high over the Cook Inlet. The master guestroom has a queen-size bed and a wonderful view of Mt. Redout (you may even catch distant glimpses of an occasional eruption). You can walk along the beach. Your host is a retired Alaska Fish & Game officer. Ask him about the best fishing spots nearby.

FAIRBANKS BED & BREAKFAST
P.O. BOX 74573, FAIRBANKS, AK 99707

Offers B&B Homes In: Fairbanks
Reservations Phone: 907/452-4967
Phone Hours: 8am to 8pm daily
Price Range of Homes: $36 and up single, $48 and up double
Breakfast Included in Price: Continental (juice, roll or toast, coffee), cereals
Brochure Available: Free
Reservations Should Be Made: Reservations accepted anytime if guaranteed with $25 deposit

Attractions Near the B&B Homes: Cruises on sternwheeler *Discovery,* Alaska Salmon Bake, mining valley at Alaskaland
Major Schools, Universities Near the B&B Homes: U. of Alaska at Fairbanks

Best B&Bs
■ This is a new two-story frame house with a large yard and deck in Fairbanks, Alaska. It's located in a quiet residential neighborhood, close to local historic houses and eight blocks from the downtown area. For

breakfast the host serves juice, rolls, and cereal. In the summertime there will be fresh fruit, honeydew melons, and pancakes. There is a TV in the room. Guests (for a donation) can use the laundry facilities. **(Top 100.)**

B&B Inns

GUSTAVUS INN
P.O. BOX 60, GUSTAVUS, AK 99826

Reservations Phone: 907/697-2254
Description: The inn combines a traditional homestead atmosphere and magnificent Alaskan setting with modern accommodations and convenient transportation. Bedrooms have queen-size or twin beds and private baths.
Amenities: Full breakfast

Nearby Attractions: Glacier Bay National Park, fishing for salmon or halibut, kayaking, biking, nature walks
Special Services: Boat tours of Glacier Bay, three meals a day served
Rates: $69.50 single, $139 double

HAWAII

B&B Reservation Services

BED & BREAKFAST HONOLULU (STATEWIDE)
3242 KAOHINANI DR., HONOLULU, HI 96817

Offers B&B Homes In: Islands of Oahu, Kauai, Maui, Hawaii, Molokai, Lanai
Reservations Phone: 808/595-7533, or toll free 800/288-4666; FAX 808/595-2037
Phone Hours: 8am to 8pm Monday through Saturday
Price Range of Homes: $30 to $250
Breakfast Included in Price: For 90% of homes

Brochure Available: Free
Reservations Should Be Made: As far in advance as possible, but
   last-minute reservations possible

Attractions Near the B&B Homes: All Hawaiian attractions
Major Schools, Universities Near the B&B Homes: U. of Hawaii (all
   campuses), Chaminade U.

Best B&Bs

■ A studio in a private residence, only 10 minutes from downtown
Honolulu, Hawaii. The studio has its own entrance, a bath with shower,
a large bedroom/sitting area with a queen-size bed and daybed, color
TV, and phone. The adjoining room has a refrigerator, table, and
chairs. No breakfast is provided. But then, the price is right.

■ Oahu home in Aiea, Hawaii, two miles from Pearl Harbor. Two
rooms are available, one with a double bed, the other with twin beds.
You will have kitchen privileges with the use of a microwave, regular
ovens, freezer, refrigerator, and range. *Note:* This B&B is not close to
a bus line. You will need a rental car if you stay here.

■ Home with an ocean view on the island of Kauai, Hawaii. You will
stay in a two-bedroom condominium. Your bedroom has a cathedral
ceiling, private bath, king-size bed, and color TV. You can walk to
Poipu Beach. Tennis court, swimming pool, and washer/dryer are on the
premises. A bargain. *Author's Tip:* If you're visiting Kauai, do not under
any circumstances miss the helicopter ride over the Waimea Canyon. It
is an incredible ride you will think about for years to come.

■ Single family Hawaiian-style pole home in Kihei, Maui, Hawaii, with
a panoramic ocean view. The home has two identical rooms for guests
on the ground floor—with cable TV, ceiling fans, twin or king-size
beds, and private baths. The ocean is only a mile from the house. You
also will have a great view of Haleakala volcano from the lanai.

■ Large home on the windward side of Oahu, Hawaii, in Laie. You will
stay in a suite (35 feet by 35 feet square) right on the beach. A Jacuzzi
is available on the private patio. You will have an ocean view of Laie
Bay from the front deck. Snorkeling and body surfing starts just outside
the front door. Only a half mile from the Polynesian Culture Center.

PACIFIC-HAWAII BED & BREAKFAST
19 KAI NANI PL., KAILUA, OAHU, HI 96734

Offers B&B Homes In: Oahu and almost all the other Hawaiian islands
Reservations Phone: 808/262-6026 or toll free 800/999-6026; FAX
  808/261-6573
Phone Hours: 24 hours a day, seven days a week
Price Range of Homes: $40 single, $45 and up double; $300 for a
  three-bedroom home on the ocean
Breakfast Included in Price: Continental with Hawaiian fruits
Brochure Available: For $2
Reservations Should Be Made: Anytime; can accept short-notice
  reservations

Attractions Near the B&B Homes: Miles of beaches, Pali Lookout,
  Queen Emma Summer Palace
Major Schools, Universities Near the B&B Homes: U. of Hawaii

Best B&Bs

■ Hillside home in Anahola, Kauai, Hawaii. A California artist has
created a unique personal "statement" with this unusual home. It is
surrounded by terraced gardens and overlooks the beautiful Anahola
Bay. The home is decorated with the artist's own paintings and objets
d'art gathered from around the world. You can stay in a separate guest
wing that features an individual lanai in the center of a redwood-
beamed living room and library. A Continental breakfast is served in
the garden courtyard amid tropical plants. This B&B is located halfway
between the Ne Pali Coast and the popular South Shore. *Insider's Tip:*
The artist/host is available for private art instruction in his studio.
Several different types of accommodations are available in this B&B.
You may want to walk around and choose what's best for you (depending on availability).

■ Spanish-style home on Oahu, Hawaii. You can stay in a Spanish
hacienda–style home and go to sleep to the sound of waves. Two
rooms and one bath have a separate entrance, with a patio leading to
a sandy beach. One room is furnished with a king-size bed, color TV,
desk, and table. The other features a double bed, a single bed, a large
refrigerator, and some outside cooking facilities (if you're in the mood
to grill a steak). You can walk to some good restaurants. *Note:* This
reservation service has several complete three-bedroom homes available;
ideal for a large family that wants privacy.

BED & BREAKFAST HAWAII
P.O. BOX 449, KAPAA, HI 96746

Offers B&B Homes In: All Hawaiian islands including Oahu, Kauai, Maui, and Lanai
Reservations Phone: 808/822-7771 or toll free 800/733-1632; FAX 808/822-2733
Phone Hours: 8:30am to 4:30pm Monday through Saturday
Price Range of Homes: $35 to $75 single, $40 to $100 double
Breakfast Included in Price: Continental (juice, roll or toast, coffee), plus such regional specialties at some homes as banana cakes, papaya and mango breads, Hawaiian French toast with coconut syrup, fresh fruit
Brochure Available: Free; Directory, guidebook, $10.95
Reservations Should Be Made: Three weeks in advance (last-minute reservations accepted if possible)

Attractions Near the B&B Homes: All national and state parks, famous zoos, historic homes, all the beauty and romance of the tropics
Major Schools, Universities Near the B&B Homes: U. of Hawaii and branches on other islands

Best B&Bs

■ An elegant oceanfront home in Kailua, Oahu, Hawaii, opens in front on a large pool with Jacuzzi and in back opens to the ocean. The home is spacious and has comfortable areas for guests to relax after a day of sightseeing. Also available to guests is a large sauna. All the bedrooms with private baths are handsomely furnished with an antique and tropical mixture. Each bedroom has a private entrance from the pool/courtyard area. A deluxe Continental breakfast is served. Treat yourself to a luxurious B&B experience. (Top 100.)

■ Located just 12 minutes from the airport in Kona, Hawaii, and 15 minutes from Kailua Village in the cool Kaloko Mauka area is this beautiful new home on five acres. It offers an attractive separate apartment at garden level with two bedrooms (one double, one twin), bath and sitting room with TV, and limited cooking facilities. Guests may choose to breakfast with their hosts or on their own. The hosts have lived in the islands some 35 years and spent several years in the Orient. Their favorite sport is golf. After a busy day of sports, shopping, or sightseeing come to cool Kaloko, and sit on your lanai high above the Kona coast with a magnificent sunset.

■ A secluded oceanfront home on beautiful Anahola Bay, Kauai, Hawaii, where guests can enjoy a large studio apartment detached from the main house. Accommodations include queen-size bed and private bath with a garden shower, color cable TV, and a mini-kitchenette. Breakfast fixings are provided for the first three days. Savor total privacy or enjoy the oceanfront amenities of the property. Occasionally, hosts will offer a "honeymoon room" in the main house that features a big deep Jacuzzi surrounded by mirrors and hanging ferns in it's own private bathroom. This beautiful room has French doors opening to a private lanai overlooking the ocean. Accommodations are a queen-size bed, cassette player, and a coffee maker for early morning coffee. Hosts serve a Continental breakfast on the lanai or by a beachside setting. You are welcome to use the kitchen as well as the other amenities of the main living area.

■ Now at Poipu Plantation, Kauai, Hawaii, a B&B is available in the plantation house with three lovely rooms each with it's own private bath. The largest of the three has a king-size bed with dressing room and full bathroom with tub and shower. The other two, one with queen and the other with two twin beds each have bath with shower. There is lots of room to relax in the large, screened-in lanai area where guests can lounge while planning their sightseeing excursions or in the living room where guests can share experiences and get to know one another. Tropical Continental breakfast is served in the formal dining room or on the lanai. Just across the street is the famous Poipu Beach Park. TV in each bedroom and a house phone are available. Two-night minimum is preferred.

■ Right on the beach and centrally located for sightseeing all of Maui, Hawaii, this large, plantation-style home is also in an exclusive neighborhood adjacent to the Maui Country Club. While one cannot see the beach from the home, a short walk (100 yards) will take you to a stretch of white, sandy beach good for walking. Usually the hosts' friendly dog will accompany you. The ocean is calm enough to do laps. The accommodation offered is a large guestroom with a private adjoining bath and a queen-size bed. No smoking in the house, please.

■ Outstanding views and a Diamond Head carriage-trade location on the edge of the beach and tourist attractions are only two of the good things to say about this Honolulu, Hawaii, house. This sprawling, two-story family residence is home to your host, her housekeeper, and two dogs. Five adult children with mates and offspring stop by for come-and-go visits. Even if some of them are "at home," there is still room for B&B guests. Two upstairs suites are reserved for B&B—each with a private bath and outdoor lanai. The "Mauka" (mountain) suite has a view of Diamond Head and a historic bed that is "larger than some economy rooms." The "Makai" (ocean) suite has two double beds and a view of the garden plus Waikiki lights from the lanai. The house is furnished with a mixture of local and American antiques. The home is an expression of some of the hosts' interests—Hawaiian history and contemporary art.

GO NATIVE . . . HAWAII
P.O. BOX 11418, HILO, HI 96721

Offers B&B Homes In: Five of the Hawaiian islands
Reservations Phone: 517/349-9598
Phone Hours: 24 hours
Price Range of Homes: $30 and up
Breakfast Included in Price: Varies at each location
Brochure Available: Free
Reservations Should Be Made: Six weeks in advance

Attractions Near the B&B Homes: All Hawaiian attractions
Major Schools, Universities Near the B&B Homes: U. of Hawaii and branches on other islands

Best B&Bs

■ Executive mansion in Hale Kai, Hawaii. Remember the movie *Black Widow* with Debra Winger and Teresa Russell? Then the private sitting room and walk-in bath with sunken tub and tropical plants may look very familiar to you. Scenes from the movie were filmed right here. This luxury home is right outside Hilo, with a dramatic view of Hilo Bay. Each room has its own private bath and private entrance. A lanai runs the entire length of the home with a view of the ocean. Each morning you will have breakfast in the dining room facing the bay. The owner's suite may be available (this is the one that was the setting for the movie). (Top 100.)

■ Restored plantation home, the Fern Grotto Inn, in the center of the Wailua River State Park, in Kauai, Hawaii. Yes, you live right in the midst of a tropical park and share a living room with TV, stereo, and library. Great view of the Wailua River.

■ A B&B gazebo at Huelo Point in Maui, Hawaii. The setting is beautiful—a two-acre oceanfront estate high on the edge of a cliff overlooking Waipio Bay. You have real privacy here in the cottage/gazebo away from the main house. It has a dining area, sitting area, kitchen, and patio. Surprises: Three 12-foot walls of sliding glass! Private half-bath with a sheltered outside shower.

■ A B&B in Pacific Heights, Honolulu, Hawaii. The view from this home is tremendous, and includes the city and the ocean. You can relax in the huge common living room. *Insider's Tip:* Head for the balcony for some great views of the sunsets. Hawaii seems to have the most beautiful sunsets in the world.

■ Home and cottage in Kailua, Kona, Oahu, Hawaii. Tropical fruit grows right outside your door. You can stay in a bedroom in the main house, which has a private bath and color TV. Or you can choose the cottage, which has a complete kitchen and TV. *Note:* Breakfast is not served in the cottage.

Canada

NOTE: All prices shown are in Canadian dollars unless otherwise indicated

──────── **B&B Reservation Services** ────────

BORN FREE BED AND BREAKFAST AGENCY
4390 FRANCIS ST., BURNABY, BC V5C 2R3, CANADA

Offers B&B Homes In: Greater Vancouver and Victoria
Reservations Phone: 604/298-8815; **FAX:** 604/298-8811
Phone Hours: 9am to 5pm Monday through Friday; answering service
   Saturday and Sunday
Price Range of Homes: $40 to $65 single, $55 to $95 double

Best B&Bs ────────────────────────────
■ The Piercey's, an old English Tudor home in Vancouver, BC. As in
many homes in this beautiful city, the garden is immaculate. The home
is right across from a park in the well-known area of Kerrisdale. Color
TV in each room.

A HOME AWAY FROM HOME B&B AGENCY
1441 HOWARD AVE., BURNABY, BC V5B 3S2, CANADA

Offers B&B Homes In: Vancouver and surrounding suburbs
Reservations Phone: 604/294-1760; FAX 604/294-0799
Phone Hours: All day, seven days a week
Price Range of Homes: $35 to $80 single, $45 to $100 double
Breakfast Included in Price: Hearty Continental
Brochure Available: Free
Reservations Should Be Made: Book early for best selections. "We
   also take same-day bookings."

AB&C BED & BREAKFAST OF VANCOUVER
P.O. BOX 66109, STN F, VANCOUVER, BC V5N 5L4, CANADA

Offers B&B Homes In: Vancouver and Victoria
Reservations Phone: 604/263-5595 *Note:* Calling this one number
   puts you in contact with three associated reservation services; FAX:
   604/298-5917

Phone Hours: 9am to 5pm daily; answering service after hours
Price Range of Homes: $40 to $55 single, $55 to $105 double
Breakfast Included in Price: Continental to full American
Brochure Available: Free
Reservations Should Be Made: As soon as possible, but last-minute reservations accepted

Attractions Near the B&B Homes: Stanley Park, Capilano Suspension Bridge, Queen Elizabeth Park
Major Schools, Universities near the B&B Homes: U. of British Columbia

OLD ENGLISH BED & BREAKFAST REGISTRY
P.O. BOX 86818, NORTH VANCOUVER, BC V7L 4L3, CANADA

Offers B&B Homes In: Vancouver, North Vancouver, West Vancouver, Victoria on Vancouver Island
Reservations Phone: 604/986-5069
Phone Hours: 9am to 5pm daily; answering machine other hours
Price Range of Homes: $40 and up single, $55 to $105 double
Breakfast Included in Price: Full breakfast
Brochure Available: Free
Reservations Should Be Made: Best to reserve ahead, although same-day calls are accepted when possible.

Attractions Near the B&B Homes: Stanley Park; Grouse Mountain, offering tramway to top; Nitobe Memorial Gardens
Major Schools, Universities Near the B&B Homes: U. of British Columbia

Best B&Bs

■ Brunswick beach house—just 40 minutes from downtown Vancouver, BC. A deluxe accommodation right on the water, offering a king-size bed in one guestroom, and a private suite. The travel-brochure setting is about all you could ask for on a vacation—with the ocean on your doorstep and the mountains behind you. Breakfast is served by Elizabeth ("hospitality plus" says the RSO). *Insider's Tip:* Right outside your door, you can catch the train to Whistler Mountain—or Lillooet in the heart of British Columbia. (Top 100.)

■ New town house in the West End of Vancouver, BC. Location, location, location. You are only one block from the English Bay Beach and two blocks from cafes, shops, and entertainment. This B&B has a queen-size bed in the bedroom and a four-piece ensuite bath. *Insider's*

Tip: Host Donald is the captain of a 27-foot Ericson Sloop, *Thorgrim.* Arrangements can be made for a cruise in nice weather.

■ B&B in North Vancouver, BC, on a large lot that has a park-like setting. Only 20 minutes from downtown Vancouver. One guestroom has a large Jacuzzi. Two other guestrooms are available with a shared bath. The host, Giselle, starts your day as if you were in a business suite of an exclusive hotel, bringing you coffee and the morning paper before serving you breakfast.

■ Private ground-level studio suite in North Vancouver, BC. This B&B has just about everything—a queen-size bed, pot-belly stove and fireplace, TV with remote—with a decor out of the old country. A view patio is right outside the room. The suite is fully self-contained. The host will leave breakfast for you to prepare at your convenience. Or if you prefer, you can join the family for breakfast. This B&B is close to Grouse Mountain and a chairlift ride to an outstanding view of Vancouver.

■ Victorian home in the lovely Kerrisdale area of Vancouver, BC. You will have a queen-size bed with private bath, a small sitting room with a fireplace adjoining your bedroom, as well as a sun deck where you can enjoy your breakfast. You will be quite close to the University of British Columbia and the university endowment lands—a natural park with trails for walking.

■ B&B with a private garden suite in North Vancouver, BC. Your room is furnished with fine antiques, and includes a fireplace, TV, stereo, and a ground-level patio. About 20 minutes from downtown Vancouver.

VANCOUVER BED & BREAKFAST LTD.
1685 INGLETON AVE., VANCOUVER, BC V5C 4I8, CANADA

Offers B&B Homes In: The Greater Vancouver area
Reservations Phone: 604/291-6147
Phone Hours: 9am to 5pm Monday through Friday
Price Range of Homes: $40 to $65 single, $60 to $95 double
Breakfast Included in Price: Continental to full American
Brochure Available: Free
Reservations Should Be Made: 48 hours in advance; minimum two-
   night stay

Attractions Near the B&B Homes: Vancouver city sights, Stanley Park,
   mountains, ocean, public markets
Major Schools, Universities Near the B&B Homes: U. of British
   Columbia, Simon Fraser U.

Best B&Bs

■ The Bavarian in Vancouver, BC. This large family home offers guests a bedroom with a comfortable queen-size brass canopy bed, a sitting area, and a full private bathroom. The bathroom contains a very pleasant surprise—a small bridge to a deluxe Jaccuzi tub. You can sink into the bubbling water with a wonderful view of the woods. Ahhh, this is living. (Top 100.)

V.I.P. BED & BREAKFAST LTD.

1786 TEAKWOOD RD., VICTORIA, BC V8N 1E2, CANADA

Offers B&B Homes In: Victoria, Sidney
Reservations Phone: 604/477-5604
Phone Hours: 7am to 10pm daily
Price Range of Homes: $30 to $35 single, $50 to $100 double
Breakfast Included in Price: Full American (juice, eggs, bacon, toast, coffee)
Brochures Available: Free
Reservations Should Be Made: Two weeks in advance (last-minute reservations accepted if possible)

Attractions Near the B&B Homes: Butchart Gardens, Provincial Museum, Craigdarroch Castle, Beacon Hill Park, Parliament Buildings
Major Schools, Universities Near the B&B Homes: U. of Victoria, Camosun College

Best B&Bs

■ The Sea Rose B&B in Victoria, BC. At first glance you may wonder why this rather modest looking bungalow made the "top" list. But first impressions can be deceiving. The reservation service picked this as their best because of the outstanding view—the ocean with the Olympic Mountains in the distance. The interior is comfortable, and the suites all have private baths and a private entry. *Insider's Tip:* Ask about the senior discount. (Top 100.)

■ Bryn Gwyn Guest House in downtown Victoria, BC. The *Milwaukee Journal* said, "Prime downtown location with a world-class breakfast." The government of Canada gave this B&B a "Tourist Ambassador Award." This turn-of-the-century home offers complimentary pickup from Inner Harbour, and a choice of vegetarian or regular breakfast.

■ Bay Breeze Manor, a Victorian Heritage Home built in 1885 in Victoria, BC. Located right on Marine Drive with a great view of

Cadboro Bay. Two guestrooms upstairs with double canopy beds and a shared bath. *Insider's Tip:* Best view is from "The Blue Room."

■ The Grahams' Cedar House Bed & Breakfast in Sidney on Vancouver Island, BC. This B&B offers two-bedroom accommodations with a full kitchen, bath, and a private entrance. The home is located in a country setting, only three minutes from Swartz Bay Ferry and seven minutes from Victoria Airport. Sidney by the Sea is an oceanside community with a superb bakery, shopping, and restaurants.

■ Seaside cottage in Victoria, BC. In the host's own words, "Our home sits on a bluff overlooking a sandy beach [Canada's Riviera]. We enjoy a friendly game of bridge. Our cat's name is Nickey. Rooms have queen-size beds. The Captain's Room and the Mate's Room overlook the ocean and have private baths."

■ The Thotl B&B in Victoria, BC. This home on a hill is right on an ocean inlet shore, close to Victoria. The host says there is no TV or stereo, but there is a large library of sea and detective stories and local guides which you can read on the large deck. Later you can walk along the shore in the company of swans, herons, geese, and ducks. The guestrooms have queen-size beds with fireplaces.

New Brunswick

ROSSMOUNT INN

ST. ANDREWS BY THE SEA, NEW BRUNSWICK E0G 2X0, CANADA

Reservations Phone: 506/529-3351
Description: A three-story manor house that resembles a European country inn
Amenities: Each of the guestrooms is furnished with antiques from around the world. The hostess, Lynda Estess, bakes breads and pastries for breakfast.

Nearby Attractions: You can wander through the little town of St. Andrews with its historic buildings, shops, and two good golf courses (green fees here are a fraction of what U.S. golfers normally would pay on their local courses).
Rates: $85 single or $95 double (breakfast is extra)

Innkeeper's Tip: "We have 87 acres," says hostess Lynda Estess. "It's a great area for bird watching. Guests have reported seeing birds they've never seen anywhere else."

The Pansy Patch is a unique B&B in St. Andrews, right across from the famous Algonquin Hotel. It looks for all of the world like a cottage lifted whole from an English village. The B&B host combines a B&B business with books and antiques which are sold in the house. You have a choice of four guestrooms. Breakfast may include waffles, muffins, biscuits, and French toast with strawberry or blueberry syrup. Open from mid-May until early October. Rates are $65 (Canadian, double). For reservations, write to the Pansy Patch at 59 Carleton St., St. Andrews, New Brunswick E0G 2X0. Or call 506/529-3834. In winter months, call 203/354-4181.

Nova Scotia

Nova Scotia is overflowing with beautiful B&Bs. The trick is to find them and make reservations. There do not seem to be any reservation agencies such as you might find elsewhere. There are many individual tourist associations that can supply information about B&Bs in their area. You can write to them for B&B brochures. However, these associations may or may not make reservations for you when you call. The reservations are often handled by the individual B&Bs in the brochures.

Based on a recent tour of Nova Scotia, here are our suggestions:

1. Pick up brochures of individual B&Bs and the associations at the tourist offices located at ferry crossings and in Halifax.
2. You can reserve some B&Bs by calling a toll-free "check-in" service —800/341-6096 (800/492-0643 in Maine).
3. You can write the Nova Scotia Farm & Country Vacation Association for a free brochure. Site 5, Box 16, RR#1, Elmsdale, NS B0N 1MD Canada. Their phone number is 002/798-5864 but it only seems to be answered sporadically in the winter months.
4. For individual B&B information for specific areas of Nova Scotia, you can write to the following.

HALIFAX

Tourism Halifax,
P.O. Box 1749,
Halifax, Nova Scotia
  B3J 3A5
  Telephone: 421-7733
  Fax No.: 421-2842

DARTMOUTH

Economic Development
  Department,
City of Dartmouth,
P.O. Box 817,
Dartmouth, Nova Scotia
  B2Y 3Z3
  Telephone: 464-2220
  Fax No.: 464-2907

CENTRAL NOVA

Central Nova Tourist
  Association,
P.O. Box 1761,
Truro, Nova Scotia
  B2N 5Z5
  Telephone: 893-8782
  Fax No.: 893-8782

CAPE BRETON

Cape Breton Tourist
  Association,
20 Keltic Drive,
Sydney River, Nova Scotia
  B1S 1P5
  Telephone: 539-9876
  Fax No.: 539-8430

PICTOU

Pictou County Tourist
  Association,
Box 782,
New Glasgow, Nova Scotia
  B2H 5G2
  Telephone: 755-5180
  Fax No.: 755-2848

YARMOUTH

Yarmouth County Tourist
  Association,
P.O. Box 477,
Yarmouth, Nova Scotia
  B5A 4B4
  Telephone: 742-5355
  Fax No.: 742-1295

ANTIGONISH-EASTERN SHORE

Antigonish-Eastern Shore
  Tourist Association,
Musquodoboit Harbour,
Halifax County, Nova Scotia
  B0J 2L0
  Telephone: 889-2362

SOUTH SHORE

South Shore Tourism
  Association,
P.O. Box 149,
Mahone Bay, Nova Scotia
  B0J 2E0
  Telephone: 624-6466
  Fax No.: 624-9734

EVANGELINE TRAIL TOURISM ASSOCIATION

E.T.T.A.
1153 Prospect Road,
New Minas, Nova Scotia
  B4N 3K5
  Telephone: 679-1645
  Fax No.: 679-2747

METROPOLITAN AREA TOURISM ASSOCIATION

Metropolitan Area Tourism
  Association,
P.O. Box 679,
Bedford, Nova Scotia
  B4A 3H4
  Telephone: 835-0677
  Fax No.: 835-8628

ONTARIO

B&B Reservation Services

BED & BREAKFAST PRINCE EDWARD COUNTY
R. R. # 1, BELLEVILLE, ON K8N 4Z1, CANADA

Offers B&B Homes In: Prince Edward County, on the north shore of Lake Ontario
Reservations Phone: 613/969-9925 or 613/969-8174
Phone Hours: 9am to 8pm daily
Price Range of Homes: $30 to $35 single, $38 to $48 double
Breakfast Included in Price: Full American, including homemade muffins, bread, tea biscuits, jams, jellies, etc.
Brochure Available: Free if you send a self-addressed envelope
Reservations Should Be Made: One month in advance in July and August (last-minute reservations accepted if possible)

Attractions Near the B&B Homes: Famous sand dunes, beaches, sailing, windsurfing, birdwatching, museums, "Bird City," bicycling, the White Chapel Meeting House, Macaulay House, Lake-on-the-Mountain, the legendary "Bottomless Lake"

Best B&Bs
■ A century-old home in Rendersville, Ontario. In a quiet location near Trenton and Belleville, this home is furnished with antiques and caters to adults. The host enjoys cooking and shares her interests in travel with

guests over fresh muffins. The home is one mile from the water and near several art galleries, an antique shop, and a tea room. Ancestors of the host built this house about 1860. (Top 100.)

■ B&B with a view of the Bay of Quinte, in Rendersville, Ontario. This spacious home is furnished with antiques. The full breakfast includes freshly picked fruits. This is a good area for cyclists and people who enjoy day trips in quiet, rural areas filled with fruit treats.

■ Century-old home on a treed village street in Bloomfield, Ontario. You have a choice of two upstairs guestrooms, both filled with antiques.

■ Farm home near Bloomfield, Ontario, and the Sandbanks. This is the place to stay if you love the beach and windsurfing. The home is decorated with a real feeling of Canada. In Bloomfield you can use the tennis courts and visit antiques and pottery shops.

■ Stone farmhouse built in 1835, in Waupoos, Ontario. The French doors open onto a wide veranda with a great view of Lake Ontario and Waupoos Island. The home is furnished with fine antiques.

■ An 1834 farmhouse in the Wellington area of Ontario. This B&B has been brought up to date with modern facilities and central air conditioning. There are two upstairs guest bedrooms. Breakfast and tea are served in the open-beamed kitchen.

THE THREE GRACES BED & BREAKFAST SERVICE—CENTRAL OTTAWA
166 WAVERLEY ST., OTTAWA, ON K2P 0V6, CANADA

Offers B&B Homes In: Central Ottawa
Reservations Phone: 613/233-0427 or 613/230-2697
Phone Hours: 9am to 11pm
Price Range of Homes: $50 single, $65 double
Breakfast Included in Price: Full American or full Continental (yogurt, croissants, cheese, fresh fruit salad, preserves, crumpets, pikelets, waffles, and more)
Brochure Available: Free

Attractions Near the B&Bs: Rideau Canal, Parliament buildings, museums, National Art Gallery, universities, Byward Market

Best B&Bs
■ B&B facing the Rideau Canal, Ottawa, Ontario. The reservation service says this is an "architectural delight surrounded by beautiful gardens." During the winter it is renowned for its ice-skating parties.

- Home on a quiet elegant street, Ottawa, Ontario. This B&B is furnished with antique show pieces.

- Centrally located home in Ottawa, Ontario. "B&B has a unique artistic flair, with an international ambience." Several languages spoken.

OTTAWA AREA BED & BREAKFAST
88 COOPER ST. OTTAWA, ON K1B 5H8, CANADA

Offers B&B Homes In: Ottawa and area
Reservations Phone: 613/563-0161
Phone Hours: 10am to 9pm preferred, but available 24 hours daily
Price Range of Homes: $40 single, $65 double
Breakfast Included in Price: Full American (juice, eggs, bacon, toast, coffee)
Brochure Available: Free
Reservations Should Be Made: Two weeks in advance (last-minute reservations accepted if possible)

Attractions Near the B&B Homes: Parliament buildings of Canada, Rideau Canal, museums, art galleries
Major Schools, Universities Near the B&B Homes: U. of Ottawa, Carleton U., Algonquin College, St. Paul's U.

Best B&Bs
- Robert's B&B in Ottawa, Ontario. You can stay in a large Heritage home within walking distance of the Parliament buildings and the museums. You'll have a choice of three guestrooms, one with a queen-size brass bed and private ensuite bath, stained-glass window, and a balcony. Two other rooms share a bath. This century-old home is full of antiques, including some unusual church chairs in the dining room. (Top 100.)

- Contemporary B&B in the Glebe area of Ontario. The large third floor guestroom has a double bed, a pull-out sofabed, and shared bath. You can walk to antiques shops, the Rideau Canal, and ethnic restaurants.

- Heritage home in Glebe, Ontario, overlooking the Rideau Canal and Brown's Inlet. Two guestrooms available, one with a double bed and another with twin beds. You will share a bathroom. Guests are welcome to use the sitting room with fireplace. The host has won two special awards from the tourist office in recognition of her friendly help to visitors.

■ Renovated home in Center Town, Ottawa. Located within walking distance of the Parliament buildings. You have a choice of a room with a double or single bed—with a balcony. Breakfast is included. *Insider's Tip:* Take a peek at the kitchen. It was created by one of Ottawa's top designers.

■ Suburban home in Ottawa. The house is furnished with country and Victorian furniture. You can walk to the Nepean Sailing Club overlooking the Ottawa River. Guests are welcome to use the in-ground swimming pool and the TV room.

■ Grain farm outside Ottawa. This B&B is located about 45 minutes from downtown Ottawa. It was built in 1867 and offers guests a variety of activities, including swimming in the in-ground pool, taking country walks, and viewing various farm animals. The breakfast "will last you all day."

BED & BREAKFAST HOMES OF TORONTO
P.O. BOX 46093, COLLEGE PARK POST OFFICE, 444 YONGE ST., TORONTO, ON M5B 2L8, CANADA

Offers B&B Homes In: Metropolitan Toronto
Reservations Phone: 416/363-6362
Phone Hours: 8am to 11pm daily
Price Range of Homes: $35 to $55 single, $45 to $70 double
Breakfast Included in Price: Juice, fresh fruit, entree, coffee or tea
Brochure Available: Free, on request
Reservations Should Be Made: At least two weeks ahead during
  summer months.

Attractions near the B&B Homes: Royal Ontario Museum, Casa Loma (98-room medieval-style castle), Hockey Hall of Fame, Marina Museum of Upper Canada, and all of the other sights of Toronto

Best B&Bs

■ This organization responded: "It is difficult for us to pick our top B&B homes. We are a cooperative rather than a registry. All members share equally in the cost and running of the association. Prospective guests are urged to deal with hosts directly." (Using the phone numbers in the free directory.) Here are several of interest picked by the author from information supplied by this association.

■ The Shaw House at College and Ossington in Toronto. The hosts are lively people. Arlene is a visual arts teacher and Wendell a yoga instructor. They recently renovated their Victorian home just steps away from the "Little Italy" section. Wendell is from Trinidad and loves to cook. Several years ago he represented Toronto in *Canadian Living* magazine's review of B&B breakfasts. For more information: 416/533-9111.

■ Newly renovated three-story Edwardian home, close to the subway at Yonge and St. Clair. (*Author's Note:* Toronto's subway system is excellent and exceptionally clean.) The Fireplace Room has leaded- and stained-glass windows and twin brass beds, plus a desk for the convenience of business travelers. For more information, call 416/962-5480.

■ "Beaconsfield" at Queen and Dufferin in Toronto was awarded the Government of Canada Tourism Ambassador Certificate and designated a heritage home by the Historical Board. With this pedigree, you can expect something special from hosts Bernie and Katya who are both active in the arts. Their 1882 Victorian home is filled with antiques, books, and plants. In season breakfast may include peaches and raspberries picked minutes before in the backyard. For more information, call 416/535-3338.

COUNTRY HOST
R.R. # 1, PALGRAVE, ON L0N 1P0, CANADA

Offers B&B Homes In: Ontario, from Toronto, northwest almost 300 miles to Tobermory; also at Point Pelee National Park area on Lake Erie (where thousands of birds migrate in spring and fall) and on Lake Nipissing at North Bay
Reservations Phone: 519/941-7633
Phone Hours: 8am to midnight daily (no collect calls)
Price Range of Homes: $35 single, $40 to $50 double
Breakfast Included in Price: Full American (juice or fruit in season, bacon or sausage, eggs, toast, coffee); real maple syrup, Canadian bacon and hot muffins, often served (lunches and dinners available in some homes if requested in advance)
Brochure Available: Free—send for personal answer, including stamped, self-addressed envelope
Reservations Should Be Made: At least one week in advance (last-minute reservations accepted if possible)

Attractions Near the B&B Homes: Bruce Trail, conservation areas, swimming, fishing, golfing, skiing, ice-fishing, snowmobiling, antiques and craft shops, wildflowers and hundreds of bird species

Best B&Bs

■ "Bruce Gables" in Wiarton, Ontario. This is a beautifully restored mansion on a hill overlooking Colpoys Bay, the gateway to Bruce County—a naturalist's paradise (over 300 species of birds are in residence until the fall migration). The owners have traveled internationally, acquiring hand-carved furniture over the years, and these unique pieces fill their home. Three large bedrooms are available upstairs. Each room has a ceiling fan. A full breakfast is served in the formal dining room. Later you can walk in the garden. World-famous Bruce Trail is nearby for hikers, or one hour away, is the ferry to Manitoulin Island or a glass-bottom boat to see the wrecks on the bottom of Georgian Bay. (Top 100.)

Prince Edward Island

B&B Inns

THE SENATOR'S HOUSE

BOX 63, TYNE VALLEY, PRINCE EDWARD ISLAND C0B 2C0
CANADA

Reservations Phone: 902/831-2071

Description: Rambling old home that once belonged to a prominent banker and senator. Offers three suites, including the Senator's Suite with a four poster queen size bed and a separate sitting room with a daybed. The V.I.P. room has has a four-poster queen-size bed. The Wing Suite is perfect for families, offering three bedrooms and two baths (one with a shower and the other with a whirlpool tub).

Amenities: Hostess serves fresh fruit, cereal, and hot breads in the morning. Ask about the honeymoon package.

Nearby Attractions: Wonderful rural scenes, including farmland punctuated by grazing sheep and wheels of hay. (Great country for photographers and artists.)

Rates: On request (Closed in the winter)

QUEBEC

———————— B&B Reservation Services ————————

MONTREAL BED AND BREAKFAST
P.O. BOX 575, MONTREAL, QUEBEC H3X, 3T8, CANADA

Offers B&B Homes In: Montreal and nearby communities (Dorval, where Dorval Airport is located; the Eastern townships; Laurentian Mountains area), also Quebec City
Reservations Phone: 514/738-9410 or 514/738-3859
Phone Hours: 9am to 9pm daily
Price Range of Homes: $30 to $45 single, $50 to $100 double
Breakfast Included in Price: Full American (juice, eggs, bacon, toast, coffee), plus regional specialties
Brochure Available: For $1
Reservations Should Be Made: Three weeks in advance, if by mail; telephone reservations accepted; deposit by VISA, MasterCard, or American Express

Attractions Near the B&B Homes: Mount Royal Park, Olympic Stadium, St. Joseph Oratory, Botanical Gardens, Place des Arts, Old Montreal, Museum of Fine Arts, Underground City
Major Schools, Universities Near the B&B Homes: McGill, U. de Montreal

Best B&Bs
■ Downtown Montreal town house at Prince Arthur Street. Your host, Brigette, loves art and antiques and it shows in her home. Come home from a day of sightseeing and relax in front of the fireplace, with a view of one of the city's most historic parks. Many "bring your own wine" restaurants nearby.

■ Condo apartment close to Montreal's great theatre complex, Place des Arts. The apartment is furnished with many personal touches and conveniences—such as a secretary table stocked with cards and stamps.

■ A house in downtown Montreal, close to the hockey arena and the city's most elegant shopping complex—Westmount Square. Original stenciled-glass windows and original woodwork add to the period character of this B&B.

■ Georgian home 15 minutes from downtown Montreal. You will stay in a chic neighborhood near St. Joseph's Oratory. This B&B has a great collection of Canadian art.

■ A nature lover's B&B—an apartment overlooking a park and the city skyline. Joyce is your host. She welcomes you to an elegantly furnished home with a fireplace.

■ A town house in Montreal's antiques district. This B&B is filled with plants. You will stay in the master bedroom with a king-size bed. You can then spend the day at nearby antiques shops and the Atwater Market.

GITE QUEBEC BED & BREAKFAST
3729 AVE. LE CORBUSIER, STE-FOY, QUEBEC G1W 4R8, CANADA

Offers B&B Homes In: Québec City and area
Reservations Phone: 418/651-1860
Phone Hours: 8am to 9pm daily
Price Range of Homes: $40 single, $60 double
Breakfast Included in Price: Full American (juice, eggs, bacon, toast, coffee)
Brochure Available: Free
Reservations Should Be Made: Two weeks in advance (last-minute reservations accepted if possible)

Attractions Near the B&B Homes: Château Frontenac, the Citadel and Governors' Promenade, Dufferin Terrace, the Plains of Abraham, Ste. Anne de Beaupré, Winter Carnival, Montmorency Falls, Île d'Orléans, Fort Museum Artillery Park, Chevalier House, Place d'Armes, Ursuline Convent and Museum

Would You Like to Become
One of Our B&B Critics-at-Large?

Have you discovered a great bed-and-breakfast home that belongs in our list of "100 Best"? Have you stayed in an elegant B&B inn that should be featured in this book?

Or have you been dissatisfied in any way with any of the homes and inns mentioned in this book?

You're invited to become one of our secret B&B critics. Just complete and send in the attached B&B *home* or B&B *inn* rating forms. There's no need to tear up the book—just photocopy as many forms as you need right from the book.

If you have been dissatisfied in any way with a B&B home, inn, or reservation service currently featured in this book, please let me know with a short note explaining the problem.

If you have really been pleased with your B&B experience, one of the nicest things you could do is send a copy of your evaluation to your host. They would be delighted to know that you thought enough of them and their home or inn to nominate them as "one of the best in North America."

Mail the completed form to:

B&B Critics
c/o Bed & Breakfast North America
Frommer Books
Prentice Hall Press
15 Columbus Circle
New York, NY 10023

Reader Nomination For
"One of the Best B&B <u>Homes</u> in North America"

Name of B&B Hosts _____

Address _____

City _____ State _____ ZIP _____

Phone _____

Criteria

(Please check one box for each category)

		Excellent	Good	Fair	Poor
1.	Quality of room and furnishings	☐	☐	☐	☐
2.	Quality of breakfast	☐	☐	☐	☐
3.	Housekeeping	☐	☐	☐	☐
4.	Friendliness/helpfulness of host and hostess	☐	☐	☐	☐

Why do you believe this home qualifies as one of the 100 best in North America? _____

_____

_____

_____

Your name _____

Address _____

City _____ State _____ ZIP _____

May we quote you by name in the next edition of this book if your nominee is selected as one of the 100 best?

☐ Yes   ☐ No

Reader Nomination For
"One of the Better B&B Inns in North America"

(*Note:* Many B&B homes also call themselves "inns." But this category is primarily for the large commercial establishments of eight rooms or more and closer in feeling to a hotel than to a private home.)

Name of B&B Inn _____

Address _____

City _____ State _____ ZIP _____

Phone _____

Criteria

(Please check one box for each category)

	Excellent	*Good*	*Fair*	*Poor*
1. Quality of room and furnishings	☐	☐	☐	☐
2. Quality of breakfast	☐	☐	☐	☐
3. Housekeeping	☐	☐	☐	☐
4. Friendliness/helpfulness of the innkeeper and the personnel of the inn	☐	☐	☐	☐
5. Quality of the public rooms	☐	☐	☐	☐

Why do you believe this home qualifies as one of the better B&B inns in North America? _____
_____
_____
_____

Your name _____
Address _____
City _____ State _____ ZIP _____

May we quote you by name in the next edition of this book if your nominee is selected as one of the 100 best?

☐ Yes   ☐ No

Index

TOP 100 B&B HOMES

ALABAMA:
Montgomery: "Red Bluff Cottage," 38

ALASKA:
Anchorage: B&B downtown, 41
Fairbanks: New home downtown, 41

ARIZONA:
Scottsdale: Spanish contemporary, Paradise Valley, 40
Sedona: Historic ranch estate, 40
  Spanish Colonial home, 41
Tucson: Hacienda in the foothills, 41

ARKANSAS:
Calico Rock: Contemporary home, 39

CALIFORNIA:
La Jolla: B&B near Pacific Ocean, 41
Napa Valley: 1852 Victorian house, 41
Pancho Palos Verdes: Colonial ranch, private beach, 41
San Francisco: B&B on Nob Hill, 41
  Queen Anne Victorian, 41
Santa Rosa: Redwood country home, 41
Whittier: B&B near Disneyland, 41

CANADA:
Ottawa: Large heritage home, 42
Rednersville: Century-old home, 42
Vancouver: "The Bavarian" large family home, 42
  Brunswick beach house, 42
Victoria: "Sea Rose" bungalow, 42
Wiarton: Restored mansion, 42

COLORADO:
Boulder: Modernized "miner's cabin," 39
Grand Lake: Hand-hewn log lodge, 39

CONNECTICUT:
Lyme: Colonial home in the woods, 34
New Haven: 1770 home, 34
Norwalk: 1898 Victorian Tudor home, 34

DELAWARE:
New Castle: Historic B&B on cobblestone street, 37

FLORIDA:
Jupiter: Contemporary, near ocean, 39
Miami: Luxury cottage, 39
Tampa: Waterfront B&B, 39

GEORGIA:
Atlanta: Home, downtown, 39
  Tudor home, off Peachtree Road, 39
Thomasville: Victorian mansion, 39

HAWAII:
Big Island: Executive mansion, 41–2
Kailua: Elegant oceanfront house, 42

ILLINOIS:
Chicago: Studio apartment, 38

IOWA:
Oelwein: B&B, Amish community, 38

KENTUCKY:
Lovington: Amos Shinkle Townhouse, 38
Midway: 1795 Federal-style house, 39

LOUISIANA:
Lafayette: Antebellum Acadian mansion, 40
New Orleans: Private guest cottages, near French Quarter, 40
  Private guesthouse, 40
  Tudor mansion, 40

MAINE:
Kennebunkport: "Oldest house in Maine," 34
Scarborough: 1779 home on the site of an old Indian fort, 34

MARYLAND:
Lutherville: Victorian home, 37
Queenstown: "The House of Burgess," 37

MASSACHUSETTS:
Auburn: Georgian farmhouse, 34
Barnstable: Barn restoration, 35
Boston: 1863 town house, Copley Square area, 35
  1828 Federal-style town house, Beacon hill, 35
Brookline: Georgian carriage house, 35
Cheshire: 1817 Mansard-style home, 35

345

NOW, SAVE MONEY ON ALL YOUR TRAVELS!
Join Frommer's™ Dollarwise® Travel Club

Saving money while traveling is never a simple matter, which is why the **Dollarwise Travel Club** was formed 31 years ago. Developed in response to requests from Frommer's Travel Guide readers, the Club provides cost-cutting travel strategies, up-to-date travel information, and a sense of community for value-conscious travelers from all over the world.

In keeping with the money-saving concept, the annual membership fee is low —$20 for U.S. residents or $25 for residents of Canada, Mexico, and other countries—and is immediately exceeded by the value of your benefits, which include:

1. Any TWO books listed on the following pages.
2. Plus any ONE Frommer's City Guide.
3. A subscription to our quarterly newspaper, *The Dollarwise Traveler*.
4. A membership card that entitles you to purchase through the Club all Frommer's publications for 33% to 40% off their retail price.

The eight-page **Dollarwise Traveler** tells you about the latest developments in good-value travel worldwide and includes the following columns: **Hospitality Exchange** (for those offering and seeking hospitality in cities all over the world); **Share-a-Trip** (for those looking for travel companions to share costs); and **Readers Ask . . . Readers Reply** (for those with travel questions that other members can answer).

Aside from the Frommer's Guides and the Gault Millau Guides, you can also choose from our Special Editions. These include such titles as **California with Kids** (a compendium of the best of California's accommodations, restaurants, and sightseeing attractions appropriate for those traveling with toddlers through teens); **Candy Apple: New York with Kids** (a spirited guide to the Big Apple by a savvy New York grandmother that's perfect for both visitors and residents); **Caribbean Hideaways** (the 100 most romantic places to stay in the Islands, all rated on ambience, food, sports opportunities, and price); **Honeymoon Destinations** (a guide to planning and choosing just the right destination from hundreds of possibilities in the U.S., Mexico, and the Caribbean); **Marilyn Wood's Wonderful Weekends** (a selection of the best mini-vacations within a 200-mile radius of New York City, including descriptions of country inns and other accommodations, restaurants, picnic spots, sights, and activities); and **Paris Rendez-Vous** (a delightful guide to the best places to meet in Paris whether for power breakfasts or dancing till dawn).

To join this Club, simply send the appropriate membership fee with your name and address to: Frommer's Dollarwise Travel Club, 15 Columbus Circle, New York, NY 10023. Remember to specify which single city guide and which two other guides you wish to receive in your initial package of member's benefits. Or tear out the next page, check off your choices, and send the page to us with your membership fee.

FROMMER BOOKS
PRENTICE HALL PRESS
15 COLUMBUS CIRCLE
NEW YORK, NY 10023
212/373-8125

Date_____

Friends: Please send me the books checked below.

FROMMER'S™ GUIDES

(Guides to sightseeing and tourist accommodations and facilities from budget to deluxe, with emphasis on the medium-priced.)

☐ Alaska	$14.95	☐ Germany	$14.95
☐ Australia	$14.95	☐ Italy	$14.95
☐ Austria & Hungary	$14.95	☐ Japan & Hong Kong	$14.95
☐ Belgium, Holland & Luxembourg	$14.95	☐ Mid-Atlantic States	$14.95
☐ Bermuda & The Bahamas	$14.95	☐ New England	$14.95
☐ Brazil	$14.95	☐ New Mexico (avail. June '91)	$12.95
☐ Canada	$14.95	☐ New York State	$14.95
☐ Caribbean	$14.95	☐ Northwest	$15.95
☐ Cruises (incl. Alaska, Carib, Mex, Hawaii, Panama, Canada & US)	$14.95	☐ Portugal, Madeira & the Azores	$14.95
		☐ Scandinavia (avail. May '91)	$15.95
☐ California & Las Vegas	$14.95	☐ South Pacific	$14.95
☐ Egypt	$14.95	☐ Southeast Asia	$14.95
☐ England & Scotland	$14.95	☐ Southern Atlantic States	$14.95
☐ Florida	$14.95	☐ Southwest	$14.95
☐ France	$14.95	☐ Switzerland & Liechtenstein	$14.95

☐ USA $16.95

FROMMER'S $-A-DAY® GUIDES

(In-depth guides to sightseeing and low-cost tourist accommodations and facilities.)

☐ Europe on $40 a Day	$15.95	☐ Israel on $40 a Day	$13.95
☐ Australia on $40 a Day	$13.95	☐ Mexico on $35 a Day	$14.95
☐ Costa Rica; Guatemala & Belize on $35 a day (avail. Mar. '91)	$15.95	☐ New York on $60 a Day	$13.95
		☐ New Zealand on $45 a Day	$13.95
☐ Eastern Europe on $25 a Day	$15.95	☐ Scotland & Wales on $40 a Day	$13.95
☐ England on $50 a Day	$13.95	☐ South America on $40 a Day	$15.95
☐ Greece on $35 a Day	$13.95	☐ Spain on $50 a Day	$15.95
☐ Hawaii on $60 a Day	$14.95	☐ Turkey on $30 a Day	$13.95
☐ India on $25 a Day	$12.95	☐ Washington, D.C. & Historic Va. on	
☐ Ireland on $40 a Day	$14.95	$40 a Day	$13.95

FROMMER'S TOURING GUIDES

(Color illustrated guides that include walking tours, cultural and historic sites, and other vital travel information.)

☐ Amsterdam	$10.95	☐ New York	$10.95
☐ Australia	$10.95	☐ Paris	$8.95
☐ Brazil	$10.95	☐ Rome	$10.95
☐ Egypt	$8.95	☐ Scotland	$9.95
☐ Florence	$8.95	☐ Thailand	$10.95
☐ Hong Kong	$10.95	☐ Turkey	$10.95
☐ London	$10.95	☐ Venice	$8.95

(TURN PAGE FOR ADDITONAL BOOKS AND ORDER FORM)

1290

FROMMER'S CITY GUIDES

(Pocket-size guides to sightseeing and tourist accommodations and facilities in all price ranges.)

☐ Amsterdam/Holland $8.95	☐ Minneapolis/St. Paul $8.95
☐ Athens. $8.95	☐ Montréal/Québec City. $8.95
☐ Atlanta $8.95	☐ New Orleans. $8.95
☐ Atlantic City/Cape May $8.95	☐ New York $8.95
☐ Barcelona. $7.95	☐ Orlando $8.95
☐ Belgium $7.95	☐ Paris $8.95
☐ Berlin (avail. Mar '91) $8.95	☐ Philadelphia $8.95
☐ Boston. $8.95	☐ Rio $8.95
☐ Cancún/Cozumel/Yucatán. $8.95	☐ Rome. $8.95
☐ Chicago $8.95	☐ Salt Lake City $8.95
☐ Denver/Boulder/Colorado Springs. . . .$7.95	☐ San Diego. $8.95
☐ Dublin/Ireland $8.95	☐ San Francisco $8.95
☐ Hawaii $8.95	☐ Santa Fe/Taos/Albuquerque. $8.95
☐ Hong Kong $7.95	☐ Seattle/Portland $7.95
☐ Las Vegas $8.95	☐ St. Louis/Kansas City (avail. May '91) . . .$8.95
☐ Lisbon/Madrid/Costa del Sol $8.95	☐ Sydney. $8.95
☐ London $8.95	☐ Tampa/St. Petersburg $8.95
☐ Los Angeles $8.95	☐ Tokyo. $7.95
☐ Mexico City/Acapulco $8.95	☐ Toronto $8.95
☐ Miami $8.95	☐ Vancouver/Victoria $7.95

☐ Washington, D.C. $8.95

SPECIAL EDITIONS

☐ Beat the High Cost of Travel. $6.95	☐ Motorist's Phrase Book (Fr/Ger/Sp) $4.95
☐ Bed & Breakfast—N. America $14.95	☐ Paris Rendez-Vous $10.95
☐ California with Kids $15.95	☐ Swap and Go (Home Exchanging). $10.95
☐ Caribbean Hideaways. $14.95	☐ The Candy Apple (NY with Kids). $12.95
☐ Honeymoon Destinations (US, Mex &	☐ Travel Diary and Record Book. $5.95
Carib). $14.95	☐ Where to Stay USA (From $3 to $30 a
☐ Manhattan's Outdoor Sculpture. $15.95	night). $13.95

☐ Marilyn Wood's Wonderful Weekends (CT, DE, MA, NH, NJ, NY, PA, RI, VT) $11.95
☐ The New World of Travel (Annual sourcebook by Arthur Frommer for savvy travelers) $16.95

GAULT MILLAU

(The only guides that distinguish the truly superlative from the merely overrated.)

☐ The Best of Chicago $15.95	☐ The Best of Los Angeles $16.95
☐ The Best of France $16.95	☐ The Best of New England $15.95
☐ The Best of Hawaii $16.95	☐ The Best of New Orleans. $16.95
☐ The Best of Hong Kong $16.95	☐ The Best of New York $16.95
☐ The Best of Italy. $16.95	☐ The Best of Paris $16.95
☐ The Best of London $16.95	☐ The Best of San Francisco $16.95

☐ The Best of Washington, D.C. $16.95

ORDER NOW!

In U.S. include $2 shipping UPS for 1st book; $1 ea. add'l book. Outside U.S. $3 and $1, respectively.

Allow four to six weeks for delivery in U.S., longer outside U.S.

Enclosed is my check or money order for $_____

NAME_____

ADDRESS_____

CITY_____ STATE_____ ZIP_____

1290